W9-DIM-039

STRIKERS and SUBSIDIES

The Influence of Government Transfer Programs on Strike Activity

Robert Hutchens
David Lipsky
Robert Stern
New York State School
of Industrial and Labor Relations
Cornell University

1989

W. E. UPJOHN INSTITUTE for Employment Research
Kalamazoo, Michigan

Library of Congress Cataloging-in-Publication Data

Hutchens, Robert M.
Strikers and subsidies : the influence of government transfer programs on strike activity / by Robert Hutchens, David Lipsky, Robert Stern.
p. cm.
Includes bibliographical references.
ISBN 0-88099-080-5. — ISBN 0-88099-079-1 (pbk.)
1. Strikes and lockouts—Government policy—United States. 2. Insurance, Unemployment—United States. 3. Labor disputes—United States. 4. Insurance, Strike—United States. 5. Trade unions—United States—Strike benefits. 6. Transfer payments—United States. I. Lipsky, David B., 1939- . II. Stern, Robert N., 1948- . III. Title.
HD5324.H79
331.89'8—dc20 89-16693
CIP

∞

THE INSTITUTE, a nonprofit research organization was established on July 1, 1945. It is an activity of the W. E. Upjohn Unemployment Trustee Corporation, which was formed in 1932 to administer a fund set aside by the late Dr. W. E. Upjohn for the purpose of carrying on ''research into the causes and effects of unemployment and measures for the alleviation of unemployment.''

The facts presented in this study and the observations and viewpoints expressed are the sole responsibility of the authors. They do not necessarily represent positions of the W. E. Upjohn Institute for Employment Research.

To our families

Authors

Robert Hutchens is professor of Labor Economics at Cornell's School of Industrial and Labor Relations. He also serves as Chairman of the Department of Labor Economics. Hutchens received his Ph.D. in economics from the University of Wisconsin in 1976, specializing in labor economics, public finance, and econometrics. He has written several papers on the economics of government transfer programs, with an emphasis on unemployment insurance and Aid to Families with Dependent Children. In 1980-81 he was a Policy Fellow at the Brookings Institution, devoting part of his time to the Department of Health and Human Services. In 1984 he was a visitor in the Department of Economics at the University of British Columbia. His current research encompasses not only government transfer programs, but also long-term implicit contracts and the market for older workers.

David Lipsky is Dean of the New York State School of Industrial and Labor Relations, Cornell University. Lipsky has been a member of the Cornell University faculty for 20 years. His field of teaching and research is collective bargaining. He has been associate dean for academic affairs at ILR, and assistant professor, SUNY, Buffalo; visiting associate professor, MIT; visiting associate professor, Boston University; Co-Director, Harvard Institute in Employment and Training Administration; adjunct lecturer, Brandeis University; and visiting scholar, University of British Columbia. He has served as Chairman of the Department of Collective Bargaining, Labor Law, and Labor History; and as Editor and Associate Editor of the *ILR Review.* He has published over 30 articles and essays and is the author or editor of 11 books, including *Collective Bargaining in American Industry* (1987), and *Paying for Better Teaching* (1984).

Robert Stern is associate professor of Organizational Behavior and Sociology at Cornell's School of Industrial and Labor Relations. He has completed extensive research on the determinants of strikes and currently works in the areas of worker participation and union-management cooperation. He has been a Fulbright Scholar at the University of Leiden, The Netherlands and a visiting professor at the School of Management and Institute of Industrial Relations at the University of California at Berkeley. Stern has written or coauthored 30 articles and 4 books, including *Employee Ownership in Plant Shutdowns, ESOPs: Benefits for Whom?* and *Worker Participation and Ownership: Cooperative Strategies for Strengthening Local Economies.*

Acknowledgements

This volume is the culmination of a research project that we conducted over the course of several years. During that period we relied on numerous people for support, advice, information, data, and assistance. The project was supported by a grant from The W. E. Upjohn Institute for Employment Research. We owe a special debt of gratitude to the Upjohn Institute, and particularly to H. Allan Hunt, Louis Jacobson, and the late Earl Wright for their encouragement, comments, and suggestions. We especially thank Lou Jacobson for providing us with valuable comments on and criticisms of the early versions of several chapters.

Charles Rehmus, former dean of the School of Industrial and Labor Relations at Cornell University, was enthusiastic about the project and encouraged us to begin: we are grateful for his support. Robert Doherty, the current dean of the ILR School, was equally encouraging and we acknowledge our gratitude to him. We also thank Ronald Ehrenberg, professor and Director of Research at the ILR School, who helped to make our research task a little easier than it might have been and offered advice at every stage of the project.

The authors conducted interviews with many government, union, and management representatives, and we thank them all for their cooperation and assistance. Through the auspices of the Interstate Conference of Employment Security Agencies, we also conducted a survey of administrators of 54 state-level employment security agencies. We wish to thank William L. Heartwell, Jr. of the ICESA for making this survey possible. Many of the survey respondents supplied us with invaluable information on the treatment of labor disputes under their unemployment insurance statutes, and we thank them all for their help. William J. Yost, Chief Hearing Officer with the Iowa employment security agency, and George A. Michaud, Chief Hearing Officer with Alaska Agency, also provided us with information on some of the important aspects of their state laws, and we appreciate their assistance.

We obtained the information and data we needed to conduct this study from individuals in a variety of federal, state, and private agencies; we benefited from having the services of several research assistants and computer programmers; we used several secretaries to type and re-type our work; and we used a crew of students to code and verify the data used in the analysis. All of these individuals are thanked by name in Appendix A. If we have inadvertently omitted from this appendix the names of people who assisted us, we apologize to them and want them to know that we are grateful. We would be remiss if we did not especially thank Tim Schmidle, who supervised the collection, coding, and verification of the data, and Nancy Hanks and Melissa Barringer, whose diligent assistance greatly improved the quality of the manuscript. Of course we must add the usual disclaimer: any errors of fact or interpretation that remain are solely the responsibility of the authors, and none of the views expressed in the volume are necessarily shared by any of the individuals acknowledged here or in Appendix A. Finally, we wish to thank our wives and families for their love and patience.

Contents

1 Setting the Stage 1
What are our current practices, where do they come from, and what is their rationale? 4
Does the provision of government transfers to strikers affect strike activity? 9
What is the proper policy? 12
Notes 13

2 Unemployment Compensation in Labor Disputes: Part I 15
Policy Development 18
What is a Labor Dispute? 20
The Establishment Rule 23
Lockouts 24
Interim Employment 31
Summary 33
Notes 33

3 Unemployment Compensation in Labor Disputes: Part II 39
Stoppage-of-Work Provisions 40
New York 46
Rhode Island 48
The New York Telephone Case 49
Innocent Bystanders 51
Grade or Class 57
The Air Traffic Controllers 59
Conclusion 68
Notes 70

4 Welfare in Labor Disputes 77
Aid to Families with Dependent Children 80
AFDC-U 1961-1981 84
Food Stamps 102
General Assistance 112
Conclusion 114
Notes 121

5 Government Transfer Programs and Strike Theories: Designing an Empirical Test . . . 133
Models of Strike Activity . . . 134
Modified Model . . . 138
Interpreting Transfer Payment Effects on Strikes . . . 141
Empirical Implementation . . . 146
Conclusion . . . 159
Notes . . . 161

6 An Empirical Analysis of the Effect of Government Transfer Programs on Strike Activity . . . 165
Labor Disputes Disqualification Policies and Strike Behavior . . . 165
The Interaction of labor Dispute Disqualification Policies and Program Generosity . . . 169
Replicating the Results . . . 174
The Effect of the AFDC, Food Stamp, and General Assistance Programs on Strike Behavior . . . 181
Conclusion . . . 183
Notes . . . 184

7 What is the Proper Policy? . . . 187
Goals for Public Policy . . . 188
Policy Options . . . 190
A Proposal . . . 198
Notes . . . 200

Appendix A: People Who Contributed to This Book . . . 203
Appendix B: Sources of Variables . . . 205

References . . . 211

Index . . . 219

Index of Cases . . . 227

Tables

5.1 Existence of Work-Stoppage and Innocent Bystander Provisions of State Unemployment Insurance Laws Regarding Strikers, 1961 143
5.2 Changes in Unemployment Disqualification of Strikers, 1961-1974 144
5.3 Work-Stoppage Historical Files, 1953-1974 Variables Available for Each Strike Observations 148
5.4 Measures of Strike Frequency 148
5.5 Means and Standard Deviations of Strike Measures Over All States and All Years, 1960-1974 152
5.6 Variables Measuring Characteristics of Transfer Programs 156
5.7 Control Variables Employed in the Analysis 160

6.1 Regressions on the Frequency, Duration, and Size of Strikes 167
6.2 Strike Frequency Regressions That Include Interaction Variables 170
6.3 Strike Regressions with Alternative Control Variables 172
6.4 Strike Frequency Regressions for Different Years 175
6.5 Strike Duration Regressions for Different Years 176
6.6 Fixed-Effects Regressions on the Frequency and Duration of Strikes, 1960-1974 178
6.7 Fixed-Effects Regressions on the Frequency and Duration of Strikes, 1960-1974, with Welfare Variables Included 182

1
Setting the Stage

One of the most controversial labor policy issues is whether strikers should be eligible for government transfer payments, such as unemployment compensation, public assistance, and food stamps. Under current policies, strikers after an extended waiting period, are eligible for unemployment compensation in two states (New York and Rhode Island) and can collect unemployment benefits in many other states under certain conditions (e.g., if a strike does not result in the employer shutting down operations). Railroad workers engaged in a lawful strike are also eligible for unemployment compensation under the federal Railroad Unemployment Insurance Act. Needy strikers may also be eligible for cash grants and other forms of public assistance made available by state and county governments.

Consider the following cases:

• In July 1971, about 38,000 workers employed by the New York Telephone Company went on strike. Under New York's unemployment insurance law, these workers were allowed to collect unemployment benefits after they had been on strike for eight weeks. Before the strike was settled in February 1972, the strikers had collected $49 million in benefits. The New York Telephone Company financed most of these benefits through payroll taxes the company subsequently paid to the state.

• In 1972, 166 workers went on strike against the Dow Chemical Company's Bay City, Michigan plant. Michigan's unemployment insurance law allows strikers to collect unemployment benefits if the strikers obtain, and are then laid off from, "bona fide interim jobs." Most of the Dow strikers obtained temporary jobs with "friendly" employers who, after a few days, laid off the strikers. The strikers then applied for, and collected, unemployment benefits for the duration of their strike. Michigan, like New York, raised Dow's unemployment insurance taxes to cover the cost of the strikers' benefits.

• During the winter of 1977-78, about 160,000 members of the United Mine Workers (UMW) staged a strike against the Bituminous Coal Operators Association. As the strike dragged on through January and February, thousands of miners applied for and received food stamps. In West Virginia, for example, 35,000 miners collected $18 million in food stamps.[1] In Pennsylvania, nearly 12,000 miners received food stamps and 2,700 received other forms of public assistance.[2] In 1981, the UMW once again struck the coal operators, and once again thousands of miners qualified for food stamps and public assistance.

• In August 1981, 12,000 air traffic controllers launched a nationwide strike against their employer, the Federal Aviation Administration. President Ronald Reagan ordered the striking controllers to return to their jobs. When they refused to do so, the president discharged the controllers for conducting an illegal strike against the federal government. Subsequently, many controllers applied for unemployment compensation. Although many states denied the controllers' claims for benefits, several allowed them to collect.

• At midnight on July 31, 1986, the collective bargaining agreement between the United Steel Workers union and the USX (formerly the United States Steel Corporation) expired. In the face of the failure to negotiate a new contract, USX shut down its plants across the country and declared a lockout. Some states ruled that the unemployed steelworkers were ineligible for unemployment benefits because of their participation in a labor dispute. Other states, however, allowed workers to collect benefits because of the lockout. In particular, nearly 800 steelworkers in Illinois and 7,500 steelworkers in Pennsylvania were allowed to collect unemployment compensation during their dispute with USX.

These are not isolated cases. Although comprehensive data on the use of public aid in strikes are lacking, it would be an easy task, using accounts in newspapers and periodicals as well as administrative and court decisions, to cite dozens of other examples. Indeed, Thieblot and Cowin, in a book published in 1972, predicted that the cost of public aid to strikers would exceed $300 million in 1973. Although that figure was probably an overestimate, it is known that in 1980 strikers received $30 million in food stamps and $5 million under the Aid to Families with Dependent Children-Unemployed Parent (AFDC-U) program.

Unfortunately, no one knows the total cost of unemployment benefits received by workers involved in labor disputes.

But the cost of public aid to strikers is only one issue of concern to policymakers and citizens. Clearly, public aid to strikers also provides benefits, not only to the strikers themselves but also to their families and, indirectly at least, to the communities in which the strikers live. Many strikers' families suffer great hardship during prolonged strikes, and the benefits associated with the alleviation of that hardship may be worth more than the costs. Moreover, an entire community may suffer as a result of a protracted strike (especially when the strikers constitute a significant proportion of the community's workforce), and subsidizing strikers with public funds may do much to bolster the community's welfare. Providing public subsidies to strikers, then, may serve an entirely suitable public interest.

The extension and liberalization of various welfare programs during the 1960s laid the foundation for the increasing use of transfer payments by strikers in the 1970s. This development did not go unnoticed by the business community. Business interests and their allies increasingly decried the use of tax dollars to subsidize strikers. For example, in 1978 Richard L. Lesher, then president of the U.S. Chamber of Commerce, said:

> our members consider it highly inappropriate that taxpayers should subsidize strikers. Such subsidies are even more incomprehensible when beneficiaries are continuing their strike outside the law. . . . In fact, our members continue to believe that taxpayers should not be required to subsidize strikers in any event, since their decision to cease working is voluntary. We believe public assistance should be available only to those who are out of work through no fault of their own.

In supporting the 1981 legislation that made strikers ineligible for food stamps, Senator Jesse Helms (Rep., N.C.), a long-time opponent of public aid for strikers, said,

> any worker who walks off the job to go on strike has given up the income from that job of his own volition. A person making such a choice, and participating in a strike, must bear the consequence of his decisions without assistance from the taxpayers.[3]

On the other hand, unions and their allies have defended the use of transfer payments in strikes as a fair and even necessary use of public funds. In 1975, the late George Meany, then president of the AFL-CIO, said, "It is our position that welfare benefits should be available to citizens who are demonstrably in need without regard for the cause of that need."[4] When the Carter administration threatened to cut off food stamp assistance to striking coal miners in 1978, Meany said the threat was an "outrage, especially for an administration dedicated to protecting and preserving human rights. . . . This attempt to force the miners to agree to an unacceptable contract by starving their wives and children is a vindictive act."[5]

In the congressional debate over the retention of striker eligibility for food stamps in 1981, Senator Carl Levin (Dem., MI) said,

> Elimination of striker participation in the food stamp program will pose hardship for the poorest of strikers. . . . The labor laws of this country protect the right to strike. The workers who choose to exercise this right should not be singled out for denial of food stamp benefits if they otherwise qualify under the Act and program regulation.[6]

While the debate over the use of government transfer payments in labor disputes continues, that debate is often characterized by rhetorical appeals to the emotions rather than analysis of hard evidence. In the hope that a more informed debate can lead to better policy, this book seeks to present a few pieces of hard evidence. The book is organized around the following questions.

(1) What are our current practices, where do they come from, and what is their rationale?

(2) Does the provision of government transfers to strikers affect strike activity?

(3) What is the proper policy?

Our answers to those questions are summarized as follows.

What are our current practices, where do they come from, and what is their rationale?

Chapters 2 through 4 address this issue. Chapters 2 and 3 examine unemployment insurance, and chapter 4 examines public assistance.

To write these chapters we not only searched through libraries, but also talked to experts in the field. We interviewed representatives of the AFL-CIO, the National Association of Manufacturers, and U.S. Department of Labor. We sent a survey to the employment security agency in each state (and conducted follow-up telephone calls) in order to obtain information on state policies and court cases. In each of these efforts we sought views on whether and how specific provisions of government transfer programs influence strike activity.

This inquiry leads us to conclude that there is considerable confusion surrounding the issue of striker eligibility for unemployment insurance benefits. First, it should be recognized that the Social Security Act of 1935, which established the unemployment insurance system, gives the states the authority to establish the rules governing claimant eligibility for unemployment benefits (provided the states meet certain minimum federal standards). Therefore, each state can determine whether, and under what conditions, workers unemployed because of a labor dispute can collect unemployment benefits.[7] Federal tolerance of state autonomy on this issue, reinforced by several key Supreme Court decisions, results in considerable diversity in the unemployment insurance eligibility rules that affect strikers.

It is widely believed, even by those with knowledge of the subject, that only two states, New York and Rhode Island, routinely permit strikers to collect unemployment benefits. Although it is true that these two states do allow strikers to collect benefits (in New York after an eight-week waiting period and in Rhode Island after a seven-week period), it is also true that *a majority of other states allow workers unemployed because of a labor dispute to collect unemployment benefits under certain conditions*. Moreover, in these states the workers are eligible to collect benefits after the normal waiting period (usually one week), or virtually from the outset of a strike. While the relevant state UI provisions take many forms, the following are particularly important.

(1) In 1984, 27 states had a "stoppage-of-work" provision, whereby strikers collect unemployment benefits if their employer continues to operate at or near normal operating levels during the course of the labor dispute. In a sense, this provision provides insurance against a failed

strike; if the strike fails to shut down the employer, then unemployment insurance benefits are available to the strikers.

(2) In 1984, 21 states qualified claimants for benefits if the labor dispute is caused by an employer lockout. For example, in the dispute between the USW and the USX Corporation in 1986-87, cited earlier, the union instructed a large number of its Pennsylvania members to report to work after the expiration of the national contract. When the corporation turned the workers away from the locked gates of its Pennsylvania steel mills, it became a near certainty that the state would allow the steelworkers to collect unemployment insurance benefits.

(3) In 1984, 44 states had an "innocent bystander" provision whereby workers obtain unemployment insurance benefits if they are unemployed because of a labor dispute but are not participating in, financing, or directly interested in the dispute. Typically, innocent bystanders are employed at the struck establishment, but are not members of either the union or the bargaining unit that is on strike.

Of course, these rules interact. Some states have none of the provisions, others have one or two, while still others have all three. Interestingly, New York—popularly regarded as a state with liberal policies on the use of unemployment benefits in labor disputes—has none of the three policies. A New York worker engaged in a labor dispute receives no unemployment insurance benefits during the first eight weeks of the strike, irrespective of whether he is a participant or an innocent bystander, and irrespective of whether the employer continues to operate or has locked strikers out. Of course, after the eight-week waiting period, the New Yorker receives full UI benefits. In contrast, Rhode Island uses a stoppage-of-work rule. Thus in Rhode Island, a striker can collect benefits after a one-week waiting period if his employer *does* continue to operate during a strike and can collect benefits after a seven-week waiting period if his employer does *not* continue to operate during a strike.

It should be clear from this brief preview that the rules governing the payment of unemployment benefits in labor disputes are complex and diverse. The variation in the rules across states means that strikers who are otherwise identical may be eligible to collect benefits in one state but not in another. Some states, particularly those with work-stoppage, lockout, and innocent bystander provisions, e.g., Georgia, Maryland, West Virginia, are relatively liberal in qualifying workers for benefits. Other states, particularly those without work-stoppage, lockout, and innocent bystander provisions, e.g., Alabama and North Carolina, are quite strict. By providing a thorough understanding of the "rules of the game," chapters 2 and 3 lay the foundation for our subsequent empirical analyses of the effect of variation in the rules on strike activity.

Chapter 4 deals with the eligibility of strikers for AFDC-U benefits, food stamps, and general assistance. For nearly 20 years, opponents of federal assistance to strikers had struggled to remove striker eligibility for AFDC-U and food stamps from the law, but without success. When Ronald Reagan became president in 1981, however, the stage was set for Congress to enact a package of sweeping budget cuts. On July 31, 1981, Congress passed the Omnibus Budget Reconciliation Act (OBRA), which cut federal expenditures by $35 billion. The Act brought about major policy changes in many domestic programs, including AFDC, Medicaid, food stamps, job training, and others.[8] Elimination of striker eligibility for AFDC-U and food stamps were only two of the many policy changes incorporated in the OBRA.

Because Congress eliminated striker eligibility for AFDC-U and food stamps in 1981, the material covered in chapter 4 is primarily historical in nature. Yet the issue of whether strikers should be eligible for welfare benefits continues to be relevant, particularly because in 1986 a federal district court ruled that the provision in the 1981 law that denies food stamps to the families of strikers violates due process and interferes with the striker's First Amendment right of freedom of association.[9] Although the Supreme Court reversed this decision in 1988, thereby ending legal challenges to the OBRA, the issue will continue to be the subject of congressional debate on public policy.[10] But in deciding on which transfer policies, if any, should be used in labor disputes, it is necessary to understand how the federal welfare system operated in the 1960s and 1970s, when strikers could qualify for assistance. Moreover, because the data gathered for our empirical analysis cover the period 1960-75, we are able to make an assessment of the effect of striker eligibility for AFDC-U and food stamps on the frequency and duration of strikes.

Until 1961, the AFDC program targeted families with children where the father was absent and the mother did not work. In 1961 Congress extended coverage under the program to dependent children in households with an unemployed father. States were given the option of deciding whether to participate in the AFDC-U program and by 1967, 21 had decided to do so.[11] Throughout the 1960s and 1970s, the payment of AFDC-U benefits to strikers remained a contentious issue, with controversy centering upon whether a striker fell within the definition of an unemployed parent. In 1977, the Supreme Court, in *Batterton v. Frances,* ruled that this definitional decision should be left to the states. Thus, the issue of whether states participating in the AFDC-U program could deny benefits to strikers' families was finally settled. By 1980, of the 26 states participating in the AFDC-U programs, 8 had chosen to deny benefits to strikers.

AFDC-U benefits were never an important source of income support for strikers. This is in part because, as noted above, many states either did not have an AFDC-U program or denied benefits to strikers. In addition, even if a participating state did permit strikers to collect benefits, a striker could only qualify if he met the same federal and state eligibility requirements imposed on all other applicants for assistance. The most salient requirements were that he was unemployed for at least 30 days, that he have a dependent child, that he could demonstrate financial need under his state's resource and income tests, and that he did not receive unemployment insurance benefits. In combination, these requirements always seriously limited the number of strikers eligible for AFDC-U. For example, since the average strike in the United States lasts about three weeks, the 30-day waiting period by itself prevented most strikers from ever becoming eligible for AFDC-U benefits.

Food stamps were a somewhat different story. The food stamp program is funded entirely by the federal government but is administered jointly by the federal government and the states under uniform federal standards. It is clear that during the 1960s and 1970s many more strikers qualified for food stamps than for AFDC-U. First, unlike the AFDC-U program, all states participated in the food stamp program. Second, there is no waiting period for food stamp benefits. Third, the resource and income tests used to qualify applicants for food stamps have been more liberal than those used in most state AFDC programs. Fourth, after 1970 the Food Stamp Act specifically provided that otherwise eligible strikers would not be disqualified from receiving food stamps.

Strikers may also benefit from the General Assistance program. General Assistance is distinguished from AFDC-U and food stamps by an absence of federal involvement. It is funded and administered by state and local governments; in some states eligibility rules differ from county to county. Since it is a very old program, there are instances where strikers have received General Assistance throughout the 20th century. Indeed, since the program was not touched by the 1981 OBRA legislation, strikers can still receive General Assistance. In most states, however, this is a small program that provides minuscule benefits to people with the lowest of family incomes. To choose an extreme example, in August, 1974, Alabama provided General Assistance benefits of $12.50 to 42 people. While we have no hard numbers, it is unlikely that many strikers benefit from this program.

Does the provision of government transfers to strikers affect strike activity?

This question is not merely "academic." It has arisen in the most practical of settings. For example, in *Grinnell Corp. v. Hackett,* a case involving the payment of unemployment compensation to strikers in Rhode Island, the first circuit court demanded an empirical burden of proof. The court said:

> [The] present record suffers from a fundamental defect. It provides no support for a causal relationship between the receipt of benefits, which unions obviously desire and often actively seek, and longer, costlier strikes. . . . [The] record lacks even a crude form of what we assume would be the most relevant and probative type of evidence—statistical comparisons of the length and cost of strikes in states granting unemployment benefits (Rhode Island and New York) and the length and cost of strikes of similar size in similar industries in other states not granting such benefits.[12]

Similarly, in *ITT Lamp Division v. Minter,* a case involving payment of AFDC-U benefits to strikers, the first circuit court called for evidence indicating,

> . . . how many states permit strikers to receive welfare; whether or not strikes tend to be of longer duration where welfare is received; and studies or expert testimony evaluating the impact of eligibility for benefits on the strikers' resolve.[13]

There exist but a handful of studies that examine the relationship between transfer payments and strike activity. Perhaps best known is a work by Thieblot and Cowin, which is primarily based on case studies.[14] A study of Great Britain by Gennard similarly relies on description, case studies, and gross cost estimates.[15] John Kennan[16] applies modern statistical methods in examining the relationship between unemployment insurance and the duration of strikes. His work, however, focuses on the New York and Rhode Island policy of providing UI benefits in very long strikes, and thereby ignores the multitude of other policies under which strikers receive government transfers.[17]

A distinguishing feature of the present work is that it uses modern statistical methods in an analysis of a broad range of government policies. Chapter 5 introduces the relevant theory, the hypotheses to be tested, the methods, and the data. Chapter 6 presents quantitative results and draws conclusions.

Chapter 5 opens with a discussion of theory. Theory is crucial to this project because it provides a bridge between the institutional details in chapters 2–4 and the quantitative results in chapter 6. Chapters 2–4 essentially tell us that in certain circumstances workers involved in strikes obtain government transfers. Theory addresses the question of whether there is a logical basis for arguing that these transfers affect strike activity. Much past work has treated this as a simple question that can be glided over in one or two sentences. In our view, that is a serious mistake for two reasons.

First, the answer is not at all obvious. Payment of government transfers to strikers will surely make it easier for workers to support themselves during a strike. But why would that result in more strike activity? The employer is presumably aware of the availability of such transfers. If government transfers strengthen the bargaining position of the union, then one might expect a rational employer to be more willing to settle without a strike, or, failing that, settle sooner rather than later. That means *less* strike activity. The point is that a concept of what starts and stops strikes necessarily underlies any claim that government transfers increase strike activity. That concept deserves critical examination; it should not be left between the lines.

The second reason for exploring theoretical issues is that empirical work always raises questions that are best answered with a theory. What explanatory variables should be included in an analysis of strike activity? What is the appropriate dependent variable? What are the key hypotheses? What is the proper interpretation of a result? Empirical work *always* requires answers to such questions. Theory helps to make the answers logically consistent and explicit rather than implicit.

Thus, chapter 5 opens with a review of theories. On the basis of this discussion it is clear that there is no general consensus on the "right" theory of strikes. Rather, there are competing and often contradictory theories. Fortunately, for our purposes a *general* theory of strike activity is not requisite. We only need a theory that links transfer policies to strike activity. That theory was found in the work of Melvin Reder and George Neumann. The fundamental proposition of the theory is that strike activity is a decreasing function of the combined (union plus management) cost of strikes. As the potential cost of a strike increases, according to Reder and Neumann, the parties have a greater incentive to develop protocols that allow them to reach peaceful settlements. From this theory we derive a series of hypotheses linking specific provisions of unemployment insurance and welfare programs to strike activity.

Those hypotheses can be tested with state level data. Transfer policies affecting strikers usually vary across but not within states. If transfer policies affect strike behavior, then that should be revealed through differences in the "average" level of strike activity across states. In consequence, we collected data on several dimensions of strike activity for the 50 states over the period 1960–1974. We also collected data on the specifics of state transfer policies ("stoppage-of-work," "innocent bystander," etc.) for the same period. Chapter 5 closes with a discussion of the nuances of data sources, variable measurement, and statistical methodology.

Chapter 6 then presents results from a sequence of regression analyses on annual cross-sections and on the full (1960–1974) panel. On the basis of the statistical evidence, we conclude that *there is a link between the unemployment insurance system and strike activity.* A more generous unemployment insurance program is related to a higher strike frequency in states that use "innocent bystander" or "stoppage-of-work" disqualification rules. Similar results were *not* obtained for other unemployment insurance provisions, e.g., the New York-Rhode Island waiting period, or other dimensions of strike activity, e.g., average duration of strikes. Finally, *our statistical models did not uncover evidence linking welfare programs to strike activity.* Either such a link is nonexistent or our methods are insufficiently precise to discern it.

What is the proper policy?

When *should* government transfers be provided to workers engaged in strikes? As discussed in chapter 7, at the heart of this question lies a philosophical problem concerning the appropriate role of the modern state in what are usually two distinct spheres: government transfers and industrial relations. The answer necessarily involves finding a balance between what are often conflicting policy goals in the two spheres. For example, a goal like government neutrality in labor relations comes in conflict with the goal of alleviating hardship and distress. Thus, the chapter begins with an examination of current policy goals and tradeoffs between those goals.

Chapter 7 ends with the authors' position on the proper policy. Briefly stated, in our opinion the present system is seriously flawed. It denies public assistance benefits to the family of a law-abiding striker irrespective of hardship. It provides unemployment insurance benefits to strikers when the involuntary nature of their unemployment is fraught with ambiguity. It places part of the burden of financing strike related transfers on the larger society, and thereby increases the level of strike activity. Chapter 7 proposes a package of alternative policies that are oriented toward the twin goals of alleviating hardship and promoting industrial peace.

NOTES

1. *Charleston Daily Mail,* April 7, 1981. See also *Charleston Evening Journal,* March 23, 1981.

2. *The Dominion Post,* April 21, 1981, p. 3-A.

3. U.S. Congress, Senate, *Congressional Record,* 97th Cong., 1st sess., 1981, 127, S9137.

4. *New York Times,* August 15, 1975, p. 36.

5. Quoted in *New York Times,* March 11, 1978, p. 12.

6. Quoted in *Daily Labor Report,* No. 114, June 15, 1981, p. A-2.

7. Railroad workers engaged in a lawful strike are also eligible for unemployment compensation under the federal Railroad Unemployment Insurance Act, 45 U.S.C.A. §352 (a), 1986.

8. Tom Joe and Cheryl Rogers, *By the Few, for the Few: The Reagan Welfare Legacy* (Lexington, Mass: Lexington Books, 1985), pp. 50-57.

9. *UAW v. Lyng,* 648 F. Supp. 1234 (D.D.C. 1986).

10. *Lyng v. UAW,* 108 S. Ct. 1184 (1988).

11. "Compilations Based on Characteristics of State Public Assistance Plans: General Provisions—Eligibility, Assistance, Administration: In Effect December 31, 1967," Public Assistance Report No. 50—1967 Edition (U.S. Dept. of Health, Education, and Welfare, Social and Rehabilitation Service, Assistance Payments Administration, 1969), p. 17.

12. *Grinnell Corp. v. Hackett,* 475 F. 2d 449 at 459 (1st Cir., 1973).

13. *ITT Lamp Division v. Minter,* 435 F.2d 989 (1st Cir., 1970); cert. denied, 420 U.S. 933 (1971).

14. Armand J. Thieblot, Jr. and Ronald M. Cowin, *Welfare and Strikes: The Use of Public Funds to Support Strikers* (Philadelphia, Pa.: University of Pennsylvania Press, 1972). This study was "funded by four industrial foundations and thirteen companies," according to Marc E. Thomas, "Strikers' Eligibility for Public Assistance: The Standard Based on Need," *Journal of Urban Law,* Vol. 52, No. 1, pp. 115-154, p. 118.

15. John Gennard, *Financing Strikers* (New York: John Wiley and Sons, 1977).

16. John Kennan, "The Effect of Unemployment Insurance on Strike Duration," *Unemployment Compensation: Studies and Research,* Vol. 2, National Commission on Unemployment Compensation, July 1980, 467-486.

17. Lewis Perl also studied the New York/Rhode Island rule using statistical methods. See Lewis J. Perl, "Statistical Analysis of Strike Activity," unpublished paper, New York: National Economic Research Associates, Sept. 11, 1974.

2
Unemployment Compensation in Labor Disputes
Part I

The unemployment compensation laws of all states contain provisions that disqualify workers if they are unemployed because of the existence of a labor dispute. State employment security agencies have the responsibility of determining, first, if a labor dispute exists and, second, if the claimant's unemployment is the result of the labor dispute. These are only threshold tests, however, in determining the claimant's eligibility for unemployment benefits. Whether workers unemployed because of a labor dispute qualify for benefits depends on the precise policies followed by a particular state—and there is considerable variation in these policies. The most common provisions are summarized for the reader's use as a reference in exhibit 2.1. We will discuss these provisions in more detail in this and the following chapter.

A fundamental distinction hinges on whether a state imposes a blanket disqualification on workers unemployed because of the existence of a labor dispute or disqualifies such workers only if the labor dispute has caused a "stoppage of work" at the establishment where the worker is employed. In the former category, approximately 20 states disqualify workers while a labor dispute is in "active progress" (or alternatively as long as the workers' unemployment continues to be the result of the dispute). In the latter category, approximately 27 states disqualify workers only if the labor dispute has caused a substantial curtailment of the employer's operations. In stoppage-of-work states, striking workers can collect benefits if their employer continues to operate at or near normal levels. In simplest terms, workers are denied benefits if their strike is a success, but are granted benefits if their strike fails.

Exhibit 2.1
Principal Labor Dispute Disqualification Provisions in Unemployment Insurance Systems

		Prevalence as of 1984
Standard provisions:		
Labor dispute disqualification	Individuals filing claims for benefits are disqualified if unemployed because of the existence of a labor dispute.	All jurisdictions
Establishment rule	A worker is ineligible for benefits if the labor dispute causing his unemployment is at the "factory, establishment, or premises at which he is or was employed."	Almost all jurisdictions
New work	Otherwise eligible claimants cannot be denied benefits for refusing to accept new work if the job vacancy was created by a strike, lockout, or other labor dispute.	All jurisdictions
Exceptions:		
Stoppage-of-work	Also referred to as the "American Rule." Striking employees are not disqualified for benefits if an existing labor dispute has not caused a cessation or substantial curtailment of operations at the plant or establishment where the strikers are employed.	27 states
Waiting period	Strikers become eligible for benefits if, after a specified period of time, the labor dispute has not ended.	Two states (New York & Rhode Island)
Innocent bystander	Workers who are unemployed because of a labor dispute may qualify for benefits if they can show that they are not participating in, financing, and/or directly interested in the dispute.[a]	Approximately 44 states
Lockout	Workers may collect benefits if their employer is withholding available work in order to bring pressure to bear in support of his bargaining position, or to resist recognition of an employee bargaining agent.	21 states
Illegal actions by employers	Benefits are paid to workers if the employer is found to be the cause of the labor dispute, by refusing to conform to the provisions of a collective bargaining contract and/or by failing to comply with federal or state laws pertaining to collective bargaining or the terms and conditions of employment.	Nine states

Exhibit 2.1 (continued)

Exceptions:		**Prevalance as of 1984**
Interim employment	Workers are eligible for benefits if, after going on strike, they obtain bona fide interim jobs from which they are then laid off.	Several states including Massachusetts, Michigan, Missouri, and Illinois
Grade or class disqualification	A worker, regardless of his own level of participation in a labor dispute, is ineligible for benefits if he was, at the time of the commencement of the dispute, a member of a grade or class of workers any one of whom participated in, financed, or had a direct interest in the dispute.	Approximately 40 states

a. Innocent bystander statutes do not uniformly include all three conditions; requirements vary across states. In some jurisdictions, for example, a worker need only prove that he did not participate in the labor dispute in order to qualify for benefits.

The remaining states, most notably New York and Rhode Island, fall outside either of these two categories. Both New York and Rhode Island disqualify strikers in the early stages of a labor dispute, but allow strikers to collect benefits if a strike lasts longer than eight weeks (New York) or seven weeks (Rhode Island).

Most states will allow workers to collect benefits if they can show that they are not actually participating in, financing, or directly interested in the labor dispute. Such workers are often called "innocent bystanders." These workers may be unemployed because of a dispute, but if they are not picketing or otherwise aiding the strikers, do not help to finance strike benefits paid to the strikers, and do not stand to benefit from a settlement growing out of the strike, they will usually be allowed to collect unemployment benefits.

About 21 states pay benefits to workers if their employer has locked them out. These states do not believe workers should be denied benefits if the labor dispute is in fact the employer's fault. The remaining states do not distinguish between strikes and lockouts, disqualifying workers regardless of which side bears responsibility for the dispute.

Policy Development

The development of most state policies regarding the eligibility of strikers for unemployment compensation began with the passage of the Social Security Act in 1935. When Congress passed the Social Security Act, it provided the impetus for the establishment of a state-administered unemployment compensation system. The Social Security Act imposed a tax of 3 percent on the payrolls of all employers of eight or more employees.[1] The Act allowed a state to avoid up to 90 percent of this tax, however, if it passed legislation providing for the payment of benefits to unemployed workers. If the state's legislation met federal standards, the state could retain the bulk of the federal tax in a state-administered unemployment compensation fund. Benefits paid to eligible unemployed workers would be financed out of the monies collected in the fund. The portion of the payroll tax retained by the federal government would be used to assist the states in the administration of their unemployment compensation laws.[2]

All states and territories that had not previously enacted unemployment compensation legislation proceeded to pass such laws in the two years following the passage of the Social Security Act. To assist the states in the development and administration of their legislation, the Social Security Act created the Social Security Board as an independent agency. The Board was also charged with the task of deciding whether state laws qualified for the tax offset and allotting the funds appropriated for the administration of the state laws.[3]

The Board drew up several "Draft Bills for State Unemployment Compensation," modeled largely on state workers' compensation laws and the British Unemployment Insurance Act of 1911.[4] One of the Board's Draft Bills became the prototype for almost all state laws that were subsequently passed.[5] According to Edwin Witte, "Each of the (state) laws had some provisions different from every other law, but all had far more similarities than differences."[6] In fact, Hetherington reports, most states simply copied most of the provisions in the Social Security Board's Draft Bill and enacted their own legislation "in great haste and without a great deal of independent study."[7]

One of the provisions contained in the Draft Bill sought to disqualify workers whose unemployment was "due to a stoppage of work which exists because of a labor dispute at the factory, establishment or premises at which he is or was last employed."[8] The Draft Bill also recommended that such workers be allowed to collect benefits if they could show that they were "not participating in or financing or directly interested in the labor dispute which caused the stoppage of work" and "do not belong to a grade or class of workers of which, immediately before the commencement of the stoppage, there were members employed at the premises at which the stoppage occurs, any of whom are participating in or financing or directly interested in the dispute."[9] Most states included this language without modification in their unemployment compensation statutes. But, given the haste with which the laws were passed, it is unlikely that many legislators understood the implications of the labor dispute qualification provisions they were adopting.

Many of the problems that the states have encountered in administering and interpreting the labor dispute disqualification provisions stem from the fact that the key terms in the Draft Bill's recommendations were left undefined. For example, what precisely is a "labor dispute"? How does a labor dispute differ from a "stoppage-of-work"? What is an "establishment"? How should a state distinguish between those workers at an establishment who are "participating in or financing or directly interested in" a dispute from those who are not? What is a "grade or class" of workers?

State agencies and courts have had more than five decades to grapple with these terms. Out of a multitude of agency and judicial decisions, some common interpretations have developed, but there is also considerable diversity in the definitions. The differences in the treatment of workers involved in labor disputes has been multiplied by numerous revisions that states have made in their unemployment compensation laws down through the years. For example, several states have amended their statutes to exclude lockouts and other employer-caused disputes from the definition of "labor dispute." These amendments have often been passed as a result of a state's experience with particular labor disputes or in response to lobbying efforts by unions, employers, and other interested parties.[10]

The remainder of this chapter will be devoted to the fundamental questions each state must answer when formulating its policy on the use of unemployment compensation in labor disputes. First, does a labor dispute exist? If it does, is the claimant's unemployment the result of that labor dispute? How have the states and the federal courts interpreted the provision that holds that the labor dispute must be at the "establishment" where the worker was last employed? To aid the reader in understanding the complexities of the rules governing the eligibility of a claimant for unemployment compensation in a labor dispute, we will, in the next chapter, use flow charts that summarize the principal questions that must be answered in determining that eligibility.

But the exceptions used to remove a claimant's disqualification are numerous, and vary from state to state. For example, is the claimant in a state with a lockout exception? How is the lockout exception applied in such states? Has the claimant had other employment during the strike? How does interim employment affect striker eligibility for unemployment compensation? These questions will be discussed in this chapter.

The next chapter discusses the three rules that later become the focus of our empirical tests: the stoppage-of-work rule, the policies followed by New York and Rhode Island, and the innocent bystander provisions. Chapter 3 will also examine the most significant Supreme Court decision regarding unemployment compensation in labor disputes, the *New York Telephone* case. In this decision, the Court gave each state wide latitude to shape its own policy regarding striker eligibility for unemployment compensation.[11] Chapter 3 concludes with a discussion of unemployment insurance cases arising out of the air traffic controllers' strike in 1981.

What is a Labor Dispute?

With the exception of Alabama, Arizona, and Minnesota, the term "labor dispute" has not been defined in state unemployment compensation statutes.[12] As a result, it has fallen upon state administrative agencies and courts to formulate definitions of the term. Without statutory guidance, agencies and courts have frequently relied upon the definitions of "labor dispute" contained in federal statutes, such as the Norris-LaGuardia Act and National Labor Relations Act, or in state labor relations statutes.[13]

The Federal Unemployment Tax Act requires, for example, that unemployment compensation be paid to otherwise eligible claimants if they have refused to accept new work because "the position offered is vacant due directly to a strike, lockout, or other labor dispute."[14] This language suggests that Congress had a broad definition of labor dispute in mind—not one confined merely to strikes and lockouts, but one that encompasses other types of labor disputes as well. Arguably, picketing, secondary boycotts, jurisdictional disputes, representational disputes, and other forms of concerted activity fall within the definition of labor dispute. Workers away from their jobs because of their involvement in such activities would not, in most jurisdictions, be eligible for unemployment benefits.

Difficult questions arise when there is an absence of concerted activity or other forms of "manifest conflict," but it is nonetheless alleged that workers are unemployed because of the existence of a labor dispute. In 1946 the United States Supreme Court had occasion to consider such a situation.[15] The case arose when a group of Alaska cannery workers were laid off at the end of the fishing season, but before a new collective bargaining agreement had been negotiated with their employers.

The canneries then announced that they would not reopen for the new season unless the workers agreed to a new contract. The workers filed claims for unemployment benefits, arguing that the term "labor dispute," in the Court's words, must be "narrowly construed to require a strike or leaving of employment which, in turn, calls for a presently existing employment relation at the time the dispute arises. According to this view, the term would not cover a situation, such as presented here, where the controversy precedes the employment."[16]

The Court, however, rejected the argument of the cannery workers, holding that "the term, 'labor dispute,' has a broader meaning than that attributed to it by the respondents."[17] Although the Court did not believe that a "labor dispute" must always be construed "as broadly as it is defined in the Norris-LaGuardia Act and the National Labor

Relations Act,''[18] nevertheless it did find that there was a ''full-scale controversy'' between the workers' union and their employers.[19] Thus, the Court ruled that the workers were not eligible for benefits, even though their employment relationship had been severed and they were not engaging in a strike or any other form of concerted activity.

On the other hand, the Supreme Court did not accept a claim that a controversy arising out of an employee's charge that her employer had committed an unfair labor practice under the National Labor Relations Act constituted a ''labor dispute'' under the state's unemployment insurance statute. Florida had disqualified a union member for unemployment benefits because she had filed a charge against her employer with the National Labor Relations Board. A Florida court ruled that the filing of the charge initiated a ''labor dispute,'' thus disqualifying the worker for benefits under the state's unemployment insurance statute. In *Nash v. Florida Industrial Commission,* the Supreme Court concluded, ''Florida should not be permitted to defeat or handicap a valid national objective by threatening to withdraw state benefits from persons simply because they cooperate with the Government's constitutional plan.''[20] *Nash* suggests that the exercise of an employee's rights under a federal statute cannot be interpreted by a state as a ''labor dispute'' that disqualifies the employee for unemployment benefits. The term ''labor dispute'' cannot be defined so broadly that it encompasses every type of disagreement between an employer and an employee.

Nevertheless, as Lewis has pointed out, '' 'Labor dispute' as a threshold concept in unemployment compensation proceedings has come to include virtually any controversy affecting the terms and conditions of the employment situation, regardless of whether the disputants stand in an employer-employee relationship. The restrictive construction of 'labor dispute' has not received judicial acceptance.''[21] The broad construction given the term ''labor dispute'' means that employers have many opportunities to challenge their employees' entitlement to benefits if their employees' unemployment is arguably the result of a labor-management controversy.

But it must be emphasized that the finding that a labor dispute exists is only the first step in determining whether a worker involved in such a dispute is eligible for unemployment benefits. All but a handful of states remove a worker's disqualification for benefits, despite the existence of a labor dispute, if the worker falls under one of several "escape clauses," which we will presently discuss.

The Establishment Rule

In almost all jurisdictions, a worker is disqualified for benefits if the labor dispute is at the "factory, establishment, or premises at which he is or was last employed." Thus, as a general rule, a worker who is unemployed because of a strike at another, separate establishment is eligible for unemployment benefits, even if the establishment is owned and operated by his employer.

States have differed, however, in their definition of "establishment." Some states have defined establishment primarily on the basis of spatial or geographical terms. An establishment, under this approach, is a distinct physical place of business where the worker was last employed.[22] Two plants belonging to the same employer but in different cities would be considered separate establishments, and workers laid off at one of the plants because of a strike at the other would be eligible for benefits. The only problem, as Milton Shadur points out, is "how small to draw the circle of physical proximity."[23]

Other states, however, dismiss the significance of physical proximity and rely instead on a test that weighs the "functional integration" of the units regardless of the distance that separates them. In one early case, the Wisconsin Supreme Court considered a situation in which workers at a Racine automobile plant set up a picket line to protest management's plan to close the plant; as a consequence, workers at the company's Kenosha plant were laid off. The Wisconsin court ruled that the workers at both plants were ineligible for benefits, even though there was technically no strike at the Racine plant and no picketing or other concerted activity at the Kenosha plant. The court held that the workers were disqualified because there was a labor dispute in active progress at the Racine plant and the Racine and Kenosha plants were functionally integrated.[24]

Taken to its limit, the functional integration test could be applied to separate plants owned by different employers or even to plants located in different states. Most jurisdictions, however, have not been willing to apply the test that broadly, but instead have limited its application to functionally integrated establishments owned by the same employer within the same state.[25]

Almost all states will allow laid-off workers to collect benefits even if they are employed in a struck establishment but are engaged in a "separate branch of work" from the strikers.[26] Suppose, for example, an employer has two businesses located on the same premises. If a strike by the employees of the one business causes the employer to lay off the employees of the other business, the laid-off workers would be eligible for benefits by virtue of their being employed in a separate branch of work. Whether workers in a separate branch of work are permitted to collect benefits depends in part, however, on whether they are truly "innocent bystanders," that is, on whether in fact they all refrain from participating in or financing the labor dispute and have no direct interest in it.

Lockouts

Although Section 7 of the Taft-Hartley Act provides unions with the right to strike or to refrain from striking, the statute does not clearly establish the right of employers to lock out.[27] The National Labor Relations Board and the courts have vacillated over the question of whether the right of the employers to lock out is the corollary of the right of unions to strike.[28]

A lockout has been defined as "the employer's withholding of available work from employees hired to perform such work in order to obtain a change, or resist a change, in terms or conditions of employment, or to resist recognition of an employee bargaining agent."[29] It has clearly been established by the NLRB and the courts that the lockout can never be used to destroy the union or the union's bargaining rights.[30] Beyond that general principle, the NLRB has said that the employer's right to lock out depends on the circumstances of the individual case:

> The nature of the measures taken, the objective, the timing, the reality of the strike threat, the nature and extent of the

> anticipated disruption, and the degree of resultant restriction on the effectiveness of the concerted activity, are all matters to be weighed in determining the reasonableness under the circumstances, and the ultimate legality, of the employer's action.[31]

The NLRB and the courts have consistently recognized the employer's right to lock out in two situations: to protect the employer against the threat of a strike that might result in "unusual economic hardship" and to preserve the institution of multiemployer bargaining. In both these situations, the lockout is considered a "defensive" weapon that may lawfully be used by employers. In the former situation, the Board has particularly been tolerant of lockouts if the parties' contract has expired and the employer is uncertain about the timing of a strike by the union. In the latter situation, the board and the courts have approved an employer lockout if the employer is a member of a multiemployer association that has traditionally bargained with the union, and the union has struck one or more of the other members of the association. Where there has been a history of multiemployer bargaining, an employer lockout in reprisal for a strike against other employers in the association has been deemed a lawful action by the Supreme Court.[32]

Several ambiguities have attended the legality of a lockout when it is used by the employer as an "offensive" weapon. In the American Ship Building case, the Supreme Court held that a single employer's right to shut down his plant "for the sole purpose of exerting economic pressure against a union and in support of a lawful bargaining position" was lawful, provided the employer had bargained in good faith to an impasse with the union.[33] The NLRB, however, has ruled that an offensive lockout becomes unlawful when an employer hires permanent replacements.[34] Moreover, although the employer's right to hire temporary replacements during a defensive lockout has been clearly established,[35] the employer's right to do so during an offensive lockout has been problematic.[36]

In recent years, however, the Board has been more tolerant of offensive lockouts and use of temporary replacements. The Supreme Court's ruling in *American Ship Building* has been extended to pre-impasse offensive lockouts.[37] Furthermore, the right to use temporary replacements during an offensive lockout was substantially expanded in *Harter Equipment.*[38] The Board, in this case, held that "an employer does not violate Section 8(a)(3) and (1), absent specific proof of antiunion motivation, by using temporary employees in order to engage in business operations during an otherwise lawful lockout, including a lockout initiated for the sole purpose of bringing economic pressure to bear in support of a legitimate bargaining position."[39] The decision has not been appealed and has been consistently applied to subsequent cases involving the use of temporary replacements during an offensive lockout.[40] The test for legality in lockout cases, then, is no longer a balance of competing interests between employers' business concerns and employees' statutory rights. An offensive lockout is currently considered lawful unless initiated in support of bad faith bargaining or if motivated by antiunion animus. Since a struck employer's right to hire permanent or temporary replacements has long been recognized,[41] limitations on the scope of similar employer behavior during a lockout suggest that under federal labor policy the employer's right to lock out is not precisely the corollary of the union's right to strike.

The distinctions that have been crafted in federal labor policy, however, have not had much influence on state policies regarding the payment of unemployment benefits to locked-out employees. As Willard Lewis has pointed out, court decisions involving unemployment insurance statutes have not been "distracted by 'offensive-defensive' or like tortious considerations of the underlying labor disputes."[42] Initially, as noted previously, state policies were principally influenced by the Social Security Board's "Draft Bill," which in turn had been based largely on the British unemployment insurance act. The British statute disqualified employees unemployed because of a labor dispute from receiving unemployment compensation, and defined "labor dispute" to cover both strikes and lockouts.[43]

Although the majority of states continue to deny unemployment benefits to employees without work because of a lockout, 21 currently pay benefits to such workers.[44] Evidently states with lockout provisions believe that workers who have been locked out are involuntarily unemployed in the sense that they are willing and able to work but are prevented from doing so by the action of their employer. Defenders of the lockout exception maintain that a state that refuses to pay benefits to locked-out employees violates the principle of state neutrality in labor-management relationships.[45] Moreover, in a state without a lockout exception, an employer facing a business downturn can avoid the increase in unemployment insurance taxes that would follow the layoff of his employees by "provoking a dispute and then locking out his employees instead of laying them off."[46] Thus, a lockout rule serves to close a loophole in the unemployment compensation tax system.

Critics of the lockout exception have argued that it is inconsistent to grant an employer the (qualified) right to lock out under federal law, but to allow his employees to collect unemployment benefits under state law if the employer uses the weapon. They have argued that such state policies frustrate the operation of the National Labor Relations Act, and that a state's attempt to distinguish between a lockout and a strike is "discriminatory, arbitrary, and capricious."[47]

Fierst and Spector, writing in 1940, thought that the effort of several states to distinguish between a strike and a lockout was "quixotic." These authors noted the "enormous" administrative difficulties of making such distinctions on a case-by-case basis.[48] On the other hand, Fierst and Spector thought that denying benefits to locked-out employees would work an inequity on employees by unreasonably enhancing the bargaining power of employers.[49] Thus, the advisability of a lockout provision depends in part on whether the difficulties of administering the provision are outweighed by the state's interest in maintaining a reasonable balance of power between labor and management.

Predictions that a lockout rule would impose heavy administrative burdens on state unemployment insurance agencies are borne out in our survey of those agencies and by an examination of the decisions of the agencies and courts. States with lockout provisions have had to grapple with a variety of vexing issues. For example, since state unemployment compensation statutes do not define "lockout," there has been extensive litigation concerning definitional issues. Cases that involve employers who have "physically" locked out their employees do not generally present major difficulties. The harder cases deal with employers who unilaterally change the terms and conditions of employment after reaching a bargaining impasse with the union. When is a unilateral change so unreasonable as to constitute a lockout? Minnesota and Pennsylvania, two states with lockout provisions, represent contrasting approaches to this question.

In 1980, Local 4-P of the United Food and Commercial Workers Union and Sunstar Foods, Inc., a beef-slaughtering and packing company in Minnesota, reached impasse in contract negotiations over the employer's demand to reduce wages by approximately 20 percent. Union members walked off their jobs after Sunstar imposed its proposed wage scale unilaterally. Because of Minnesota's lockout provision, most of the workers then filed claims for unemployment benefits.

The claims deputy for the Minnesota Department of Employment Security determined that the claimants were ineligible for benefits because they were participating in a labor dispute. The Appeals Tribunal affirmed the decision of the claims deputy. But the workers then appealed the determination to the commissioner of the DES, and he reversed the ruling of the Appeals Tribunal. In his view, the workers were separated from their employment because of a lockout. The case went to the Minnesota Supreme Court, where Sunstar argued that since it had offered work to the employees, albeit at a substantially lower wage, there had been no lockout. The employees argued that the unilateral imposition by Sunstar of employment terms so unreasonable that the employees had no alternative but to leave did indeed constitute a lockout.

The Minnesota Court examined a large number of judicial decisions in jurisdictions with lockout provisions, seeking guidance on the question of whether Sunstar's action had been so harsh as to constitute a lockout. In an earlier decision by the Minnesota Court, for example, an employer's unilateral wage cut of 2 to 4 percent had not been ruled a lockout.[50] But in cases in other states involving employer wage reductions of 15, 20, and 25 percent, the Courts had found the employers to be engaged in a lockout and permitted the claimants to collect benefits. The Minnesota Court seemed to suggest that if a unilateral wage reduction amounted to less than 15 percent, the ensuing work stoppage should not be considered a lockout. But if the wage reduction were greater than 15 percent, the employer's action was so unreasonable that it had to be considered a lockout.[51]

Clearly, such a rule may be administratively convenient but it is also highly arbitrary. It gives no weight to whether the employer and the union had bargained in good faith (an issue that was never raised in the *Sunstar* case) or to whether the employer's action was or was not justified by his financial condition. Moreover, the Minnesota Court probably overestimated its ability to find a general rule on wage reductions in the decisions of other state courts; we have found state practice to vary so greatly on this issue that seeking a general standard is probably a chimera.

Arguably, Pennsylvania interprets the lockout rule more liberally than any other state.[52] It not only insists that the employer bargain in good faith, but also requires that if the parties' contract has expired, the terms and conditions that existed under the contract must be maintained until a new agreement is reached. According to the acting executive director of Pennsylvania's Office of Employment Security, "If the employer withholds work or fails to honor all of the terms and conditions of the prior agreement, the resultant stoppage is a lockout."[53] Thus, in Pennsylvania, a work stoppage that results from any unilateral change of the wage scale by the employer following the expiration of a contract would be considered a lockout, and the affected employees would be deemed eligible to collect unemployment benefits.[54]

In a leading Pennsylvania case, a union of oil refinery workers failed to reach agreement with the Sun Oil Company before the expiration of an existing contract. For five weeks after the termination of the contract the parties worked on a day-to-day basis. When a federal mediator certified that an impasse had been reached, Sun Oil began to implement its contract proposals unilaterally. Union members responded by walking off their jobs. The Unemployment Compensation Board of Review held that a lockout had occurred because of the company's "unreasonable" action and the refinery workers collected unemployment benefits. Sun Oil took the case to the United States Supreme Court, which dismissed the appeal "for want of a substantial, federal question."[55]

According to one authority, "Pennsylvania has adopted a position both difficult to understand and difficult to justify."[56] Our Pennsylvania correspondent notes that as a result of his state's definition of a lockout, "union members have become more successful in gaining benefits in . . . work stoppages at any time. This has created serious problems for service industries, light manufacturers, and . . . school districts."[57] Clearly Pennsylvania's broad definition of a lockout differs substantially from the treatment of lockouts by the NLRB and the federal courts. Yet, given the Supreme Court's decisions in the *Sun Oil* and *New York Telephone* cases, the Court obviously intends to tolerate such diversity.

Related to the lockout rules in unemployment insurance laws are those statutory provisions that pay benefits to workers if the employer is found to be the cause of the labor dispute. Seven states pay strikers benefits if the employer has refused to conform to the provisions of a collective bargaining contract. Seven states pay benefits if the employer has failed to comply with any federal or state laws pertaining to collective bargaining or the terms and conditions of employment. (Five of these states—Alaska, Arizona, Maine, Minnesota, and New Hampshire—have both of these provisions in their statutes.[58]) Lewis has written, "Such exclusions from the labor dispute definition on the basis of illegal actions by employers leaves the state employment security agency charged with the double duty of policing the collective agreement and interpreting federal law. This makes possible inconsistent interpretations of the same law by federal and state courts."[59] Our research, however, suggests that these provisions are considered neither particularly significant nor a cause of much concern.[60] No doubt this view stems in part from the fact that so few states have such provisions. Also, the use of contract grievance procedures and arbitration has dramatically reduced the number of strikes occurring because of employer violations of collective bargaining agreements. On the other hand, one might expect that the growth of federal regulation of the workplace would have resulted in more strikes over alleged employer violations of federal law. The parties, however, generally avoid the use of economic weapons to resolve disputes over their adherence to federal regulations, preferring instead to use their own grievance procedures or to have the appropriate agencies and the courts settle such issues.[61]

Interim Employment

Several states, including Massachusetts, Michigan, Missouri, and Illinois, pay unemployment benefits to employees who, after going on strike, obtain *bona fide* interim jobs from which they are then laid off.[62] In several states the courts have wrestled with the problem of drawing the line between interim (or temporary) and permanent jobs. In Florida, for example, a striker took a job that, in "good faith," he expected to be permanent. Nine months later he was laid off. The court then ruled that he qualified for jobless pay.[63]

In other states, attempts by strikers to obtain unemployment benefits after a period of temporary employment have been unsuccessful. The courts in most states seek to determine whether a striker who obtains new work has severed his employment relationship with the struck employer. Most courts have ruled that obtaining new work does not by itself indicate that the striker has severed his prior employment relationship. They have ruled instead that a striker's unemployment following an interim job is actually due to the labor dispute and not to the layoff by the new employer.[64]

In 1968 Michigan developed a contrary rule in *Great Lakes Steel Corp. v. Michigan Employment Security Commission*.[65] There the court interpreted the Michigan statute to allow strikers to collect benefits even when they had worked on interim jobs for as little as one day and their labor dispute with their regular employer had yet to be resolved.[66] In 1974 the Michigan statute was amended in an attempt to clarify the meaning of "*bona fide* interim employment." The Michigan statute now holds that a striker's disqualification for unemployment benefits is terminated by the striker "performing services in employment in at least two consecutive weeks falling wholly within the period of the individual's total or partial unemployment due to the labor dispute."[67]

In a letter to the authors, the director of the Bureau of Unemployment Insurance, Michigan Employment Security Commission, offered his interpretation of the state's interim employment rule: "In each consecutive week the individual must earn wages in excess of [his] potential weekly benefit rate based on wages earned with the labor dispute employer."[68] Thus, it would appear possible for a striker in Michigan to work as little as one day in each of two consecutive weeks on an interim job to qualify for unemployment benefits.

Two strikes against the Dow Chemical Company illustrated how the Michigan rule operates in practice. In 1972, 166 workers represented by District 50, Allied and Technical Workers Union, went on strike against Dow's Bay City plant. (The Bay City local later became part of the United Steelworkers Union.) At first the strikers were declared ineligible for unemployment benefits. "But, at the urging of their local, many immediately took advantage of the 1968 court decision that held that any striker who takes an interim job and is then laid off can qualify for compensation—even if he works only one day. Of 166 who struck, at least 135 took jobs with 'friendly' employers, many in local bars, earning as little as $1 to $18 to qualify for weekly benefits."[69]

In 1974, workers at Dow's Midland, Michigan plant went on strike and once again the union urged the strikers to obtain interim jobs with "friendly" employers. Most of the strikers did so, were laid off, and then collected unemployment benefits for the duration of the strike. The strike lasted 26 weeks and was settled precisely at the point when most strikers' eligibility for benefits was about to expire. In an *amicus* brief submitted to the Supreme Court in the *New York Telephone* case, Dow charged, "This utilization of benefits was not fortuitous or unplanned but was, in fact, a part of the Steelworkers' comprehensive strike and defense program used by its local affiliates, in conjunction with allotments from the [Steelworkers'] Strike and Defense Fund, to aid local members in withstanding the financial pressure of a strike situation."[70]

Under Michigan's experience rating provisions, only a proportional part of the strikers' benefits was assessed against their interim employers. Therefore, almost all of the benefits paid to the Dow strikers were charged to that company. As a result, Dow was ordered to pay most of the $3,400,000 that had been disbursed to the strikers in Bay City and Midland.[71] Dow challenged the Michigan law in the courts, arguing that payment of unemployment benefits to striking workers who had obtained and then been laid off from temporary jobs interfered with the employer's "federally protected right to bargain collectively."[72] The suit was dismissed by the district court, but the court retained jurisdiction and ordered that Dow not be charged with the expense of the unemployment benefits.[73]

Summary

In this chapter we have provided an overview of the development of public policy with respect to the use of unemployment compensation in labor disputes. We have also discussed the fundamental issues that all states consider in determining striker eligibility for unemployment benefits, including the definition of a "labor dispute" and the interpretation of the establishment rule. Last, we examined two sets of circumstances that some states consider adequate to remove the disqualification of strikers for unemployment compensation. The first set of circumstances involved lockouts and other employer-caused disputes; the second set involved strikers who obtain, and are then laid off from, interim jobs.

A theme of the chapter is the diversity across states in the treatment of workers away from their jobs because of a labor dispute. Although all states define a labor dispute in broad terms, they otherwise vary in their treatment of the establishment rule, lockouts, and interim employment. This theme is carried over into the next chapter where we take up the three unemployment insurance provisions that are arguably the most important rules affecting striker eligibility for benefits.

NOTES

1. 49 Stat. 620 (1953), 42 U.S.C. §301 (1940); William Haber and Merrill G. Murray, *Unemployment Insurance in the American Economy* (Homewood, Ill.: Richard D. Irwin, 1966), pp. 76-89; Edwin E. Witte, "Development of Unemployment Compensation," *Yale Law Journal*, Vol. 55, No. 1 (December 1945), p. 32. Five states passed unemployment compensation legislation prior to the passage of the Social Security Act. Wisconsin passed its unemployment compensation statute in 1931. California, Massachusetts, New Hampshire, and New York adopted unemployment compensation laws shortly before the passage of the Social Security Act. See *Baker v. General Motors Corp.*, 106 S.Ct. 3129 at 3136, n.25 (1986).

2. Ibid.

3. Witte, pp. 32-35.

4. U.S. Social Security Board, *Draft Bills for State Unemployment Compensation of Pooled Funds and Employer Reserve Account Types,* Washington, D.C., 1936; W. Joseph Hetherington, "Federal Preemption of State Welfare and Unemployment Benefits for Strikers," *Harvard Civil Rights and Civil Liberties Law Review,* Vol. 12, No. 2 (1977), pp. 455-456; Milton I. Shadur, "Unemployment Benefits and the 'Labor Dispute' Disqualification," *The University of Chicago Law Review,* Vol. 17, No. 2 (Winter 1950), pp. 294-295.

5. Witte, pp. 33-34.

6. Ibid., p. 34.

7. Hetherington, pp. 455-456.

8. U.S. Social Security Board, "Draft Bill," §1 (5) (1936).

9. Ibid.

10. Our surveys and interviews with union and employer representatives and with state employment security agency officials uncovered numerous accounts of these efforts.

11. *New York Telephone Co. v. New York State Department of Labor,* 440 U.S. 519 (1979).

12. U.S. Department of Labor, Employment and Training Administration, *Comparison of State Unemployment Insurance Laws,* Washington, D.C., 1984, p. 4-12 (hereafter cited as *Comparison*); see also, Willard A. Lewis, "The Concept of 'Labor Dispute' in State Unemployment Insurance Laws," *Boston College Industrial and Commercial Law Review,* Vol. 8, No. 1 (Fall 1966), pp. 29-54.

13. Lewis, "Concept of 'Labor Dispute,'" pp. 30-33.

14. 26 U.S.C. §3304 (a) (5) (1976). For a discussion of this "struck work" provision, see Brian R. Whitehead, "Unemployment Benefits, Laid-Off Workers, and Labor Disputes: The Unemployment Benefit Conflict," *Willamette Law Review,* Vol. 19 (Fall 1983), pp. 737-756.

15. *Unemployment Compensation Commission v. Aragon,* 329 U.S. 143, 91 L.ed. 136 (1946).

16. Ibid. at 142.

17. Ibid. at 143.

18. Ibid. at 143.

19. Ibid. at 143.

20. *Nash v. Florida Industrial Commission,* 389 U.S. 235 (1967) at 239.

21. Lewis, "Concept of 'Labor Dispute,'" p. 53.

22. See, for example, *Ahne v. Department of Labor and Industrial Relations,* 53 Ha. 185, 489 P. 2d 1397 (1971); *In re Curatala,* 10 N.W. 2d 10, 176 N.E. 2d 1397 (1971); *In re Ferrara,* 217 N.Y. 2d 11, 176 N.E. 2d 43 (1961); *Northwest Airlines, Inc. v. App. Bd.*, 378 Mich. 119, 142 N.W. 2d 649 (1966); *Abuie v. Ford Motor Co.*, 194 N.E. 2d 136 (1963).

23. Shadur, p. 321.

24. *Spielman v. Industrial Comm'n.*, 236 Wis. 240 N.W. 1 (1940).

25. The two major exceptions are Michigan and Ohio. Michigan defines establishment to include any employing unit within the United States that is functionally integrated with an employing unit where a strike is occurring. Ohio defines establishment to include any employing unit located in the United States that is owned or operated by the employer. See *Comparison,* p. 4-12. See also, *Chrysler Corp. v. Smith,* 297 Mich. 438, 298 N.W. 2d 87 (1941); *Adamski v. BUC,* 161

N.E. 2d 907 (Ohio, 1959). In 1966, ground crews conducted a nationwide strike against the major airlines, causing the layoff of flight personnel. A Michigan court ruled, however, that the flight personnel were not part of the same "establishment" as the ground crews and could therefore collect unemployment benefits. See, *McAnallen v. ESC,* 26 Mich. App. 621, 182 N.W. 2d 753 (1970). See also, *Park v. ESC,* 353 Mich. 613, 94 N.W. 2d 407 (1959).

26. Shadur, pp. 323-324.

27. Benjamin J. Taylor and Fred Witney, *Labor Relations Law,* 4th ed. (Englewood Cliffs, N.J.: Prentice-Hall, 1983), pp. 484-489; Willard A. Lewis, "The 'Lockout as Corollary of Strike' Controversy Reexamined," *Labor Law Journal,* Vol. 23, No. 11 (November 1972), pp. 659-670.

28. Ibid.

29. Lewis, "The 'Lockout as Corollary of Strike'," p. 660.

30. Taylor and Witney, p. 484.

31. *Betts Cadillac-Olds, Inc.*, 96 NLRB 268 (1951).

32. *NLRB v. Truck Drivers Local Union No. 449 (Buffalo Linen Supply Co.),* 353 U.S. 85 (1959). See also, Taylor and Witney, pp. 485-487 and Lewis, "The 'Lockout as Corollary of Strike'," pp. 660-662.

33. *American Ship Building Co. v. NLRB,* 380 U.S. 300 (1965). See also, Lewis, "The 'Lockout as Corollary of Strike'," pp. 661.

34. *Johns-Manville Products Corp.*, 223 NLRB 189 (1976). Recall that "offensive" lockouts are usually those that occur in single-employer bargaining relationships or where the employer does not face unusual hardship.

35. *NLRB v. Brown, et al. d/b/a Brown Food Store, et al.*, 380 U.S. 278 (1965).

36. In *Inland Trucking Company v. NLRB,* 440 F.2d 562 (1971), the court ruled that an employer who locked out his employees after reaching a bargaining impasse with the union and hired temporary replacements was in violation of the NLRA.

37. See, e.g., *Darling & Co.*, 171 NLRB 801 (1968); *Lane v. NLRB,* 418 F.2nd 1208 (1969).

38. *Harter Equipment,* 280 NLRB 77 (1986).

39. Ibid. at 11-12.

40. See, e.g., *Birkenwald, Inc.*, 282 NLRB 130 (1987).

41. *NLRB v. MacKay Radio and Telegraph Co.*, 304 U.S. 333 (1938).

42. Lewis, "The 'Lockout as Corollary of Strike'," p. 668.

43. Lewis, "Concept of 'Labor Dispute'," pp. 29-31. Comment (by David R. Confer), "Pennsylvania's Lockout Exception to the Labor Dispute Disqualification from Unemployment Compensation Benefits: Federal Challenges and Issues," *Dickinson Law Review,* Vol. 80 (1975), p. 72.

44. In two of the 21 jurisdictions, the payment of benefits has been mandated by judicial decisions. In the other 19, the state's unemployment insurance statute contains a lockout exception. See, *Comparison,* p. 4-12 and Table 405; James T. Carney, "The Forgotten Man on the Welfare Roll: A Study of Public Subsidies for Strikers," *Washington University Law Quarterly,* Vol. 1973, No. 3 (Summer 1973), p. 499.

45. Herbert A. Fierst and Marjorie Spector, "Unemployment Compensation in Labor Disputes," *The Yale Law Journal,* Vol. 49, No. 3 (January 1940), pp. 479-481; Leonard Lesser, "Labor Disputes and Unemployment Compensation," *Yale Law Journal,* Vol. 55, No. 1 (1945), pp. 172-176.

46. Carney, p. 488.

47. This was the argument made by the employer in *Holland Motor Express, Inc. v. Michigan Employment Security Commission,* 42 Mich. App. 19, 201 N.W. 2d 308 (1972). The court, however, rejected the argument and held that the state's distinction between strikes and lockouts was not an irrational classification.

48. Fierst and Spector, p. 479. Carney, p. 499, called the administrative problem a "nightmare."

49. Fierst and Spector, pp. 480-481.

50. *Hessler v. American Television and Radio Co.*, 258 Minn. 541, 104 N.W. 2d 876 (1980).

51. *Sunstar Foods, Inc. v. Uhlendorf,* 310 N.W. 2d 80 (1981).

52. Confer, p. 75.

53. Letter from Wendel K. Pass, acting executive director, Office of Employment Security, Pennsylvania Department of Labor and Industry, to the authors, December 17, 1981.

54. See, e.g., *Lee National Corp. v. Board of Review,* 187 Pa. Super. 96, 211 A.2d 124 (1965); *Mackintosh-Hemphill Div., E.W. Bliss Co. v. Board of Review,* 205 Pa. Super. 9, 106 A.2d 23 (1965); *Penn Manufacturing Corp. v. Board of Review,* 215 Pa. Super. 310, 264 A.2d 126 (1969); *Vrotney Unemployment Compensation Case,* 400 Pa. 440, 163 A.2d 91 (1960). See also Confer, pp. 73-76.

55. *Sun Oil Co. of Pennsylvania v. Unemployment Compensation Review Board,* 440 U.S. 977, 100 LRRM 3055 (1979). See also, *Local 730 v. Unemployment Compensation Review Board,* 480 A.2d 1000 (1984).

56. Confer, p. 75.

57. Letter from Pass to authors.

58. *Comparison,* p. 4-12 and table 405.

59. Willard A. Lewis, "The Law of Unemployment Compensation in Labor Disputes," *Labor Law Journal,* Vol. 113, No. 2 (February 1962), p. 183.

60. Hetherington, pp. 487-488, expresses a similar view.

61. For a discussion of how unions and employers use joint committees and grievance procedures to resolve possible violations of the Occupational Safety and Health Act, see Thomas A. Kochan, Lee Dyer, and David B. Lipsky, *The Effectiveness of Union-Management Safety and Health Committees* (Kalamazoo, Mich.: W.E. Upjohn Institute, 1977).

62. *Comparison,* table 405: Brief for the New York State Department of Labor at 8, *New York Telephone Co. v. New York State Department of Labor,* 440 U.S. 519 (1979) as reprinted in *New York Telephone Co. v. New York State Department of Labor, Petitions and Briefs,* Law Reprints Labor Series (1978-1979 Term). For example, the Missouri statute reads, in part, that a claimant shall be ineligible for benefits if his unemployment is "due to a stoppage of work which exists because of a labor dispute . . . provided, that in the event he secures other employment from which he is separated during the employment as a permanent employee for at least the major part of each of two weeks in such subsequent employment to terminate his ineligibility." Missouri

Employment Security Law, Chapter 288.040, §5 (1). (December 1980). Illinois' interim employment rule was promulgated by the state's Supreme Court in *Dienes v. Holland,* 78 Ill.2d 8, 397 N.E.2d 1358 (1979). The Employment Security Administrator of the Illinois Bureau of Employment Security commented on this decision: "Prior to *Dienes* . . . all employment, absent a bona fide severance from the disqualifying employer, was looked upon as an intervening, 'stop-gap' measure, something to tide the worker over until he could return to his regular employer. We have interpreted *Dienes* to mean that employment elsewhere (and then layoff therefrom) within the period of the work stoppage due to the dispute will be curative of the labor dispute disqualification if that intervening employment can be shown to have been: (a) for a minimum of one full calendar week; and (b) substantially full time." Letter from Agaliece W. Miller, Employment Security Administrator, Illinois Bureau of Employment Security, to the authors, December 11, 1981.

63. *Bruly v. Ind. Comm.*, 100 So.2d 22 (Fla. 1958). Florida also allowed a striker who had been employed on a new job for two months to collect unemployment compensation. *Labinsky v. Ind. Comm.*, 167 So.2d 620 (Fla. 1964).

64. Carney, p. 502. See, e.g., *Cruz v. Department of Employment Security,* 22 Utah 393, 453 P.2d 894 (1969); *Evans v. Ind. Comm.*, 361 S.W.2d 332 (Mo. 1962); *Scott v. Unemployment Comp. Comm'n.*, 141 Mont. 230, 376 P.2d 733 (1962); *Brechner v. Ind. Comm'n.*, 148 So.2d 567 (1963); *In re Hatch,* 130 Vt. 218, 290 A.2d 180 (1972); *Mark Hopkins, Inc. v. Employment Comm'n.*, 24 Cal.2d 744, 151 P.2d 229 (1944); *McAllister v. Board of Rev.*, 197 Pa. Super. 552, 179 A.2d 121 (1962).

65. 381 Mich. 249, 161 N.W.2d 14 (1968).

66. Ibid. See also, Carney, p. 502.

67. MESA §29 (8). Letter from Thomas S. Malek, director, Bureau of Unemployment Insurance, Michigan Employment Security Commission, to the authors, January 29, 1982.

68. Letter from Malek.

69. "Loopholes Give Extra Aid to Strikers," *Business Week,* September 9, 1972, p. 36. See also, Carney, pp. 502-503, 511, and "How Your Tax Dollars Support Strikes," *Nation's Business,* March 1973, p. 25.

70. Brief Amici Curiae on Behalf of Dow Chemical Co., *et al.* at 15, *New York Telephone Co. v. New York State Department of Labor,* 440 U.S. 519 (1979).

71. Ibid. at 15-17.

72. *Dow Chemical Co. v. Taylor,* 57 F.R.D. 105 at 107 (1972).

73. Ibid. See also, Carney, p. 311.

3
Unemployment Compensation in Labor Disputes
Part II

One of the most common misconceptions about unemployment compensation in labor disputes is that only two states—New York and Rhode Island—have provisions authorizing payment of benefits to workers unemployed because of a strike. Even putative experts on this topic sometimes maintain the fiction that the practice is confined to two states. For example, one authority made the case against the payment of unemployment benefits to strikers in the following terms:

> The only redeeming factor of programs calling for unemployment compensation to persons involved in a labor dispute is that they are the practice in only two states. The misguided policy of two state legislatures has created an inequitable, albeit legal, arrangement that does injustice to employers and to the collective bargaining process as well.[1]

Quite apart from this author's normative judgments about the practice, he simply errs in believing other jurisdictions never pay unemployment benefits to strikers. We have already examined, in the previous chapter, some of the conditions under which workers in labor disputes will qualify for benefits. In this chapter, we will first discuss the most important exception to the general rule that "strikers never collect benefits": the stoppage-of-work provision, which is in the statutes of more than half the states. Although many authorities seem to believe that the little-known stoppage-of-work provision is a statutory oddity of little consequence, we will argue in this chapter and later, on the basis of our empirical results, that the provision is critically important.

This chapter next examines the policies of New York and Rhode Island. We maintain that it is another misperception to believe that New

York has the most liberal policy regarding striker eligibility for unemployment compensation. On the contrary, we will argue that New York's policy is *less* liberal than the policies of many other states, particularly those that have lockout, interim employment, stoppage-of-work, and innocent bystander provisions. Since New York does not use such qualifying provisions, and since very few strikes last longer than eight weeks, only a small minority of strikers ever collect benefits under New York's law.

A large majority of states recognize an obligation to protect workers who are unemployed because of a labor dispute but are not involved in the dispute. Accordingly, the next section of this chapter analyzes "innocent bystander" provisions. It is particularly important to understand these provisions because of the role they will play in our empirical tests. We also examine "grade or class" provisions, which to some extent dovetail with innocent bystander rules.

In 1981 the nation's air traffic controllers went out on strike, in violation of a federal law prohibiting strikes by federal employees. When the striking controllers refused to obey President Reagan's order that they go back to work, the president discharged them. Subsequently, many of these controllers filed claims for unemployment compensation. The treatment of these claims by state agencies and the courts is considered in the last section of this chapter. The story of the air traffic controllers graphically illustrates the disparate experience of strikers under our unemployment insurance statutes.

Stoppage-of-Work Provisions

Approximately 27 state unemployment compensation statutes contain so-called stoppage-of-work provisions.[2] These provisions allow strikers to collect benefits if an existing labor dispute has not caused a cessation or substantial curtailment of operations at the plant or establishment where the strikers are employed. Eligible strikers in work-stoppage states can collect benefits from the outset of a strike (or, more precisely, after the normal waiting period, which in most states is one week after the claimant has filed for benefits). In the statistical analysis contained in this study (see chapter 6), we will provide evidence that the work-stoppage rule does affect the level of strike activity in a state.

It is therefore particularly important to consider the implications of a work-stoppage provision.

In effect, such provisions allow strikers to collect unemployment compensation if their strike has failed—that is, if the strikers have been unable to shut down their employer or otherwise cause a significant decrease in the level of his operations. As the figure 3.1 shows, in work-stoppage states, if a strike succeeds in forcing employers to close down or to reduce the scale of their operations significantly, the strikers cannot collect unemployment benefits (unless the state has other "exceptions" that remove the strikers' disqualification). But if employers hire replacements (or strike-breakers) or are able to use supervisors or other nonstriking employees to continue to operate at or near normal levels, the strikers can collect benefits. Thus, in work-stoppage states, unemployment benefits become a kind of insurance against a failed strike.[3]

Under British law it had been established that the clause did not pertain to a stoppage-of-work by an individual employee; rather the law had been construed by the British Tribunal and British courts to pertain to a stoppage-of-work at the establishment where the striker was employed.[4] Using British precedents, most states adopted this interpretation of the work-stoppage rule.[5] In addition, most work-stoppage states will qualify strikers for benefits even if the plant or establishment is operating at only 75 or 80 percent of normal levels.[6] Hetherington has discussed the rationale for the work-stoppage rule:

> [The] state interest in granting benefits to strikers is greater in cases where the strikers have failed to shut down their employer. For in these cases the employer ordinarily prevents a shutdown by hiring replacements for the strikers, and the fact of replacement represents a drastic change in the strikers' employment status. While they are technically still employees under the NLRA, they often have little prospect of getting their jobs back. Thus they are in essentially the same position as workers who have permanently lost their jobs because the employer has replaced them with machines or gone out of business. A state would have good reason, then, for giving them the same compensation as it provides those workers.[7]

In adopting the work-stoppage rule, the initial motivation of British and American lawmakers may have been to protect striking employees in cases where the employer had broken their strike by hiring permanent replacements. But in recent years an increasing number of employers have been able and willing to operate during strikes without depending on replacements to do so. Automation and other forms of new technology have given many employers the technical capacity to operate during strikes. The increasingly competitive markets in which many American companies conduct business have also strengthened employers' resolve to protect their sales, revenues, and profits by operating during a strike. Plant operation during strikes also grew in part because of high unemployment rates during the 1970s and early 1980s: struck employers wishing to hire replacements had a large, available pool of workers from which to draw new employees. The erosion of union strength and solidarity is also related to the increase in the number of employers who operate during strikes (although in this regard cause and effect are difficult to disentangle). Finally, some employers have been influenced by the perceived success of the federal government in operating the nation's air traffic control system despite a walkout in 1981 by virtually all of the controllers in the country.[8] We will give this strike a closer look at the end of this chapter.

It can be assumed that a company's decision to operate during a strike may give it the bargaining power it needs to force the union to accept a settlement on (or close to) the employer's terms. It is perhaps the case that the growing number of employers who operate during a strike may choose to do so out of a desire to "break the strike" or even "break the union." But recent research suggests that employer decisions in this regard are primarily motivated by strategic considerations related to the employer's market position. This assertion is demonstrated by the fact that most employers who operate during strikes nowadays consider the hiring of permanent replacements only as a last resort. As Perry, Dramer, and Schneider conclude, "For the most part . . . plant operation has not been perceived or practiced as a weapon to enable an employer to break a union."[9]

In the past, employer operation during a strike was a rarity in American labor relations. In the immediate post-World War II period the practice was largely confined to high technology industries such as oil refining, telephones, and broadcasting. In recent years, however, the practice has spread to more labor-intensive industries, such as newspapers, hotels, paper, and shipbuilding.[10] The trend to employer operation during strikes magnifies the importance of the work-stoppage rule. Such provisions may have had little practical significance in the era when employers routinely shut down their plants during strikes. But in work-stoppage states, it is probably the case that the growth of plant operation during strikes has resulted in growth in the number of strikers collecting unemployment benefits. Moreover, the use and cost of unemployment compensation under work-stoppage provisions should have a growing influence on the parties' relative bargaining power and hence on the frequency and duration of strikes.[11]

Curiously, most authorities on this topic have failed to recognize the significance of the work-stoppage rule. For example, Hetherington speculated that the work-stoppage rule was likely to have less impact than other rules allowing strikers to collect unemployment benefits:

> In pre-strike bargaining, for instance, [the work-stoppage rule] is not likely to have much influence on either the employer or the employees; for both, the prospect of the employees collecting unemployment benefits at the employer's expense will be balanced by the knowledge that this prospect will be realized only if the strike fails. Nor is there likely to be much of an effect on either side after a strike has begun and failed: at this point the relative bargaining power of employer and employees will be fixed by the failure of the strike, not by the availability of unemployment benefits to the strikers.[12]

Hetherington, however, does not supply any evidence to support his view. A contrary view is that, in fact, unions and their members can make informed estimates of the likelihood of employers operating during strikes, particularly in industries such as telephones and oil refining where the practice is routinely followed, and that the payment of unemployment benefits to strikers does alter the relative bargaining power of the parties. In states with work-stoppage provisions, employees may be more prone to strike because they know that if their strike fails they will not suffer a cessation of income. In addition, if struck employers bear none or only a small part of the expense of the unemployment benefits, which is frequently the case under experience rating provisions, and if they know continued operation will serve to protect their market position, they may not have much incentive to avoid strikes. Clearly, empirical evidence on the effect of work-stoppage provisions on strike activity is needed to assess the validity of the two contrary points of view.

Down through the years the work-stoppage rule has been the subject of considerable litigation. For example, in *Kimbell, Inc. v. Employment Security Commission,* the Supreme Court dismissed, for want of a substantial federal question, an appeal that involved New Mexico's work-stoppage provision; the plaintiff in the case had contended that the retroactive post-strike award of unemployment benefits to strikers was preempted by federal labor law.[13] Apparently Oklahoma is currently the only state with a work-stoppage provision in which the state's highest court has held that the provision refers to a stoppage-of-work by the employee, and not the employer.[14] Since 1975, the highest courts of four additional states have ruled that the work-stoppage provision allows strikers to collect benefits so long as their activities have not substantially curtailed the operations of their employer.[15]

The most recent of these decisions dealt with a 1980 strike by the Oil, Chemical and Atomic Workers Union against the marketing division of Chevron U.S.A., Inc. in Anchorage, Alaska. In response to the strike, Chevron hired replacements, reassigned nonstriking employees, and used subcontractors to take over the work normally performed by the strikers. As a result, Chevron had no difficulty making all of its deliveries and meeting its customers' demands during the strike. Using Alaska's work-stoppage provision as the basis for their claim, 39 strikers applied for unemployment benefits.

The director of the Alaska Division of Employment Security, in correspondence with the authors, noted that Alaska had always tacitly followed the lead of other states in holding that "stoppage-of-work" referred to the work carried on at the employer's establishment, and not the work of the individual employee. "Accordingly, we would pay benefits to strikers who did not bring about a substantial curtailment of their employer's operations."[16] But when the Chevron strikers filed for benefits, the Division of Employment Security decided to deny their claim. According to the director, "We [found] that the courts of other jurisdictions were frequently ill-informed in the subject matter, and that they had a tendency to rely upon the stare decisis principle (the decisions of the courts of other states) without seriously weighing public policy considerations, the legislative intent or history of their own states, or even the rationale of the courts upon which they place their reliance."[17] The Alaska agency decided to use the Chevron strike to create a legal test of the interpretation of the state's work-stoppage provision.

The initial denial of benefits to the Chevron strikers was upheld by the assistant director of the Division, a referee for the Department of Labor, and the Commissioner of Labor, who overruled his prior interpretations of the work-stoppage provision. The Commissioner's decision was affirmed by the Alaska Superior Court in 1981. The Chevron workers appealed to the state's Supreme Court, which reversed the lower court's ruling.[18]

In reviewing the history of the stoppage-of-work provision in Alaska and other states, the Supreme Court found that the great majority of states had interpreted the provision to mean a stoppage-of-work at the employer's plant or establishment, not a stoppage-of-work by the individual employee. In Alaska, this interpretation had prevailed for 27 years. During that period the Alaska legislature had, on several occasions, amended the state's unemployment compensation statute but had never tried to alter the standard meaning of the work-stoppage provision. The Court took the inaction of the legislature as a sign that it acquiesced in the Employment Security Division's formerly consistent interpretation of the provision.

The Employment Security Division maintained that the standard interpretation of the work-stoppage provision forced the state to take sides with the employee in a labor dispute, thereby placing the employer "in the ridiculous position of having to finance the strike against him through his direct reimbursement of the [unemployment insurance] fund, or through taxes paid into the fund.''[19] The superior court agreed that the work-stoppage rule compromised the state's neutrality in labor disputes. But the state's Supreme Court disagreed:

> This statute can be seen as attempting to chart a neutral course between two absolute approaches to the payment of unemployment benefits. If compensation were always paid to striking workers, the state would abolish the labor dispute disqualification entirely and could be viewed as always siding with the striker. If compensation were never paid to strikers . . . the state could be viewed as seriously interfering with the right to strike and thus siding with management.
>
> The legislature, by enacting the ''stoppage of work'' language has avoided these positions, and called upon the [Employment Security Division] to refrain from passing on the merits of the dispute in evaluating benefit claims. Strikers who do not stop the employers' operations qualify for benefits while those who succeed in curtailing production do not. Employers whose operations continue must therefore contribute to the fund while employers whose work is stopped do not. We do not find this scheme to be without some measure of logic.[20]

The Alaska court then found that the OCAW strike in fact had not caused a stoppage-of-work at Chevron's Anchorage facility; therefore the strikers were entitled to receive unemployment benefits.

New York

New York passed its unemployment compensation law in April 1935, before Congress enacted either the National Labor Relations Act or the Social Security Act. New York legislators, therefore, could not know whether their treatment of strikers would be consistent with the subsequent recommendations of the Social Security Board. The New York law was drafted by a tripartite committee, consisting of employer, union, and public representatives.[21] The committee recommended that workers unemployed because of a labor dispute (called an ''industrial controversy'' in New York law) be paid benefits after a 10-week waiting period, and the New York legislature adopted this recommendation. In April 1941, the legislature reduced the waiting period to eight weeks.[22]

In contrast to the great majority of states, New York disqualifies not only strikers but also innocent bystanders during the first eight weeks of a labor dispute.[23] Thus, New York uses a "no-fault" approach, disqualifying all workers unemployed because of a labor dispute in its early stages, and qualifying them for benefits thereafter.[24]

The New York State Department of Labor has explained the state's unique approach in the following terms:

> New York's provision reflects a "hands-off" policy in industrial controversies. Once the fact of an industrial controversy has been established, the state does not examine the issues or the merits of the dispute. It does not determine who is "participating in," "financing," or "interested in" the dispute or who belongs to the same "grade or class of workers" involved in the dispute. It does not decide whether the dispute is a "lockout" or a "strike," or whether it is legal or illegal.[25]

The committee that drafted the New York law believed that any attempt to affix responsibility for a labor dispute would be administratively cumbersome. For example, the committee thought that it is often impossible to distinguish strikes from lockouts. If eligibility for unemployment compensation depended on such distinctions, the committee maintained, unions and employers would end up blaming each other for the existence of a labor dispute, and administrators and judges would be burdened with the task of resolving the parties' competing claims. To prevent "manipulation" by either employers or unions, the committee recommended that New York's statute "require no administrative adjudication as to the cause of the industrial dispute or the nature of the participants."[26]

From the start, the New York law has been the focus of controversy. Proponents acknowledge that it is "a rough sort of compromise," which "may have seemed desirable for administrative and social reasons."[27] They argue that when a strike has dragged on for an extended period, it becomes difficult to determine whether a striker is voluntarily or involuntarily unemployed. To retain his or her eligibility for benefits, a striker in New York is required to seek and accept suitable temporary jobs—and, according to the law's proponents, this requirement has been strictly enforced.[28] Thus, it is argued, the unemployment of a worker involved in an extended strike may be more a consequence of the state of the labor market than of the existence of the labor dispute.

Employers have regularly lobbied for changes in New York's law, arguing that it encourages unions to strike and prolongs the duration of existing disputes, violates the principle of state neutrality in labor disputes, interferes with the federally established policy of "free collective bargaining," constitutes an unnecessary drain on the state's unemployment insurance fund, and, because employer unemployment insurance taxes are experience rated, forces employers to finance strikes against themselves.[29] Through the years, numerous amendments to change the law have been introduced in the New York legislature, but proponents of the law have always been able to prevent their passage.[30]

Rhode Island

Rhode Island's law, passed in 1936, pays benefits to strikers after seven (rather than eight) weeks.[31] A major difference between the New York and Rhode Island laws is that the latter pays benefits to innocent bystanders after a one-week waiting period. Another major difference is that Rhode Island does not adversely adjust an employer's experience rating because his or her employees have collected benefits during a strike. Finally, Rhode Island has a stoppage-of-work provision that allows strikers to collect jobless pay after a one-week waiting period if their employer's operations have not been substantially curtailed by the labor dispute.[32] Under these various qualifying provisions, Rhode Island potentially allows more workers unemployed because of a labor dispute to collect benefits than any other state.

In the past, at least five other states (Alabama, Louisiana, Pennsylvania, Tennessee, and New Jersey) have allowed strikers to collect unemployment benefits after a waiting period of from three (Pennsylvania) to eight (Alabama and Louisiana) weeks.[33] All of these laws were repealed, according to Carney, "as a result of public pressure."[34]

The question of whether federal labor policy prohibits New York (or any other state) from paying unemployment compensation to strikers remained unresolved until the United States Supreme Court issued a definitive ruling in *New York Telephone Co. v. New York Department of Labor.*

The New York Telephone Case

On July 14, 1971, the Communications Workers of America, AFL-CIO, launched a nationwide strike against the Bell System.[35] Four days later the parties reached an agreement in principle, subject to ratification by the union's members, and the CWA ordered all of its members to return to work. In New York, however, about 38,000 workers employed by the New York Telephone Co. (Telco), the Western Electric Co., and AT&T's Long Lines Department defied their union's order and remained on strike. The New York workers continued to strike because they objected to their settlement being in line with the pattern settlement on wages, fringe benefits, and other so-called "national issues" that applied to Bell System employees throughout the rest of the country. CWA members in New York wanted to "break the pattern" by holding out for a larger settlement. The New York Telephone Co. resisted its employees' demands because it felt that yielding would lead to "labor turmoil throughout the Bell System."[36]

At first the international union opposed continuation of the strike in New York, but eventually the union lent its support.[37] After the eight-week waiting period, the New York Telephone workers began to collect unemployment compensation and continued to do so until their strike ended in February 1972.[38] The strike was settled when Telco agreed to "a modest, but precedentially significant increase in wage benefits" above the national pattern.[39] For a five-month period, 33,000 New York Telephone workers collected $49 million in unemployment insurance benefits; the average benefit paid to a claimant was about $70 per week.[40]

At the start of the strike, Telco's unemployment insurance account had credits of about $40 million. Collection of unemployment benefits by the striking New York Telephone workers nearly exhausted this account. Moreover, during the two years that followed the settlement of the strike, Telco's tax payments to the state were increased by about $16 million over what they would have been had the strike never occurred.[41]

Subsequently, Telco brought suit in a federal district court against the New York Department of Labor, seeking a declaration that the New York statute authorizing the payment of unemployment compensation to strikers was invalid because it conflicted with the policy of "free collective bargaining" established in federal labor laws. The district court, in its decision in the suit, concluded that the availability of unemployment compensation was a substantial factor in the workers' decision to remain on strike and had a "measurable impact on the progress of the strike."[42] Judge Owen, in his decision, wrote

> I regard it as a fundamental truism that the availability to, or expectation of a substantial weekly, tax-free payment of money by a striker is a substantial factor affecting his willingness to strike or, once on strike, to remain on strike, in the pursuit of desired goals. This being a truism, one therefore would expect to find confirmation of it everywhere. One does.[43]

On appeal to the circuit court, however, the New York Department of Labor succeeded in getting the district court's decision overturned. The Second Circuit considered the issue of whether federal labor policy had preempted the states from paying unemployment compensation to strikers. Noting that the question had been a political "hot potato" since the early 1930s, the circuit court conducted a review of congressional intent as manifested in the legislative history of the National Labor Relations Act, the Social Security Act, and other relevant statutes, and concluded that there was "no clear preemptive intent" on the part of the Congress. "Indeed, virtually all the evidence is to the contrary."[44] Judge Meskill, writing for the court, said,

> The conflict between New York's statute and the broad federal policy of free collective bargaining does not render the State statute unconstitutional. The conflict is one which Congress has decided to tolerate.[45]

The stage was thus set for the Supreme Court's hearing of the case. The Court, in a six-to-three decision, upheld the constitutionality of the New York statute, even though it agreed with the district court's finding that the New York law "altered the economic balance between labor and management."[46] It quoted with approval its own finding in an earlier case concerning the payment of welfare benefits to strikers in New Jersey: "It cannot be doubted that the availability of state welfare assistance for striking workers in New Jersey pervades every work stoppage, affects every existing collective-bargaining agreement, and is a factor lurking in the background of every incipient labor contract."[47]

Despite its view that the payment of unemployment compensation to strikers had a deleterious effect on collective bargaining, the Court declared that the ultimate resolution of the case depended on congressional intent. In its examination of the legislative history of the relevant federal statutes, the Court found that Congress had been silent on the issue when it passed the NLRA and Social Security Act in 1935, but on several subsequent occasions had explicitly addressed the matter. "On none of these occasions," the Court said, had Congress suggested that "such payments were already prohibited by an implicit federal rule of law. Nor, on any of these occasions, has it been willing to supply the prohibition."[48] Concluding, Justice Stevens, the author of the plurality opinion, said,

> In an area in which Congress has decided to tolerate a substantial measure of diversity, the fact that the implementation of this general state policy affects the relative strength of the antagonists in a bargaining dispute is not a sufficient reason for concluding that Congress intended to pre-empt that exercise of state power.[49]

By upholding the constitutionality of the New York statute in the New York Telephone case, the Supreme Court virtually validated all existing state laws that pay unemployment benefits to strikers.[50]

Innocent Bystanders

"Innocent bystanders" are workers who are not (1) participating in a labor dispute by picketing or refusing to cross a picket line,

(2) financing the dispute (e.g., through the payment of union dues that are used to finance strike benefits), or (3) directly "interested" in the dispute (in the sense of benefiting from a settlement that grows out of a dispute). Suppose, for example, that a unionized group of production workers strike their employer, causing the employer to lay off his non-union office personnel; can the office workers collect unemployment benefits? Approximately 44 states would consider the office workers to be innocent bystanders and would therefore allow them to collect benefits. The remaining states, however, do not distinguish innocent bystanders from actual strikers, and therefore disqualify both groups.[51]

Ohio, for example, is one of a handful of states that denies unemployment benefits to innocent bystanders. The constitutionality of Ohio's statute was tested in a case that illuminates the anomalous consequences of state control over these matters. In 1974, the United Mine Workers union staged a nationwide strike that shut down a large proportion of the nation's coal mines, including those operated by U.S. Steel and Republic Steel. Shortages of coal resulting from the UMW's strike caused the two corporations to lay off over 1200 employees at their steel plants in Ohio. These workers were represented by the United Steelworkers union. As the district court pointed out, "The steelworkers were in no way involved in the disqualifying labor dispute between the coal miners and the steel companies nor did they benefit from that dispute."[52]

In short, the steelworkers were innocent bystanders. Many of the laid-off steelworkers applied for unemployment benefits but were notified by the Ohio Bureau of Employment Services that their claims were disallowed. One of the steelworkers, Leonard Hodory, filed a class action suit on behalf of himself and the other laid-off workers. Hodory challenged the constitutionality of the Ohio law on the grounds that it had been preempted by the Social Security Act of 1935, denied him and his fellow workers equal protection of the laws as guaranteed by the 14th Amendment to the U.S. Constitution, and bore "no real and substantial relation" to the purpose of unemployment insurance legislation.[53]

Hodory pointed out that he was unemployed through no fault of his own. It was clear that, but for Ohio's labor dispute disqualification provisions, he would have been eligible for unemployment benefits. It was the purpose of unemployment insurance legislation, Hodory argued, to provide benefits to persons whose unemployment was involuntary. Since his unemployment was indisputably involuntary, to deny him benefits, Hodory maintained, frustrated the fundamental purpose of both Ohio's unemployment compensation statute and the Social Security Act.[54] Indeed, one of the anomalous consequences of Ohio's statute was that it allowed employees who were locked out to collect benefits but it denied benefits to innocent bystanders. Hodory thought that this was an arbitrary distinction that served to deny him equal protection under the law.

But the State of Ohio in the Hodory suit argued that denying innocent bystanders unemployment benefits was not an arbitrary measure, but one that did indeed serve a suitable government interest. The state argued that granting benefits to innocent bystanders would, because of experience rating, place an added financial burden on the struck employers. In effect, Ohio argued that if the steelworkers were allowed to collect benefits that were ultimately financed by the steel companies, the companies would be placed at an unfair disadvantage in their negotiations with the coal miners. Moreover, Ohio argued that paying innocent bystanders could seriously drain the state's unemployment compensation fund, and thus denying such workers benefits was not arbitrary but helped to achieve a legitimate purpose, namely, protecting the fiscal integrity of the compensation fund.[55]

Although Hodory won his case in the lower courts, the Supreme Court sided with the State of Ohio, holding that the state's denial of unemployment benefits to innocent bystanders (while granting them to locked-out employees) was not so arbitrary that it violated the equal protection clause of the Constitution. Nor was the state's policy preempted by the Social Security Act or other federal legislation, a holding that foreshadowed the Court's conclusion in the *New York Telephone* case.[56]

In states with innocent bystander provisions, determining which workers are or are not participating in, financing, or directly interested in a labor dispute has often been the source of thorny problems. Once again it is difficult to find consistent interpretations in the decisions of the employment security agencies and the courts. Suppose, for example, that a nonunion, white-collar worker arrives at her place of employment only to find that the unionized production workers have gone on strike and established a picket line around the establishment. If the white-collar worker refuses to cross the picket line and report to her job, she risks the displeasure of her employer. If she crosses the picket line, she not only risks the displeasure of the strikers but possibly her own physical safety. In innocent-bystander states, if she crosses the picket line but finds that the employer has no work for her to perform, she will probably be able to collect unemployment benefits. If she refuses to cross the picket line and then discovers that she has been laid off because of the strike, she will probably be ineligible for benefits. Despite the layoff, her refusal to cross a picket line will be considered "participation" in a labor dispute.[57]

But suppose further that the white-collar worker genuinely fears that if she crosses the picket line she will be physically harmed. What if the picketers are brandishing clubs or making verbal threats or have actually harmed another worker who attempted to cross the line? If the white-collar worker refuses to cross the picket line under these conditions, will she be ineligible for unemployment benefits?

Only four state statutes specifically deal with the issue of innocent bystanders who have failed to cross a picket line. Three—Colorado, Kansas, and Texas—appear to impose a blanket disqualification on such workers, regardless of extenuating circumstances. One—Illinois—takes a contrary approach, holding that "an individual's failure to cross a picket line . . . shall not, in itself, be deemed to be participation by him in the labor dispute."[58] In Illinois, the Bureau of Employment Security will disqualify innocent bystanders for benefits if they have refused to cross a picket line and have also engaged in other behavior the agency believes constitutes participation in the strike, such as "bringing food and coffee to the pickets, helping [to] man strike headquarters, and deciding as a group and not as individuals not to cross the picket line."[59]

In other jurisdictions, the courts have generally ruled that innocent bystanders who have refused to cross a picket line "must show a fear of personal injury" to be eligible for unemployment benefits.[60] The burden of proof in such cases is placed on the claimants; they must prove to the court that their fear is "reasonable," "well-founded," or "justifiable."[61] It has been said that this burden "is often very heavy."[62] For example, rumors of picket-line violence,[63] or even a showing that actual acts of violence occurred[64] have not persuaded some state courts that claimants should be paid benefits. As a result of these and other decisions, Gross has pointed out, "Many nonstrikers who in fact have a 'reasonable fear' for their personal safety may be denied benefits unless they actually suffer bodily injury."[65]

How much latitude do states have to disqualify claimants because they have helped to finance a strike conducted by other workers? The Supreme Court addressed this question in *Baker v. General Motors Corp.*[66] In October, 1967, while the UAW was conducting a national strike against Ford, the union held a special convention to authorize "adequate strike funds to meet the challenges of the 1967 and 1968 collective bargaining effort."[67] In effect, the convention doubled regular monthly dues (from $20 to $40 per member) for a two-month period. Shortly thereafter the strike against Ford was settled, and in December the union reached a national agreement with General Motors. The emergency dues were waived by the union in December and January, reverting to the regular rate.

But in January, three UAW locals went on strike at three GM foundries. During these strikes UAW members collected strike benefits from the fund in which the emergency dues had been deposited. As a consequence of the foundry strikes, "operations were temporarily curtailed at 24 other functionally integrated GM plants, idling more than 19,000 employees."[68] Most of these laid-off employees applied for unemployment benefits, basing their claims, in effect, on the premise that they were innocent bystanders.

Their claims were denied by the Michigan Supreme Court on the ground that the emergency dues payments constituted "financing" of the foundry workers' strikes. The claimants then took their case to the Supreme Court, where they argued that Michigan's action had to be rejected because it infringed on the claimants' federal rights under the National Labor Relations Act.

The high court did not accept the argument of the claimants, however. The Court defined the parameters within which the case fell:

> *New York Telephone Co.* makes it clear that a state may, but need not, compensate actual strikers even though they are primarily responsible for their own unemployment. And, on the other hand, *Hodory* makes it equally clear that a state may refuse, or provide, compensation to workers laid off by reason of a labor dispute in which they have no interest or responsibility whatsoever. In between these opposite ends of the spectrum are cases in which the furloughed employees have had some participation in the labor dispute that caused their unemployment. This is such a case.[69]

The Court was troubled by the fact that the claimants' payment of emergency dues occurred before the foundry workers decided to strike, raising the question of whether the claimants could have possibly anticipated that their dues would be used to finance the strikes. But the Court was persuaded that there was "a meaningful connection between the decision to pay the emergency dues, the strikes which ensued, and ultimately their [i.e., the claimants] own layoffs."[70] The Court maintained that the claimants' unemployment was not actually involuntary but was, indeed, entirely foreseeable because of their payment of the extra dues. Disposing of this issue, it then ruled that Michigan's treatment of the laid-off UAW members was not preempted by federal law. Rather, Michigan had to be accorded the same latitude in these matters as New York had been in the *New York Telephone* case and Ohio in the *Hodory* case.

Writing for the Court, Justice Stevens also noted, "We of course express no opinion concerning the wisdom of one policy choice or another."[71] And he added a caveat, "We have no occasion to consider the circumstances, if any, in which individuals might be disqualified solely because they paid regular union dues required as a condition of their employment."[72] Many states currently disqualify claimants merely because their *regular* dues have been used to finance a strike by their fellow union members, but Justice Stevens' caveat suggests that the constitutionality of such a practice is still an open question.[73]

Grade or Class

Even if an innocent bystander can prove that he did not personally participate in, finance, or have a direct interest in a labor dispute, he may still be disqualified for unemployment benefits if he was, at the time of the commencement of the dispute, a member of a grade or class of workers *any one of whom* participated in, financed, or had a direct interest in the dispute. The "grade or class" disqualification was included in the Social Security Board's Draft Bill and was subsequently adopted by approximately 40 states.[74] In these states, a nonstriking claimant must not only prove his own "innocence," he must prove the innocence of all of his nonstriking co-workers who are in the same grade or class.

Three arguments have been advanced in support of the grade-or-class disqualification. First, the provision is intended to discourage so-called "key man" strikes. Suppose a small number of workers strike and shut down a plant; in some cases, a walkout by one "key man" might be enough to halt production. In the absence of a grade-or-class provision, the other workers might be able to collect benefits if they can show that they were innocent bystanders. But if all workers in the same grade or class are disqualified for benefits, there is less reason for key-man strikes to occur.[75]

Second, grade-or-class provisions are said to benefit unions "by discouraging defections from their ranks."[76] According to Ahrens, "Workers, knowing they would be disqualified on the grounds of participation or financing if they belonged to a union which called the strike, would seek to avoid union membership in order to gain unemployment benefits if a strike were called. Disqualifying the entire grade or class of workers would destroy this incentive not to join unions."[77]

Third, it is said that grade-or-class provisions ease the administrative burdens of employment security agencies. Whereas the determination of whether a claimant's participation in, financing of, or direct interest in a labor dispute must be made on an individual basis, the disqualification of an entire grade or class will follow a showing that a single claimant in a grade or class did not have the status of an innocent bystander.[78] According to Ahrens, "The grade or class provision is useful to administrators, then, because it allows the decision of benefit claims on a group, rather than individual basis, and because it permits them to avoid difficult fact determination in some cases."[79]

There has been, however, considerable variation in the definition of grade or class in the decisions of the courts. In some jurisdictions, membership in a grade or class depends on the type of work performed, e.g., whether it is office work or production work.[80] In other jurisdictions, membership in a grade or class depends on whether the type of work performed is functionally or operationally integrated.[81] In still other jurisdictions, workers who are members of the same union[82] or the same group of unions negotiating jointly with an employer[83] are considered to be members of the same grade or class.

A court decision in the state of Washington provides an example of how the definition of grade or class can significantly affect the eligibility of workers for unemployment benefits. Prior to 1980, the employment security agency, using the functional integration test, would disqualify all construction workers at a given site if a strike by one trade caused the layoff of workers in other trades working at the same site. But in *Abbott v. Employment Security Department,* a state court ruled that union membership, and not the functional integration of work, should be the primary test in determining the boundary of a grade or class.[84] Since that decision, according to the Commissioner of Washington's Employment Security Department, "Some trades have struck without posting pickets, resulting in a job shutdown without requiring participation in the dispute by other trades. Trades sent home by the employer when all possible work is completed have been ruled to have met the exception tests of the law since they have not participated in the dispute nor have they any direct interest in its outcome. This has resulted in payment of benefits to individuals who would have been denied as little as five years ago."[85]

Grade-or-class provisions have been criticized on two grounds. On the one hand, most of the workers who are disqualified for benefits would also be disqualified under innocent bystander provisions. For example, in the case of key-man strikes it would probably be difficult for nonstriking workers who are in the same grade or class as the striking workers to show that they are not directly interested in the outcome of the strike or, if they are dues-paying members of the same union, that they are not helping to finance the strike. Thus, in most cases, the inclusion in a statute of both innocent bystander and grade-or-class provisions is a redundancy. On the other hand, in those cases where nonstriking workers are members of the same grade or class as striking workers but are truly innocent bystanders, it may be inequitable to deny them benefits. Grade-or-class provisions, then, may be desirable solely because of their administrative convenience.[86]

To clarify the questions that must be answered to determine whether a claimant will qualify for unemployment benefits, we construct the flow charts that appear here.

In this and the previous chapter, we discussed a number of court decisions affecting the eligibility of employees involved in labor disputes for unemployment insurance benefits. We conclude this section of our discussion with a summary of the key cases, which is contained in exhibit 3.1.

The Air Traffic Controllers

On August 3, 1981, nearly 12,000 air traffic controllers represented by the Professional Air Traffic Controllers Organization (''PATCO'') walked off their jobs. A few hours after the strike began, President Reagan personally announced that ''any striker who was not back on the job within 48 hours would be discharged and could not be reemployed by any federal agency.''[87] The Federal Aviation Administration continued to operate the nation's air traffic control system, using nonstriking controllers, military personnel, supervisors, controllers brought back from retirement, and trainees from the FAA's Air Traffic Service Academy. The President carried out his threat to discharge the striking controllers, but their replacements managed to return the air traffic control system to near-normal operating levels within the next several weeks.[88]

Figure 3.1

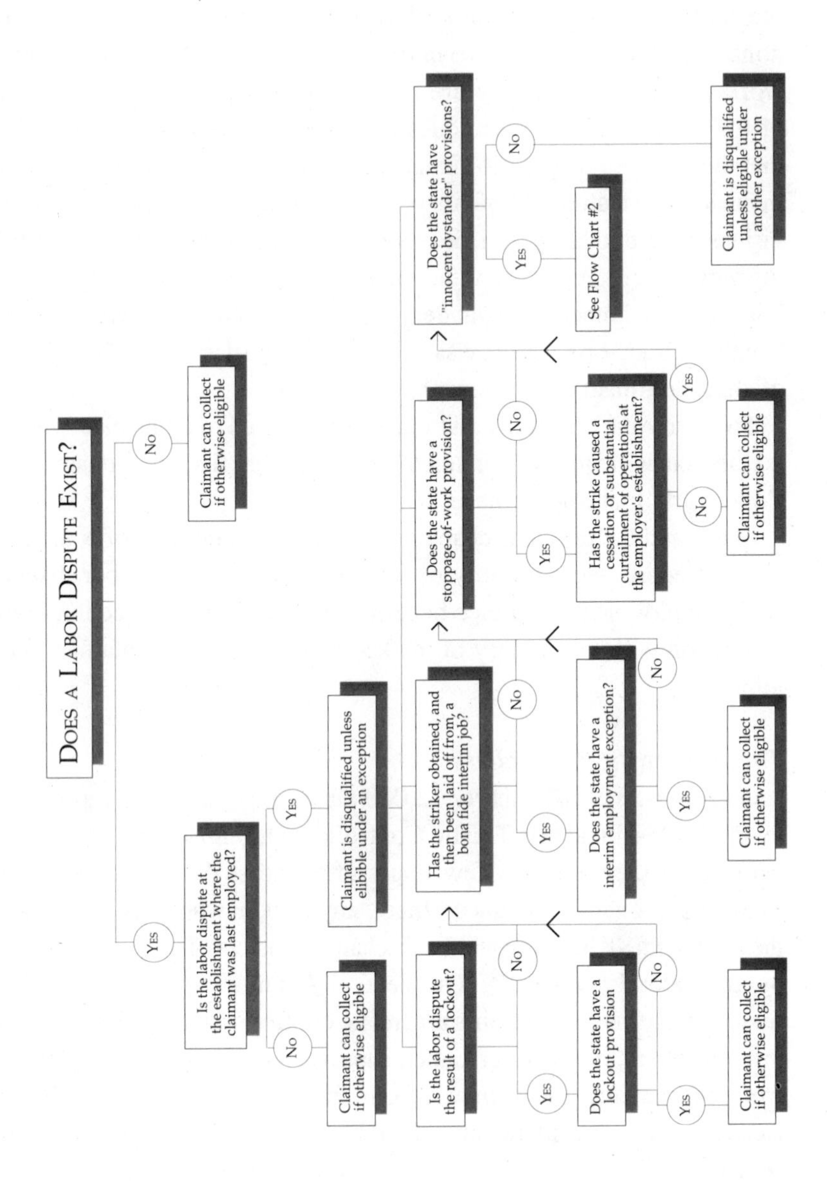
Does a Labor Dispute Exist?
No
Claimant can collect if otherwise eligible
Yes
Is the labor dispute at the establishment where the claimant was last employed?
No
Claimant can collect if otherwise eligible
Yes
Claimant is disqualified unless elibible under an exception
Is the labor dispute the result of a lockout?
Yes
Does the state have a lockout provision
Yes
Claimant can collect if otherwise eligible
No
No
Has the striker obtained, and then been laid off from, a bona fide interim job?
Yes
Does the state have a interim employment exception?
Yes
Claimant can collect if otherwise eligible
No
No
Does the state have a stoppage-of-work provision?
Yes
Has the strike caused a cessation or substantial curtailment of operations at the employer's establishment?
No
Claimant can collect if otherwise eligible
Yes
No
Does the state have "innocent bystander" provisions?
Yes
See Flow Chart #2
No
Claimant is disqualified unless eligible under another exception

Figure 3.2

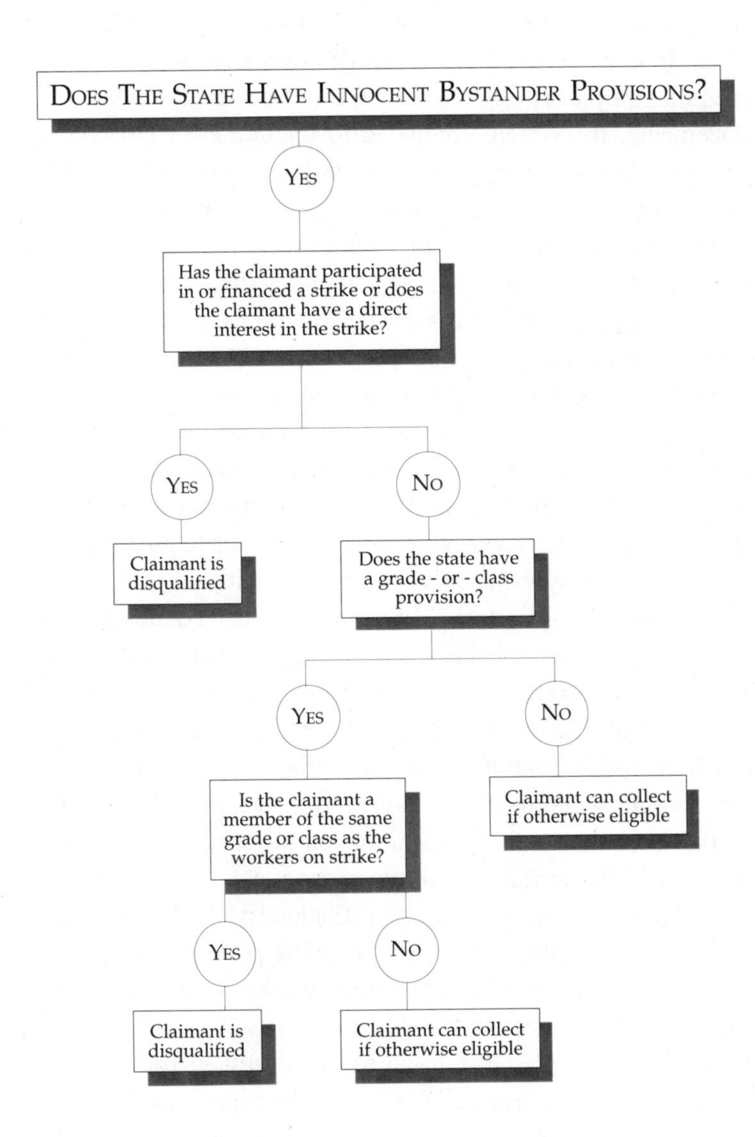
DOES THE STATE HAVE INNOCENT BYSTANDER PROVISIONS?
YES
Has the claimant participated in or financed a strike or does the claimant have a direct interest in the strike?
YES
NO
Claimant is disqualified
Does the state have a grade - or - class provision?
YES
NO
Is the claimant a member of the same grade or class as the workers on strike?
Claimant can collect if otherwise eligible
YES
NO
Claimant is disqualified
Claimant can collect if otherwise eligible

In the days and weeks that followed their walkout, many PATCO members filed claims for unemployment compensation. Although the majority of states denied the controllers' claims, a handful granted them benefits. In some of the states with work stoppage provisions, controllers argued that they were eligible for benefits because the FAA had hired replacements, the system continued to operate at or close to normal levels, and—implicitly at least—their strike had failed. In other states with lockout provisions controllers claimed benefits on the ground that they had been locked out by their employer, the FAA.

The air traffic controllers' case illustrates the difficulties that arise when state agencies and courts are faced with the problem of reconciling labor dispute disqualification provisions with other potentially conflicting disqualification provisions in unemployment insurance statutes. All statutes contain provisions that require disqualification of claimants who were terminated by their employer because of misconduct connected with their work. Both the definition of misconduct and the period of disqualification, however, vary from jurisdiction to jurisdiction. Thus, for example, Pennsylvania only disqualifies claimants if they have been guilty of "willful misconduct." Pennsylvania then requires the claimants to earn six times their weekly unemployment benefit amount on a new job before they become requalified for benefits; Connecticut, which also uses a "willful misconduct" standard, requires that claimants earn 10 times their weekly benefit amount on a new job. Most of the remaining states disqualify claimants for milder forms of misconduct. Many adjust the period of disqualification on a case-by-case basis, depending upon the seriousness of the misconduct; others impose a fixed period of disqualification; still others disqualify claimants for the duration of their unemployment or longer. The period of disqualification for misconduct can be as short as three weeks in Alabama, or as long as 52 weeks in Florida.[89]

In most states, the fact that the air traffic controllers had been discharged by the federal government for misconduct (i.e., for their participation in an illegal strike) was deemed to take precedence over the controllers' involvement in a labor dispute. These states held that the controllers' discharge terminated their employment relationship with the

Exhibit 3.1
Principal Judicial Decisions Pertaining to Labor Dispute Disqualification Provisions

Case	Issue	Findings	Effect on Provisions
Unemployment Compensation Commission v. Aragon, 329 U.S. 143 91 L.ed. 136 (1946)	Interpretation of the term ''labor dispute.''	Denial of benefits to cannery workers based on their involvement in a labor dispute was upheld, even though their employment relationship had been severed and they were not engaging in a strike or any other form of concerted activity. Court found that there was a ''full-scale controversy'' between the workers' union and their employers.	Labor dispute disqualification does not require a strike or leaving of employment, or a currently existing employment relation at the time the dispute arises. ''Labor dispute'' may be defined very broadly by agencies determining claimant eligibility.
Nash v. Florida Industrial Commission, 389 U.S. 235 (1967)	Interpretation of the term ''labor dispute.''	The Supreme Court reversed a Florida Court's ruling that a union member's filing of an unfair labor practice charge against her employer initiated a ''labor dispute'' and thus disqualified her for unemployment benefits.	The exercise of an employee's rights under a federal statute cannot be interpreted by a state as a ''labor dispute'' that disqualifies the employee for unemployment benefits. The term ''labor dispute'' cannot be defined so broadly that it encompasses every type of disagreement between an employer and an employee.

Grinnell Corp. v. Hackett 475 F.2d 449 (1st Cir., 1973)	Federal preemption of Rhode Island statute authorizing payment of unemployment benefits to strikers.	The Court of Appeals remanded the case to the federal district court since the record was not sufficient to determine whether the statute infringed upon federal labor policy.	States have wide latitude to determine eligibility of strikers for unemployment benefits. One of several cases in which federal courts ruled that state law in this area was not preempted by federal policy. The court wanted empirical evidence that the payment of benefits affected strike activity.
Kimbell, Inc. v. Employment Security Commission, 429 U.S. 804 (1976)	Federal preemption of work-stoppage provisions.	The U.S. Supreme Court dismissed, for want of a substantial federal question, an appeal of a decision by the Supreme Court of New Mexico allowing payment of benefits under a work-stoppage rule.	States can pay unemployment benefits to strikers if their strike has not caused a cessation or a substantial curtailment of production at their employee's establishment. The federal preemption argument was rejected by the Court.
Hodory v. Ohio Bureau of Employment Services, 431 U.S. 471 (1977)	Federal preemption of state policy denying unemployment benefits to innocent bystanders.	The Supreme Court upheld the state's denial of benefits to steelworkers who were innocent bystanders in a strike by UMW. The Court held that the state's policy did not violate the equal protection clause, nor was it preempted by federal legislation.	States may refuse benefits to workers who have been laid off as a result of a labor dispute in which they are not participating, are not financing, and in which they hae no interest. The federal preemption argument was once again rejected by the Court.

New York Telephone v. New York Dept. of Labor, 440 U.S. 519 (1979)	Federal preemption of New York statute authorizing the payment of unemployment benefits to strikers.	The Supreme Court upheld the constitutionality of the statute, despite its view that the payment of benefits to strikers had a harmful effect on collective bargaining.	The decision validated all existing state laws that pay unemployment benefits to strikers and gave each state wide latitude to shape its own policy regarding striker eligibility. The Court definitively rejected the argument that federal policy preempted state law in this area.
Sun Oil Co. of Penn. v. Unemployment Compensation Review Board, 440 U.S. 977 (1979)	Interpretation of the term "lockout."	The Supreme Court dismissed the appeal of a lower court court ruling that union members who had walked off their jobs were eligible for benefits since the employer's "unreasonable" action constituted a lockout.	State lockout provisions may be subject to broad interpretation.
Baker v. General Mobis, 106 S.Ct. 3129 (1986)	Interpretation of the term "innocent bystander."	The State of Michigan denied unemployment benefits to union members who had been laid off as a result of strikes at sister foundries, arguing that claimants' payment of emergency strike dues constituted "financing" of the foundry workers' strikes. The Supreme Court held that claimants had, by paying the special dues, financed the labor dispute that caused their unemployment and ruled that the state's policy was not preempted by federal law.	States may disqualify claimants if they have helped a strike conducted by other workers. The decision applies to the payment of emergency union dues, and does not address issue of whether states may disquality claimants whose regular dues have been used to finance a strike by other workers.

FAA and thus their participation in a labor dispute. The issue of whether there had or had not been a lockout or stoppage of work at the airports where the controllers worked was accordingly not a matter that affected the eligibility of the controllers for benefits.

Thus, for example, New Jersey disqualified the controllers for six weeks, but then permitted them to collect benefits for the duration of their unemployment.[90] Arkansas disqualified the controllers for eight weeks.[91] Iowa also disqualified the controllers for misconduct. But a group of Sioux City controllers appealed the initial determination to a Hearing Officer. At the hearing, the FAA chose not to appear and the controllers, who realized that a strike against the federal government can be considered a felony, pleaded the Fifth Amendment and refused to testify. Because the burden of proving misconduct in Iowa falls on the employer, and since neither the FAA nor the controllers presented any evidence at the hearing, the Hearing Officer had to make his decision on the presumption that the controllers were innocent of misconduct, and thus he ruled them eligible for benefits. The case went to the Iowa Supreme Court, which upheld the Hearing Officer's decision.[92]

Michigan, on the other hand, found that the labor dispute provisions took precedence over the misconduct disqualifier. The Michigan Employment Security Board of Review refused to disqualify the strikers for misconduct, saying,

> A finding of misconduct necessarily implies an evaluation of the claimants' behavior. Here, there is no behavior to examine except for the claimants' participation in a peaceful strike. If that participation was misconduct because it was allegedly "wrong", then it must be concluded the strike itself was wrong. However, the Michigan Courts have long embraced a policy of neutrality in labor dispute situations, a policy which precludes the Board from examining the merits of a dispute. [93]

Michigan, however, appears to be the only state that qualifed the air traffic controllers on this basis.

In Connecticut, the employment security agency found that even though the controllers had been discharged, they had not been guilty of either "felonious misconduct" or "repeated willful misconduct," which are the kinds of behavior Connecticut required before it would deny discharged employees their claim for unemployment benefits.[94] Accordingly, Connecticut initially allowed all of the controllers who filed claims to collect benefits. The FAA, however, appealed the employment security agency's determination, and the Connecticut Supreme Court overruled the agency's decision in 1985.[95] The Connecticut court held that the controllers had been guilty of felonious misconduct under the laws of the United States (but not Connecticut), and therefore should have been disqualified.

In another case in Montana, the state's Supreme Court held that "the misconduct provision of Montana's Unemployment Insurance Act applies to the PATCO strike and disqualifies the PATCO members from benefits because the unemployment resulted from an unlawful strike."[96] The dissenting opinion, however, emphasized that the strikers had already received unemployment compensation, "and we all recognize the impossibility of recovering the benefits from the individual air controllers."[97]

In Hawaii, 135 air traffic controllers filed claims, arguing that they were eligible for unemployment benefits under the state's work-stoppage provision. The FAA countered that striking controllers had been properly discharged for misconduct. The state agreed with the FAA, but allowed the controllers to collect benefits for five weeks.[98]

Of all the state courts' decisions, only Louisiana ordered payment of benefits because the FAA had "failed to sustain its burden of proving that former air traffic controllers were engaged in willful misconduct at time of strike." The Supreme Court of Louisiana reasoned that the FAA had allowed the controllers to join a union (PATCO) and to be represented by PATCO in collective bargaining. The controllers, therefore, did not commit "willful misconduct" since they "reasonably believed in the legality of the strike because of representations by the bargaining agent recognized by the FAA."[99]

At the time of this writing, several states were still wrestling with the claims of the air traffic controllers. The controllers' cases, however, clearly illustrate, as one of our respondents noted, the "division of authority throughout the country" over the treatment of misconduct in labor disputes.[100] It is unlikely that the resolution of the controllers' claims by the courts will serve to harmonize the misconduct and labor dispute disqualification provisions in state unemployment insurance laws.

Conclusion

At this point it should be abundantly clear that state policies regarding striker eligibility for unemployment compensation are far from uniform. Although common patterns of practice are detectable, whether workers unemployed because of a labor dispute qualify for benefits depends not only on a state's unemployment compensation statute but also on the application and interpretation of the statute by the state's employment security agency and courts. State autonomy in determining whether strikers should or should not receive unemployment pay was upheld by the Supreme Court in the *New York Telephone* case. Although the Court clearly believed that the payment of benefits to strikers could affect the balance of power in collective bargaining—and inferentially the incidence and duration of strikes—it decided that Congress intended to tolerate such practices.

State autonomy has meant that workers unemployed because of a labor dispute who may be otherwise identical will be eligible for benefits in some states but denied them in others. Diversity of treatment may result in anomalies and inequities, but that may be a price worth paying to enjoy the presumed benefits of state autonomy. One of the benefits, it can be argued, is that each state has the opportunity to tailor labor dispute disqualification policies that best meet the needs of its work force and employers and are consistent with its political philosophy.

Conceptually, states can be ranked on the basis of how generously they treat workers unemployed because of a labor dispute. It is certainly not self-evident, however, that New York should be ranked at the top of the list. Only a small proportion of strikes in New York last longer than eight weeks. The New York Department of Labor estimated that over the period 1947-78 about 13 percent of all strikers were involved in disputes lasting more than eight weeks. These strikers collected unemployment benefits amounting to less than 1 percent of the total benefits paid to all unemployed beneficiaries. Although the average duration of strikes lasting longer than eight weeks in New York was 14.8 weeks, the average duration of the payment of benefits to strikers was only 4.4 weeks.[101] Clearly, only a small minority of strikers in New York ever become eligible for benefits and the cost of the benefits disbursed to strikers is nominal. In other respects, New York has more restrictive policies regarding the payment of benefits to workers involved in labor disputes than do most other states. It does not have a stoppage-of-work provision, it does not have a lockout provision, and it only pays benefits to innocent bystanders after the eight-week waiting period. In a later chapter we will present empirical tests that show that the effect of New York's law on strike activity is statistically insignificant. Recognition that New York's law is actually more restrictive than the laws of most other states may help explain this result.

In contrast, strikers in stoppage-of-work states can collect unemployment benefits virtually from the outset of a strike. Given the increasing number of employers who are choosing to operate during a strike, it is likely that the number of strikers who are taking advantage of stoppage-of-work provisions is growing. Arguably, those states with stoppage-of-work provisions are more "generous" than those states without them, including New York.

The most generous states may be those that have stoppage-of-work, lockout, and innocent bystander provisions. In 1984, there were nine states that had all three of these provisions.[102]

Curiously, most of the states falling into this category do not have strong labor movements (Pennsylvania, Rhode Island, and West Virginia are the exceptions). In a later chapter, we will test the proposition that a state's generosity is related to its level of strike activity. We will show that lockout provisions have no discernible effect on a state's level of strike activity, perhaps because lockouts are a relatively rare phenomenon. But we will also show that states with comparatively high benefit levels and both stoppage-of-work and innocent bystander provisions have significantly higher levels of strike activity than states without those provisions.

NOTES

1. Marc E. Thomas, "Strikers' Eligibility for Public Assistance: The Standard Based on Need," *Journal of Urban Law,* Vol. 52, No. 1 (1974), p. 131. It is probably unfair to cite only one author on this score. See also, Stephen G. Eisenberg, "Policy Considerations Underlying the Payment of Unemployment Insurance to Strikers," *New York State Bar Journal,* Vol. 56, No. 5 (July 1984), p. 30 for a similar misstatement of fact. It should be noted that both the Thomas and Eisenberg articles contain much of value to students of the subject.

2. U.S. Department of Labor, Employment and Training Administration, *Comparison of State Unemployment Insurance Laws,* Washington, D.C., 1984, p. 4-13 and Table 405 (hereafter cited as *Comparison*).

3. For a discussion of the stoppage-of-work rule see, U.S. Social Security Board, "Issues Involved in Decisions on Disputed Claims for Unemployment Benefits," *Social Security Yearbook,* 1940, Washington, D.C., June 1941, pp. 65-69; Herbert A. Fierst and Marjorie Spector, "Unemployment Compensation in Labor Disputes," *The Yale Law Journal,* Vol. 49, No. 3 (January 1940), pp. 483-486; Willard A. Lewis, "The 'Stoppage of Work' Concept in Labor Dispute Disqualification During Industrial Disputes," *Monthly Labor Review,* Vol. 51, No. 6 (December 1940), pp. 1380-1382; W. Joseph Hetherington, "Federal Preemption of State Welfare and Unemployment Benefits for Strikers," *Harvard Civil Rights and Civil Liberties Law Review,* Vol. 12, No. 2 (1977), pp. 458-459.

4. K. Pribran, "Compensation for Unemployment During Industrial Disputes," *Monthly Labor Review,* Vol. 51, No. 6 (December 1940), pp. 1380-1382. In *Ahne v. Department of Labor and Industrial Relations,* 53 Hawaii 185 at 188, 489 P.2d 1397 (1971) it was noted, "The British courts, however, quickly interpreted the phrase, 'stoppage of work to refer not to the cessation of the workmen's labor, but to a stoppage of work carried on in the factory."

5. According to Shadur, "It is hardly surprising that the overwhelming majority of appellate decisions in the United States have adopted the same interpretation." Milton I. Shadur, "Unemployment Benefits and the 'Labor Dispute' Disqualification," *The University of Chicago Law Review,* Vol. 17, No. 2 (Winter 1950), p. 308. See, e.g., *Lawrence Baking Co. v. Michigan Unemployment Compensation Commission,* 308 Mich. 198, 13 N.W.2d 260 (1944), cert. denied, 323 U.S. 738 (1944). But in *Hawaii Telephone Co. v. Hawaii Department of Labor and Industrial Relations,* 405 F.Supp. 275, 90 LRRM 2854 at 2863 (1975), the Court said American judicial decisions had resulted in an "almost inescapable overbroadening of the British rule." In its analysis of British precedents, the court pointed out that for a claimant to terminate his disqualification in Great Britain, he must show that his job had been filled by a replacement. American courts have not imposed this requirement on striking claimants. The court went on to say that under the American interpretation of the stoppage-of-work rule the strikers' position "becomes one of 'heads I win, tails you lose'!" It held that Hawaii's stoppage-of-work provision "irreconcilably intrudes into the federal process of free collective bargaining," and invalidated the provision. 90 LRRM at 2865. The Hawaii case was being appealed at the time the *New York Telephone* case was decided.

6. The District Court reviewed several decisions bearing on this question in *Hawaii Telephone Co. v. Hawaii Department of Labor and Industrial Relations,* 90 LRRM at 2862-2863. In *Magner v. Kinney,* 141 Neb. 122, 2 N.W.2d 689 (1942), for example, the court ruled that a strike that caused an employer to reduce his operating level to less than 70 percent of the normal level had caused a stoppage-of-work; therefore, claimants were not eligible for unemployment benefits.

On the other hand, in *Meadow Court Dairies v. Wiig,* 50 Hawaii 225, 437 P.2d 317 (1968), strikers were allowed to collect benefits under a stoppage-of-work provision where their employer continued to operate at 80 percent of his normal level. According to the Unemployment Insurance Director in Nebraska, "The Nebraska Appeal Tribunal has followed the policy for many years that a substantial stoppage of work occurs when operations have been reduced below 25 percent. So if employment levels remain at 75 percent and production levels equal 75 percent, there is no substantial stoppage of work existing." Letter from Eldon E. Peterson, Unemployment Insurance Director, Division of Employment, Nebraska State Department of Labor, to the authors, November 25, 1981. American courts look primarily at production levels, not employment levels, to determine whether a stoppage-of-work has occurred. See, *Hawaii Telephone Co. v. Hawaii Department of Labor and Industrial Relations,* 90 LRRM at 2863. Using the level of operations maintained by the employer during a strike to determine whether a stoppage-of-work has occurred was called the "American Rule" by the Supreme Court in the *New York Telephone* case, 100 LRRM at 2901, n. 24.

7. Hetherington, p. 489.

8. See Charles R. Perry, Andrew M. Dramer, and Thomas J. Schneider, *Operating During Strikes* (Philadelphia, Pa.: Industrial Relations Unit of the Wharton School, University of Pennsylvania, 1982).

9. Ibid., p. 125.

10. Ibid., pp. 1-2.

11. We will present evidence to support this proposition in chapter 6.

12. Hetherington, p. 489.

13. 429 U.S. 804 (1976).

14. *Board of Review v. Mid-Continent Petroleum Corporation,* 141 P.2d 69 (Okla. 1943). See also, *Aero Design and Engineering Co. v. Board of Review,* 356 P.2d 344 (Okla. 1960).

15. *Continental Oil Co. v. Board of Labor Appeals,* 582 P.2d 1236 (Mont. 1978); *Albuquerque-Phoenix Express, Inc. v. Employment Security Commission,* 544 P.2d 1161 (N.M. 1975); *Shell Oil Co. v. Brooks,* 567 P.2d 1132 (Wash. 1977); *Oil, Chemical and Atomic Workers Union, Local 1-1978 v. Employment Security Division,* 659 P.2d 583 (Alas. 1983). See also, *Warner Press, Inc. v. Review Board,* Ind. App., 413 N.E.2d 1003 (Indiana 1980); *Employment Sec. Adm'n v. Browning-Ferris, Inc.,* Md., 438 A.2d 1356 (Md. 1982).

16. Letter from A.G. Zillig, Director of the Alaska Division of Employment Security, to the authors, December 9, 1981. We obtained additional information on this case from George A. Michaud, Chief Hearing Officer for the Alaska Employment Security Division, in telephone interviews and correspondence in December 1984 and January 1985.

17. Ibid.

18. *Oil, Chemical and Atomic Workers Union, Local 1-1978 v. Employment Security Division,* 659 P.2d 583 (Alaska 1983).

19. Ibid. at 590-591.

20. Ibid. at 591.

21. See the discussion in Brief for the New York State Department of Labor at 33, *New York Telephone Co. v. New York State Department of Labor,* 440 U.S. 519 (1979) as reprinted in *New York Telephone Co. v. New York State Department of Labor, Petitions and Briefs,* Law Reprints Labor Series (1978-1979 Term).

22. Ibid., pp. 32-38; see also, New York State Department of Labor, *The Industrial Controversy Provision of the New York State Unemployment Insurance Law,* 1935-1975, Labor Research Report No. 1, April 1976, p. 2.

23. N.Y. Labor Law §592 (McKinney Supp. 1978); *Comparison,* pp. 4-13 to 4-14. Section 592.1 of the New York statute reads as follows:

> 592. Suspension of accumulation of benefit rights. 1. Industrial controversy. The accumulation of benefit rights by a claimant shall be suspended during a period of seven consecutive weeks beginning with the day after he lost his employment because of a strike, lockout, or other industrial controversy, including concerted activity not authorized or sanctioned by the recognized or certified bargaining agent of the claimant, and other concerted activity conducted in violation of any existing collective bargaining agreement in the establishment in which he was employed, except that benefit rights may be accumulated before the expiration of such seven weeks beginning with the day after such strike, lockout, or other industrial controversy was terminated.

Note that the waiting period is actually eight weeks since strikers, like other claimants in New York State, must wait an additional week after filing a claim to collect benefits.

24. For one court's discussion of New York's philosophy, see *Matter of Heitzenrater,* 19 N.Y.2d 1 (1966). See also, *Matter of Burger,* 277 App. Div. 234 (Third Dept.), aff'd. 303 N.Y. 654 (1950).

25. New York State Department of Labor, *The Industrial Controversy Provision,* p. 3.

26. Brief for the New York State Department of Labor at 33.

27. New York State Department of Labor, *The Industrial Controversy Provision,* p. 4; see also, *Matter of Heitzenrater,* 19 N.Y.2d 1 (1966).

28. Brief for the New York State Department of Labor at 36.

29. See, for example, Brief for the New York Telephone Company, *New York Telephone Co. v. New York State Department of Labor,* 440 U.S. 519 (1979) as reprinted in 12 *New York Telephone Co. v. New York State Department of Labor, Petitions and Briefs,* 1, Law Reprints Labor Series (1978-1979 Term). See also the amicus curiae briefs submitted by the U.S. Chamber of Commerce, the Center on National Labor Policy, the Rochester Telephone Corp., *et al.*, and the Dow Chemical Corp., *et al.* reprinted in the same source.

30. New York State Department of Labor, *The Industrial Controversy Provision,* pp. 5-15, discusses these proposed amendments.

31. 1935-36 R.I. Public Laws 848 (1936); see also, *Grinnell v. Hackett,* 475 F.2d 449; *cert. denied,* 414 U.S. 858 (1973).

32. *Comparison,* table 405, pp. 4-43 to 4-45; interview with Robert Langlais, Rhode Island Department of Employment Security, February 21, 1985.

33. Hetherington, pp. 54-56; James T. Carney, "The Forgotten Man on the Welfare Roll: A Study of Public Subsidies for Strikers," *Washington University Law Quarterly,* Vol. 1973, No. 3 (Summer 1973), p. 499.

34. Carney, p. 499. The dates of passage and repeal for these states are as follows: Alabama, 1939 and 1941; Louisiana, 1938 and 1946; Pennsylvania, 1945 and 1947; Tennessee, 1939 and 1947; New Jersey, 1967 and 1968.

35. At the time, the Bell System consisted of the American Telephone and Telegraph Co., AT&T's 21 operating companies, the Western Electric Co., and the Bell Telephone Laboratories, Inc., *New York Telephone Co. v. New York Department of Labor,* 440 U.S. 519, 100 LRRM 2896 (1979).

36. *New York Telephone Co. v. New York State Department of Labor,* 434 F.Supp. 810, 95 LRRM 2487 at 2489 (1977).

37. 100 LRRM at 2897 n. 1.

38. Ibid.

39. Ibid.

40. Ibid. at 2897. The maximum weekly benefit at the time was $75, which was payable to any eligible claimant whose base salary was at least $149 a week. Most of the telephone workers qualified for the maximum weekly benefit.

41. Ibid.

42. Ibid.

43. 95 LRRM at 2489.

44. *New York Telephone Co. v. New York State Department of Labor,* 566 F.2d 388 (2d Cir. 1977), 96 LRRM 2921 at 2925-2926.

45. Ibid. at 2926.

46. 100 LRRM at 2900.

47. Ibid. n. 20, quoting *Super Tire Engineering v. McCorkle,* 416 U.S. 115 at 123-124, 85 LRRM 2913 (1974).

48. Ibid. at 2904-2905.

49. Ibid. at 2905.

50. This is not to say that all state actions that grant or deny unemployment compensation to strikers will be approved by the federal courts. Where there is a direct conflict between the state's granting or denial of benefits and the employee's rights under federal labor law, federal law must prevail. In *United Steel Workers of America v. Meierhenry,* 608 F.Supp. 201 (1985), for example, the district court refused to approve a decision by the South Dakota Department of Labor that denied benefits to union members who went on strike against the Homestake Mining Company, while it granted benefits to nonunion employees who were part of the same bargaining unit. The court noted, "While a neutral unemployment benefit policy which does not conflict with any specific provision of the NLRA may not be preempted, it can hardly be argued that Congress intended to allow states power to administer their unemployment programs in such a manner as to directly interfere with express rights guaranteed under [the NLRA]. For these reasons, the court does not consider its decision here controlled by *New York Telephone Co.*" Ibid. at 205.

The *New York Telephone Co.* decision is one of a long line of cases in which the Court has grappled with the problem of determining when state actions are preempted by federal labor law. The leading decision on federal preemption is *San Diego Building Trades v. Garmon,* 359 U.S. 236 (1959), where the Court held that "in the absence of compelling congressional direction, we could not infer that Congress had deprived the states of the power to act." Ibid. at 244. On the significance of the *New York Telephone* decision to the doctrine of federal preemption, see Comment (by Michael E. Cutler), "Balancing in Labor Law Preemption Cases: New York Telephone Co. v. New York State Department of Labor," *Stanford Law Review,* Vol. 32 (April 1980), pp. 827-844, and Comment (by Lisa Kretzschmar), "New York Telephone Co. v. New York State Department of Labor: Limiting the Doctrine of Implied Labor Law Pre-Emption," *Brooklyn Law Review,* Vol. 46 (Winter 1980), pp. 297-320.

51. *Comparison*, pp. 4-13 to 4-14 and table 405.

52. *Hodory v. Ohio Bureau of Employment Services*, 408 F.Supp. 1016 at 1018 (1976).

53. Ibid. at 1017.

54. Ibid. at 1017-1018.

55. Ibid. at 1021-1022.

56. *Ohio Bureau of Employment Services v. Hodory*, 431 U.S. 471 (1977).

57. Note (by Thomas Brian Gross), "A Possible Cure for a Case of Mistaken Identity: Unemployment Benefits for Nonstriking Workers Who Have Failed to Cross a Picket Line," *University of Pittsburgh Law Review*, Vol. 42 (Fall 1980), pp. 94-99.

58. 48 Ill. Ann. Stat. 434 (1980); see also, *Nestle v. Johnson*, 68 Ill. App. 3d 17, 385 N.E.2d 793 (1979) and Gross, pp. 93-94.

59. Letter from Agaliece W. Miller, Employment Security Administrator, Illinois Bureau of Employment Security, to the authors, December 11, 1981.

60. Gross, pp. 95-96 and cases cited therein.

61. Ibid., pp. 96-97.

62. Ibid., p. 97.

63. *Unemployment Compensation Board of Review v. G.C. Murphy Co.*, 19 Pa. Commw. Ct. 572, 339 A.2d 167 (1975).

64. *Ex parte McCleney*, 286 Ala. 288, 239 So.2d 311 (1970).

65. Gross, p. 105. For a discussion of the "direct interest" disqualification, see Note (by Robert David Ray), "Unemployment Compensation During Labor Disputes: Qualifying the 'Direct Interest' Disqualification," *Missouri Law Review*, Vol. 46 (Summer 1981), pp. 694-707. See also, Note (by James M. Ringer), "Effect of Participation in a Labor Dispute Upon Continuation of Unemployment Benefits," *Cornell Law Quarterly*, Vol. 52 (Spring 1967), pp. 738-752 and Note (by James A. Arnold III), "Unemployment Compensation: Denial of Benefits for Participation in a Labor Dispute," *Arkansas Law Review*, Vol. 30 (Winter 1977), pp. 551-556.

66. *Baker v. General Motors Corp.*, 106 S. Ct. 3129 (1986).

67. Ibid., at 3131.

68. Ibid., at 3133.

69. Ibid., at 3137.

70. Ibid., at 3138.

71. Ibid., at 3139.

72. Ibid.

73. In a strongly worded dissent, Justice Brennan argued that Michigan's statute was clearly preempted by the NLRA. Moreover, he stated flatly that "a disqualification based upon the payment of ordinary dues would seriously interfere with basic organizational rights protected by the NLRA," and would thus be preempted. Ibid. at 3142.

74. Note (by Richard A. Ahrens), "Labor Dispute Disqualification: The Function of 'Grade or Class' Provisions in State Unemployment Compensation Statutes," *St. Louis University Law Jour-*

nal, Vol. 18, No. 4 (Summer 1974), pp. 629-640; Willard A. Lewis, "The Law of Unemployment Compensation in Labor Disputes," *Labor Law Journal,* Vol. 113, No. 2 (February 1962), pp. 193-195; U.S. Social Security Board, "Issues Involved in Decisions on Disputed Claims," pp. 72-73.

75. Ahrens, p. 633; Lewis, "The Law of Unemployment Compensation in Labor Disputes," p. 194; U.S. Social Security Board, "Issues Involved in Decisions on Disputed Claims," p. 72.

76. Ahrens, p. 633.

77. Ibid.

78. Ibid., pp. 634-636.

79. Ibid., p. 636.

80. See, e.g., *Outboard Marine and Manufacturing Co. v. Gordon,* 403 Ill. 523, 87 N.E.2d 610 (1949).

81. See, e.g., *Bethlehem Steel Co. v. Board of Review (In re Rusynko),* 402 Pa. 202, 166 A.2d 871 (1961). This test has been specifically rejected by some courts. See, e.g., *Haley v. Board of Review,* 106 N.J. Super. 420, 256 A.2d 71 (1969); *Wilson v. Employment Security Commission,* 74 N.M. 3, 389 P.2d 855 (1963).

82. *Burgoon v. Board of Review,* 100 N.J. Super. 569, 242 A.2d 847 (1968); *Copen v. Hix,* 130 W. Va. 343, 43 S.E.2d 382 (1947); *Iron Workers' Union v. Ind. Comm'n.,* 194 Utah 242, 139 P.2d 208 (1943).

83. *Borchman Sons v. Carpenter,* 166 Neb. 322, 89 N.W.2d 123 (1958); *Dravo Corp. v. Bd. of Rev.,* 187 Pa. Super. 246, 144 A.2d 670 (1958); *In re Kennecott Copper Corp.,* 13 Utah 262, 372 P.2d 987 (1962); *Operating Engineers Local No. 3 v. Ind. Comm'n,* 7 Utah 2d 48, 318 P.2d 336 (1957).

84. 27 Wash. App. 619, 621 P.2d 734 (1980).

85. Letter from Norman J. Brooks, Commissioner, Washington State Employment Security Department, to the authors, December 14, 1981.

86. Ahrens, pp. 633-634, 639-640; Lewis, "The Law of Unemployment Compensation in Labor Disputes," pp. 194-195.

87. Herbert R. Northrup, "The Rise and Demise of PATCO," *Industrial and Labor Relations Review,* Vol. 37, No. 2 (January 1984), p. 178.

88. Ibid., p. 177.

89. *Comparison,* pp. 4-7 to 4-8.

90. Information supplied by Joseph Sieber, Member of the New Jersey Unemployment Insurance Board of Review, in an interview, December 10, 1984.

91. Letter from Cecil L. Malone, Director, Unemployment Insurance, Arkansas Employment Security Division, to the authors, December 2, 1981.

92. The Sioux City case was described by William Yost, the Hearing Officer in the case, in a telephone interview, December 10, 1984. See also, *Department of Transportation, Federal Aviation Administration v. Iowa Department of Job Services,* 341 N.W. 2d 752 (Iowa Sup. Ct. 1983).

93. *Conway v. Federal Aviation Administration,* unpublished decision of the Michigan Employment Security Board of Review, appeal Docket Nos.UCF81-89419-R01-94173 through

UCF81-89630-R01-94343, February 15, 1985. The Michigan board's decision allowed approximately 200 air traffic controllers in Michigan to collect unemployment benefits retroactively. *Detroit Free Press,* February 20, 1985, p. 96.

94. Information supplied by Charles McGlew, Assistant Director, Unemployment Compensation, Connecticut Department of Labor, in a telephone interview, December 10, 1984.

95. As a direct consequence of the air traffic controllers' case, the Connecticut state law was amended in 1982 to include ''participation in an illegal strike as determined by state and federal laws or regulations'' as a disqualifier for unemployment insurance. See, *Federal Aviation Administration v. Administrator, Unemployment Compensation,* 494 A.2d 564 (Conn. 1985) at 566.

96. *Federal Aviation Administration v. Montana State Department of Labor and Industry,* 685 P.2d 365 (Mont. 1984) at 368.

97. Ibid.

98. *New York Times,* November 28, 1981, Section 1, p. 23.

99. *Charbonnet v. Gerace,* 457 So.2d 676 (La. 1984) at p. 679. Three other state courts have considered the claims of air trafic controllers: *Ramone v. Department of Employment Security, Board of Review,* 474 A.2d 748 (R.I. 1984) (denied claims of air traffic controllers because participation in an illegal strike constituted misconduct); *Swiecicki v. Dept. of Employment Security,* 667 P.2d 28 (Utah 1983) (failure of air traffice controller to report to work in face of presidential order requiring him to do so was tantamount to voluntary quit); *Wolf v. FAA,* 461 N.Y.S.2d 573 (N.Y. 1983) (denied claim of air traffic controller because his participation in an illegal strike constituted misconduct).

100. Letter from Miller to the authors.

101. New York State Department of Labor, *The Industrial Controversy Provision,* p. 24; interview with Roger Gerby, New York State Department of Labor, Division of Research and Statistics, October, 1981. (Mr. Gerby prepared the statistics presented in this paragraph for use in the *New York Telephone* case.)

102. Georgia, Iowa, Maryland, Mississippi, Oklahoma, Pennsylvania, Rhode Island, South Dakota, and West Virginia. See, *Comparison,* table 405.

4
Welfare in Labor Disputes

Before the depression of the 1930s, the welfare system in the United States was financed and administered by state and local governments. As Carney notes, "The federal government had no role in public assistance except to provide veterans' pensions and disaster relief."[1] State and local welfare agencies provided relief to needy persons unable to work because of physical or mental disabilities, to victims of disasters, and to the blind, the aged, and dependent children.

Mass unemployment during the depression, however, caused the existing welfare system to collapse. According to Schlesinger, a quarter of the labor force in 1933 was "subsisting wanly and desperately on relief" on an average stipend of about 50 cents per day per family.[2] State and local governments simply lacked the resources to meet the needs of the millions of able-bodied workers who, unable to find work, coped with destitution.

Within the first month of taking office, President Roosevelt sent a message to Congress requesting the establishment of the Federal Emergency Relief Administration (FERA). By the end of that first month, Congress had complied with his request, establishing FERA and authorizing it to distribute $500 million to bankrupt state and local relief agencies. Roosevelt then picked Harry Hopkins to be FERA's administrator. Hopkins—who would become one of Roosevelt's chief advisors and closest confidantes—moved quickly to disburse FERA's funds to local agencies.[3]

In May 1933, Hopkins received a letter from the executive director of the Pennsylvania State Emergency Relief Board asking for instruction on whether FERA would permit certain strikers in Montgomery County to receive federal relief payments. Hopkins issued the following statement:

> The Federal Emergency Relief Administration is concerned with administering relief to the needy unemployed and their

> families. Each case applying for relief to the local emergency relief agencies should be treated on its merits as a relief case wholly apart from a controversy in which the wage earned may be involved.
>
> The FERA will not attempt to judge the merits of any labor dispute. State and Federal agencies, as well as courts, exist which are duly qualified to act as arbiters and adjusters in such disputes.
>
> Unless it be determined by the Department of Labor that the basis for relief is unreasonable and unjustified, the FERA authorizes local relief agencies to furnish relief to the families of striking wage earners after careful investigation has shown that their resources are not sufficient to meet emergency needs.[4]

Although Hopkins said that FERA would not authorize public assistance for strikers if the Department of Labor found that the basis for a strike was "unreasonable and unjustified," in fact the Department of Labor never developed a means of making such a determination.[5] Nevertheless, Hopkins's policy was subsequently reaffirmed in statements issued by FERA in October 1933, and again in September 1934.[6]

Thus, when 12,000 agricultural workers went on strike in October 1933 against cotton growers in California's San Joaquin Valley, the federal government authorized relief to all needy strikers. The 1933 cotton strike, which Daniel has called "the zenith of the New Deal's larger program of permanently altering the economic power relationship between government and farm employers," was marked by violent confrontations between growers and workers.[7] The federal administrator of the National Recovery Act in California, George Creel, acting without formal authority, intervened in the strike in an attempt to stem the violence and bring about a settlement. When the growers attempted to "starve out" the strikers, California Governor James Rolph, after receiving approval from FERA officials, authorized the state's Emergency Relief Administration to provide food and other supplies to all needy strikers. Creel then threatened to exclude the growers from the New

Deal's farm support programs unless they agreed to submit their dispute to a fact-finding commission. At the same time, the strikers were told by state officials that federal relief would be denied them unless they, too, agreed to fact-finding and returned to work.[8]

> The state's plan to condition the distribution of federal relief on the strikers' return to work failed miserably. When strikers learned that strings were attached to the relief supplies offered to them, they refused to accept them. . . . Finally, when several strikers' children died of malnutrition and a public scandal seemed imminent, state officials relented. . . . By October 21 [the seventeenth day of the strike] the strikers were receiving relief without conditions attached. The sudden shift in the state's policy prompted angry growers to complain that relief workers were now dispensing aid to strikers on condition that they remain off the job.[9]

In the event, both sides agreed to Creel's fact-finding proposal. The fact-finding commission, after two days of hearings, produced a recommendation for settling the strike. When both sides denounced the recommendation, Creel once again used the lever of relief payments to force them to change their minds. On the one hand, he promised the growers that if they accepted the fact-finders' recommendation, all federal relief to the strikers would be terminated. On the other hand, he warned the workers that if they did not accept the recommendation and return to work, they would no longer receive federal relief. Still the strikers did not yield.[10] According to Daniel, "The stalemate was finally broken not by strikers clamoring to return to work . . . but by [their] union's Communist leaders, who concluded that the strike had caused enough suffering and that neither the strikers nor the union could gain anything by prolonging it further.[11]

Bernstein has said that the San Joaquin Valley strike was "perhaps the first time in American history that strikers were fed at public expense, the cause of bitter criticism."[12] Moreover, the authors know of no instance in later years of a public official using welfare assistance in such a direct and aggressive manner to coerce striking workers and their employers to accept a settlement.

Criticism of FERA's policy of authorizing relief for needy strikers intensified in 1934. In late August, newspapers across the country reported that members of the United Textile Workers, who were set to begin a strike the following month, would receive public relief. These reports "raised a storm of protest."[13] An attorney representing textile manufacturers in Georgia wrote to President Roosevelt, saying that "the strike never would have been called . . . without the financial support from the Federal Government."[14] Bowing to pressure, the Alabama Relief Administrator ordered relief payments to the strikers to be terminated, a move that "apparently contributed to the defeat of the union."[15]

The arguments surrounding FERA's policy of authorizing public aid to strikers have persisted to this day. Hopkins contended that providing public subsidies to strikers would not affect the number or duration of strikes and would cost the government very little. Moreover, Hopkins believed public subsidies to strikers would reduce the potential for violence during strikes, thus contributing to law and order, and would be consistent with the New Deal philosophy of encouraging collective bargaining through the enhancement of union bargaining power.[16]

Those opposing FERA's policy generally disagreed with the New Deal's prounion philosophy and also maintained that public subsidies would increase the incidence and duration of strikes. The strikes by the agricultural workers and the textile workers provided evidence, opponents believed, of the pivotal role that public relief could play in affecting a union's propensity to strike. In both cases, the threat or actual termination of relief seemed to lead to the capitulation of the union.[17] Despite the controversy, FERA's policy, as Brown pointed out, "had a strong influence on the position of the officials in the later permanent state and local welfare agencies when it became necessary for them to deal with similar situations."[18]

Aid to Families with Dependent Children

The Social Security Act, passed in 1935, established two categories of income maintenance programs. In one category are social insurance programs, such as old age insurance and unemployment compensation.

These programs base benefit payments on an individual's past earnings and on tax contributions. In the other category are public assistance programs, which provide aid to the elderly, the blind and the disabled, and to families with dependent children. These are based on need alone.

The program now called Aid to Families with Dependent Children (AFDC) was established by the Social Security Act to provide assistance to children in need because of the death, incapacity, or continued absence of a parent. Congress has given the states considerable discretion in setting AFDC benefit levels. Each state determines its own standard of need and then the family's income and resources are compared to this standard. In principle, "the monthly AFDC cash payment is the difference between the family's standard of need and the amount of family income and other resources. However, in most states, the actual cash benefit paid is below the state's standard of need because of statutory and administrative limits on maximum benefits and the failure of many states to keep their need standards up-to-date based on current living costs."[19] There has always been considerable variation across states in the amount of monthly benefits paid. For example, in 1983, the maximum monthly benefit for a family with three children ranged from $120 in Mississippi to $751 in Alaska.[20]

It was not originally the purpose of AFDC to assist needy children simply because of the unemployment of a parent. AFDC's aim was to assist female-headed households with no other means of support. As the U.S. Supreme Court has noted, "The original conception of AFDC was to allow widows and divorced mothers to care for their children at home without having to go to work, thus eliminating the practice of removing needy children in situations of that kind to institutions."[21] When the program was established, "female household heads with small children were usually considered to be unemployable."[22] In practical terms, given the chronic job shortage that existed during the depression years, AFDC mothers were unlikely to be able to find jobs even if they made an effort to do so. In addition, it was assumed that unemployment compensation would be the principal means of supporting those with a labor market attachment who were without work.[23]

Consequently, in the early years of the Social Security Act, Congress never considered the issue of whether needy strikers should receive

AFDC benefits. The matter was left to the states to decide.[24] Thieblot and Cowin assert that many state welfare officials "were not only guided by the precedents established by Harry Hopkins and the Federal Emergency Relief Administration, but were themselves sympathetic to unions and their aims. In the absence of congressional direction to the contrary, welfare aid to strikers was not only assured in most states, but on some occasions even promised beforehand."[25] As an illustration, Theiblot and Cowin note that in 1936, the secretary-treasurer of the United Mine Workers told a meeting of the Steel Workers Organizing Committee that workers employed by U.S. Steel could "count on public relief if S.W.O.C. called a strike."[26]

Even though the Social Security Act did not prohibit the payment of AFDC to needy strikers, it is unlikely that, prior to the 1960s, many strikers ever received such benefits. In previous research on this topic, it is reported that strikers received welfare assistance in the 1940s and 1950s in a number of noteworthy labor disputes. But in almost all of these reported cases, strikers received general assistance under state programs, rather than AFDC. For example, some autoworkers in Michigan received welfare assistance during the UAW's strike against General Motors in 1945; steelworkers received assistance during a strike against the basic steel companies in 1946; and electrical workers on strike against a General Electric plant in Erie, Pennsylvania received assistance in 1948.[27] According to Chamberlain and Kuhn, "in the long steel strike of 1959, federal, state, and local benefits and relief provided the striking steelworkers with at least $22,750,000 worth of aid."[28] I.W. Abel, then the secretary-treasurer of the United Steel Workers, estimated that the total amount of public aid received by steelworkers during the 1959 strike was $45 million.[29] Whichever estimate is closer to the truth, it is clear that most of the public aid was in the form of unemployment compensation and general assistance, rather than AFDC.[30]

In the majority of cases, needy strikers did not receive AFDC during the 1940s and 1950s simply because they did not meet the program's strict eligibility criteria. Almost all AFDC recipients during this period were needy families in which a female head was unlikely to have had any work experience at all. It is true that if a striker "deserted" his family, his children could obtain AFDC assistance, provided his family met the other eligibility requirements. But there is no evidence that many strikers were willing to leave their homes to achieve this result. As long as the focus of the AFDC program was the needy children of "unemployable" mothers, the issue of paying AFDC to strikers had no practical significance.[31]

As early as World War II, the labor movement began to establish ties with public relief organizations. The Congress of Industrial Organizations (CIO) established the Community Services Program in 1946, headed by Leo Perlis, to further this effort. "It was the CIO that first officially adopted the Community Services program, and it was CIO affiliated unions which Leo Perlis described as being the first to approach the use of public aid during a strike in an organized manner."[32] In 1956, shortly after the merger of the AFL and CIO, the AFL-CIO Department of Community Services was established. Perlis became the director of the new department, which was charged with promoting the union movement's involvement in local agencies, such as the united fund, local community chests, and other charitable organizations. Through the activities of the Community Services Department, "unions have become active participants in community welfare organizations and, accordingly, have become knowledgeable of the services and policies of these agencies. As a result, the availability of public funds as strike benefits has become an integral part of organized labor's strike planning."[33]

Over the years, AFDC eligibility criteria were significantly broadened, leading to a growing number of recipients. In 1937, for example, about half a million children were receiving AFDC; by 1960 the number had grown to 2.4 million. The cause of their dependency also changed: in the late 1930s about 40 percent of the dependent children received assistance because of the death of the father, 25 percent because the father was incapacitated, and 35 percent because the father was absent from the home. By the early 1960s, however, only 6 percent received assistance because of the death of the father, 20 percent because of the incapacity of the father, and 65 percent because of the father's absence. The remaining 9 percent were in a new category: they received AFDC because of the unemployment of the father.[34]

As the nature of the AFDC population changed through these years, new concerns were voiced about the program's operation. In the years after World War II, the number of female labor force participants grew dramatically. The belief that "a woman's place is in the home" was called into question, no less for welfare mothers than for other women. The growing number of job opportunities for women constituted a challenge to the original premise of the AFDC program: that women with needy children should not work and were, in any event, unemployable. Yet welfare mothers were positively discouraged from working because any dollar a woman earned from work would be subtracted from her family's benefit. As the role of women in American society changed, this "100 percent tax" on benefits was increasingly criticized.[35]

In addition, the growing number of AFDC recipients who qualified for benefits because of the father's absence drew attention to the possibility that the AFDC program was contributing to the breakup of the family. Most state programs during this period disqualified a family from receiving AFDC if an able-bodied man was living in the house, even if he was unemployed. This rule encouraged fathers who were unable to support their families to leave home so that their wives and dependents might qualify for AFDC. "Proponents of welfare reform claimed that this eligibility requirement forced many fathers into real or pretended abandonment of their families."[36] Many critics charged that the growing rate of divorce, separation, and desertion was at least partly attributable to AFDC eligibility rules.[37]

Moreover, renewed concern in the 1960s with the problem of poverty in America further fueled criticism of the adequacy and effectiveness of the AFDC program.[38] As a consequence, the AFDC program was significantly restructured and liberalized during the 1960s. In the wake of these changes, strikers in large numbers became eligible for benefits under the AFDC program for the first time.

AFDC-U 1961-1981

To remedy the possibility that AFDC eligibility criteria were causing fathers to abandon their families, Congress amended the program in

1961 to provide assistance to the needy children of unemployed parents (AFDC-U).[39] Although it is not clear that Congress intended to create a new source of public assistance for strikers when it established the AFDC-U program, by its action Congress opened the door for states to provide AFDC-U benefits to strikers' families.[40] The new program made it possible for strikers and their families to qualify for AFDC assistance without the necessity of the striker "deserting" his spouse and children.[41]

Accordingly, the AFDC-U program quickly became a possible source of support for workers on strike. It is well to keep in mind, however, that to receive AFDC-U assistance, a striker had to meet all of the AFDC eligibility requirements. Although Congress changed these requirements from time to time, generally they consisted of the following:

- A striker had to have one or more dependent children living in his household.
- The children had to be under a certain age. For example, in 1981, just prior to the passage of the Omnibus Budget and Reconciliation Act, states had the option of paying benefits to children through the age of 18 or to children through the age of 21 if the children were regularly attending a school, college or university or a vocational or technical training course.
- The striker and his family had to meet a strict needs test. In 1981, before the passage of the OBRA, a family was ineligible for benefits if it had property or financial assets in excess of $2,000. The value of the family's home, personal effects, and one automobile was excluded from this calculation.
- The striker had to have been unemployed for at least 30 days prior to the receipt of benefits. A striker was considered unemployed if he or she had worked less than 100 hours in the preceding month. The striker could not have refused without good cause, within that 30-day period, a "bona fide" offer of employment or training. Of course, states that allowed strikers to collect AFDC-U did not consider the availability of work at a struck establishment a "bona fide" offer of employment.
- If the striker was eligible for unemployment compensation, he or she had to apply for and accept such benefits. The unemployment compensation benefits were then counted as part of the striker's income.[42]

Congress gave the states the option of participating in the AFDC-U program. The number of states participating in the program has varied but is usually around 25. States that elect to participate must operate their programs under federal standards and regulations, but otherwise have considerable administrative control and discretion.

Strikers receipt of AFDC-U benefits was a source of considerable litigation throughout the 1960s and 1970s. In general the courts found that in the absence of an explicit legislative or regulatory prohibition otherwise eligible strikers could receive AFDC-U. Of course, the relevance of this litigation is currently in abeyance because Congress provided an explicit prohibition on strikers receiving AFDC-U in 1981. Nevertheless, a review of the litigation is useful because the issues addressed in these cases are fundamental in any consideration of appropriate policy in this area.

It should also be noted that many of the court cases that dealt with striker receipt of AFDC-U also dealt with striker receipt of General Assistance (GA). In part this is because strikes that lead to the receipt of AFDC-U also often lead to the receipt of GA. Moreover, although the AFDC-U and GA programs differ in their administrative structures (the former is administered jointly by the federal government and the states, while the latter is administered strictly by the states), the legal issues associated with the payment of program benefits to strikers are quite similar. For the sake of simplicity of exposition, however, we focus here on litigation involving payment of AFDC-U to strikers. In doing so, however, we discuss some themes that have also emerged in GA litigation.

Legal debates over the payment of AFDC-U to strikers largely dealt with three issues. First, did states have the option, under the Social Security Act or regulations issued by the Secretary of Health, Education, and Welfare, to grant (or deny) AFDC-U benefits to strikers? Second, was the granting of such benefits violative of the public policy of state neutrality in labor disputes? Third, in the absence of an explicit prohibition in federal or state statutes on the payment or welfare benefits to strikers, did other provisions in those statutes *imply* a prohibition? Of particular concern in this regard were the provisions in the Social

Security Act stating that an individual is ineligible for AFDC-U if he is out of work "without good cause" or if he has refused a "bona fide offer of suitable employment." Parallel or related provisions in state welfare codes have also been the centerpiece of litigation over the payment of general assistance to strikers.

The first question was considered in a series of cases that culminated in the Supreme Court's decision in *Batterton v. Francis* in 1977.[43] Until 1968, the definition of "unemployment" under the AFDC-U program was left to the states, which meant that the states had the option of deciding whether strikers did or did not fall within the definition of an unemployed parent.[44] In 1968, however, Congress amended the Social Security Act, withdrawing "some of the definitional authority delegated to the States."[45] The 1968 amendments required a participating state to provide AFDC-U where a needy child "has been deprived of parental support or care by reason of the unemployment (as determined in accordance with standards prescribed by the secretary) of his father."[46]

Accordingly, in 1969 the Secretary of Health, Education, and Welfare promulgated a regulation that included a definition of unemployment, but was silent on the issue of whether strikers fell within the definition.[47] Acting under this regulation, Maryland's Department of Employment and Social Services issued a rule that denied AFDC-U benefits to families in which the father was out of work for reasons that disqualified him for unemployment compensation. Grounds for disqualification for unemployment compensation in Maryland included voluntarily leaving work without good cause, gross misconduct, and participation in a labor dispute (other than a lockout).

In *Francis v. Davidson* (referred to as *Francis I*), a federal district court held that the Maryland rule was invalid.[48] The case arose out of a class action suit brought by two subclasses: fathers who had been denied AFDC-U benefits in Maryland because they had been on strike, and fathers who had been denied benefits because they had been discharged for misconduct. The district court found that the Maryland rule was invalid because it clearly went beyond the HEW regulation, which had defined unemployment strictly in terms of hours worked. The court maintained, "A man out of work because he was discharged for cause by his employer *is unemployed.* There can be no two ways about that conclusion.''[49] The court also believed that a man out of work because of a labor dispute was also ''unemployed,'' and therefore held that the Maryland rule was in conflict with the HEW regulation.

Reacting to the decision in *Francis I,* the Secretary of Health, Education, and Welfare issued a new regulation in 1973 that, for the first time, explicitly gave the option to the states to exclude from eligibility for AFDC-U fathers whose unemployment resulted from their participation in a labor dispute.[50] *Francis I* had focused significant attention on the issue of striker eligibility for AFDC-U. For example, the Senate Finance Committee, in considering 1972 welfare reform proposals, specifically proposed overturning *Francis I* and eliminating striker eligibility by federal statute.[51] Business opposition to welfare for strikers was also mounting, fueled in part by the publication of the book by Thieblot and Cowin in 1972.[52] Moreover, the Nixon administration had come into office in 1973, determined to implement a ''New Federalism,'' under which states would have more discretion to administer a large number of joint federal/state social programs.[53] It was in this atmosphere that Nixon's Secretary of Health, Education and Welfare sought to overturn *Francis I* by issuing a new regulation.

After the 1973 regulation was issued, Maryland again tried to implement its rule, petitioning the district court to dissolve the injunction that had been issued as a result of *Francis I.* But Maryland officials were again frustrated when the court refused to dissolve the injunction. That Court, in a case that is known as *Francis II,* recognized that ''the conflict between the federal and the Maryland regulation ended after the former was amended,'' but continued the injunction on the grounds that giving states the option of denying benefits to strikers and their families violated the *statutory* requirement that the Secretary of Health, Education, and Welfare had to establish the standards concerning the definition of unemployment. *Francis II* held that the Secretary did not have the authority to delegate this responsibility to the states.[54]

Francis II was then consolidated on appeal with a similar case and the circuit court affirmed the decisions of the two district courts in an unpublished *per curiam* decision.[55] The Supreme Court then granted *certiorari.* In *Batterton v. Francis,* the court overturned *Francis I* and *II* by holding that the 1973 HEW regulation and, by inference, the contested Maryland rule were valid. The court did not agree with the district court's view on *Francis II* that the term "unemployment" was unambiguous. The Supreme Court said that "Congress itself must have appreciated that the meaning of the statutory term was not self-evident, or it would not have given the Secretary the power to prescribe standards."[56] The Court acknowledged that the Secretary "could not . . . adopt a regulation that bears no relationship to any recognized concept of unemployment or that would defeat the purpose of the [AFDC-U] program. But the regulation here at issue does not even approach these limits of delegated authority."[57] The Court stressed that it had been the intent of Congress to aid the families of the *involuntarily* unemployed, and that it was perfectly consistent with that intent for the Secretary to permit the states to deny benefits to strikers, whose unemployment arguably was involuntary.[58]

In *Francis II* the district court had invalidated the HEW regulation in part because the court believed the regulation did not serve the purpose of providing a uniform national standard for determining AFDC-U eligibility of those participating in labor disputes. But the Supreme Court held that, even though one purpose of the 1968 amendments to the Social Security Act was to foster uniform national standards of eligibility, this purpose did not preclude the Secretary of HEW from recognizing local policies. The Court said that "the goal of greater uniformity can be met without imposing identical standards on each State."[59] The Court therefore held that the 1973 HEW regulation "adequately promotes the statutory goal of reducing interstate variations in the [AFDC-U] program. In this respect, the regulation is both reasonable and within the authority delegated to the Secretary."[60] The issue of whether states participating in the AFDC-U program could be given the option of denying benefits to strikers' families was thus settled. By 1980, eight of the 26 states participating in the program had chosen to deny benefits to strikers.[61]

The second issue addressed in AFDC-U and GA cases was whether the payment of welfare benefits to strikers violated the principle of state neutrality in labor relations and, especially, in labor disputes. The issue of state neutrality has always been a central concern in the debate over whether strikers should be eligible for government transfer payments.[62] The debate sharpened after the passage of the Taft-Hartley Act in 1947, a statute that made the policy of state neutrality in labor relations much more explicit than it had ever been before. During the debate in the Senate that preceded passage of the Act, Senator Taft explained the purpose of the legislation of which he was cosponsor:

> Our aim should be to get back to the point where, when an employer meets with his employees, they have substantially equal bargaining power so that neither side feels it can make unreasonable demands and get away with it.[63]

The philosophy of the Taft-Hartley Act was to establish a statutory framework for collective bargaining that favored neither employers nor unions. Within that framework the parties would be free to fashion the precise terms of their relationship through collective bargaining. Nothing in that framework dictated that the parties had to reach agreement. They were, within broad limits, free to disagree and to use economic weapons (strikes, lockouts, and other forms of concerted activity) against one another.[64] In the larger debate over striker eligibility for public assistance, and in a number of court cases dealing with that issue, the question of whether the eligibility for and receipt of AFDC-U and GA benefits by strikers upset the balance of bargaining power between the unions and employers and placed the government squarely on the side of the strikers was a central concern.

For example, in the 1972 Senate debate over a proposed amendment to the Social Security Act to eliminate striker eligibility for AFDC-U, Senator Russell Long (Dem., La.) said. "The Senator from Louisiana feels that the Government should be neutral between labor and management in a labor dispute, and to pay welfare benefits to people who are on strike is not being neutral."[65] Senator Jacob Javits (Rep., N.Y.) responded, "One thing the Senator from Louisiana has said is quite proper: The Government should be neutral. But the Government should not hurt children whose father happens to be on strike. That is not being neutral either."[66]

A leading case in which the court's decision hinged in part on its view of whether the payment of AFDC-U and GA to strikers violated the policy of state neutrality in labor disputes is *Strat-O-Seal Manufacturing Co. v. Scott.*[67] Strat-O-Seal sought to enjoin the Illinois Department of Public Aid from paying welfare benefits to strikers. The company contended that the payment of AFDC-U and GA benefits "is contrary to the announced policy of our State to remain neutral in labor disputes."[68] Because of a desire to maintain neutrality in labor disputes, Strat-O-Seal argued, Illinois had a policy of refusing to pay unemployment compensation to strikers.[69] It would be inconsistent, Strat-O-Seal argued, for Illinois to refuse to pay strikers unemployment compensation, but not AFDC-U and GA.

But the Illinois court disagreed, rejecting the analogy between unemployment compensation and public assistance. The court pointed out that strikers in Illinois had been paid public assistance for 16 years. The Illinois legislature certainly knew about this practice, but had chosen to do nothing about it. The court was not prepared to overturn an existing practice, an action it thought was more properly the prerogative of the legislature.[70]

Moreover, the court did not agree that the payment of welfare benefits to strikers violated the principle of state neutrality in labor disputes. On the contrary, the court expressed the following view:

> Labor union membership or activity and the right to strike in proper cases and under proper circumstances is an accepted fact in our industrial community. Plaintiffs would ask us to exact by judicial interpretation as the price of exercising that right a forfeiture of the benefits available to others under the Public Assistance Code. By so doing, we exact a quid pro quo and impose economic sanctions not specifically required by the code. The strong arm of the State is thus employed to strangle authorized activity and State neutrality ends.[71]

Other state courts, following the lead of the Illinois court in *Strat-O-Seal,* also found that the payment of welfare benefits to strikers did not violate the policy of state neutrality in labor disputes. For example, one series of cases in New York State grew out of the efforts of the Social

Services Commissioner in Onondaga County (in which the city of Syracuse is located) to prevent strikers in the county from receiving GA. In the first case in this series, *Lascaris v. Wyman* (known as *Lascaris I*), County Commissioner Lascaris brought an action for a declaratory judgment against the State Commissioner of Social Services seeking a judicial interpretation of the state's social welfare law as it applied to striking employees. At the time the case arose, in 1969, New York counties had been paying general assistance to needy strikers for at least 17 years, even though there had never been an explicit provision in the state welfare law that either forbade or required such payment. County Commissioner Lascaris accordingly sought judicial approval of his intention to deny benefits to strikers in his county. But the court in *Lascaris I* was no more anxious to overturn a long-standing practice in the state than the court in *Strat-O-Seal* had been.[72] Closely following the reasoning in the *Strat-O-Seal* case, the *Lascaris I* court held that denying welfare benefits to strikers would amount to a forfeiture of the employees' right to strike, which was guaranteed by New York's labor law.[73]

After *Lascaris I*, the New York legislature, in 1971, passed an amendment to the Social Services Law elaborating on the circumstances in which a person would be deemed "employable" and therefore ineligible for GA. Employees participating in a labor dispute were not included in the amendment's definition of an employable person.[74] Then, in the summer of 1971, the Communication Workers of America began the strike against the New York Telephone Company that, as we have seen, resulted in the company challenging the payment of unemployment compensation to strikers under New York's unemployment insurance statute.[75] Some of the striking telephone workers in Onondaga County applied for welfare benefits under New York's Social Services Law, but once again County Commissioner Lascaris sought judicial approval of his determination that the telephone workers were ineligible for GA.

Lascaris brought an action in the State's Supreme Court (the lower court in New York) seeking declaratory judgment to confirm his determination. The Supreme Court granted summary judgment to the plaintiff,[76] but the Appellate Division of the Supreme Court reversed.[77]

Lascaris then appealed to New York's highest court, the Court of Appeals. In this case, known as *Lascaris II,*[78] the Court of Appeals held that strikers were eligible to receive GA, provided they registered with the state employment office and did not refuse suitable employment. The court said that "a person on strike does not, simply because he is on strike, 'refuse' to accept employment."[79] In the court's view, the 1971 amendment to the Social Services Law had not affected striker eligibility for GA. In fact, the court believed that the amendment should be regarded as legislative approval of New York's long-standing practice of paying GA to otherwise eligible strikers.[80]

But did the payment of welfare benefits to strikers violate the state's policy of neutrality in labor disputes? The court, in strongly worded language, held that it did not:

> It may be fairly said that in cases such as this the policy of government neutrality in labor controversies is, in reality, little more than an admirable fiction. Although, on the one hand, the State may not be acting in a strictly neutral fashion if it allows strikers to obtain public assistance, it may not, on the other hand, be seriously maintained that the State adopts a neutral policy if it renders strikers helpless by denying them the public assistance or welfare benefits to which they would otherwise be entitled. Indeed, it seems manifest that public assistance serves a purpose different from and, by that token, not in conflict with that which underlies the State's policy of neutrality.[81]

Quoting the decision of the First Circuit Court of Appeals in *ITT v. Minter,* the court in *Lascaris II* pointed out that "welfare programs, supplying unmet subsistence needs to families without time limitation, address a more basic social need then does unemployment compensation," which is based on prior earnings and not on demonstrated need.[82] Given its view that the 1971 amendment had not affected striker eligibility for GA and that payment of GA did not violate the policy of state neutrality in labor disputes, the court in *Lascaris II* ruled that public assistance should be paid to otherwise eligible strikers.[83]

Thus, attempts to deny strikers either state general assistance or (before 1981) AFDC-U on the grounds that such assistance should be regarded as state subsidization of strikes in violation of the public policy of government neutrality in labor disputes have not found favor in the courts. Some scholars have criticized the courts on this point. For example, Carney has written, "Although the claim that inaction, as well as action, affects the fortunes of the combatants has a certain philosophical merit, it tends to obscure the fact that provision, rather than denial, of subsidies to strikers represents a change in the status quo and thus, from an historical standpoint, constitutes a governmental intervention."[84] The courts have acknowledged that paying welfare benefits to strikers constitutes a form of government intervention in labor disputes, but they have rejected the argument that paying benefits interferes with the policy of "free collective bargaining," not only for the reasons previously discussed but also because the claim was not supported by empirical evidence. As the court in *Lascaris II* put it, "It is not at all clear—there is no evidence in the record on the point—exactly what impact public assistance grants have on the system of collective bargaining."[85] Arguably the *Lascaris II* court would have taken a dimmer view of paying public assistance to strikers if it had been possible to show that such payments increased the frequency and duration of strikes.

The third question addressed by the courts was whether, in the absence of an explicit statutory ban on the payment of welfare benefits to strikers, other provisions in federal and state statutes implied a prohibition. For example, the Social Security Act, as noted, denied AFDC-U to applicants who had refused without good cause a bona fide offer of employment. Similarly, most state codes require that an applicant for general assistance register for employment at a state employment agency and accept offers of suitable employment or training. In some welfare cases it was contended that, by participating in a labor dispute, strikers had left their jobs without good cause and, by not returning to their jobs at the struck establishment, strikers were refusing offers of suitable employment. Courts have rejected such arguments, recognizing that the imposition of such strictures on strikers would be tantamount to denying them the right to strike.

In other cases it was contended that, even though strikers should not be forced by statutory work requirements to abdicate their right to strike, strikers who registered for employment were not truly interested in accepting jobs offered by other employers, and their lack of interest in alternative jobs amounted to a refusal to accept suitable employment. In general courts have rejected this contention as well.

For example, in *Strat-O-Seal* the court dealt with the claim that merely participating in a strike constituted a refusal to accept suitable employment. Provisions in the Illinois Public Assistance Code made benefits available to "persons who for unavoidable causes are unable to maintain a decent and healthful standard of living" and denied benefits to "any employable person who refuses suitable employment or training for self-support work."[86] The plaintiff in *Strat-O-Seal* argued, first, that the strikers' need arose from an avoidable cause—namely, the strike itself—and that, second, their unwillingness to return to their jobs constituted a refusal to accept suitable employment. The Illinois court rejected both arguments. In the court's view, "The need for aid does not arise solely and initially from participation in a strike. It arises either from the refusal to help oneself or the inability to do so."[87] Refusal to help oneself, the court pointed out, is an avoidable cause of need and therefore a bar to public assistance. The inability to help oneself is an unavoidable cause and therefore qualifies applicants for public assistance. Some strikers had the economic resources to help themselves, could not refuse to use their resources, and were therefore ineligible for public assistance. But other strikers had exhausted their resources and could help themselves only "by abdicating the right to participate in a proper strike or by remaining on the job in the struck plant."[88] But, the court held, to require needy strikers to abandon their strike "is to place the hangman's noose over an existing right when the legislature has not specifically done so."[89] Thus, need that arises out of an employee's participation in a bona fide strike and his refusal to return to his employer was not held by the *Strat-O-Seal* court to be a bar to public assistance.

In *Lascaris I* striking General Electric employees in Onondaga County had applied for general assistance. The company remained open during the strike for those employees who desired to work. The county commissioner contended that by refusing to return to their jobs the strikers had refused to accept suitable employment and should therefore be denied general assistance. The court had to interpret provisions of the New York Social Services Law that required an applicant for benefits to register with the nearest employment agency, report for interviews at the agency when requested to do so, accept referrals to jobs, and report for employment when a suitable job was available. But the statute was silent on whether a striking employee could qualify for benefits if he refused to go back to work for his employer. The court held, "Where an employee loses employment by reason of a bona fide strike, lockout or other industrial controversy, this will not be a bar to the employee in obtaining welfare assistance if he otherwise qualifies. Strict and narrow application of [the statutory requirements] cannot be used to force the employee back to work and forfeit his rights under the Labor Law."[90]

Not content with the decision in *Lascaris I,* the county commissioner raised the same argument in *Lascaris II* (which, of course, arose after the Social Services Law had been amended). Again the court had to rule on whether a striking employee's refusal to work for his employer during the strike constituted a refusal to accept suitable employment. The Appellate Division pointed out that a union member who returns to work for his employer during an authorized strike could be fined, or even expelled, by his union. Therefore, the Appellate Division said, "A refusal by a union member to work for his employer can hardly be viewed as a 'voluntary act,'"[91] and accordingly the court concluded that mere participation in a strike did not constitute a refusal to accept suitable employment and thus was not a bar to public assistance. But, although the issue was raised, the Appellate Division did not address directly the contention that strikers should be disqualified because they had also refused suitable jobs offered by other employers.[92]

When the case was heard by the Court of Appeals, the plaintiff more forcefully pressed the argument that the strikers were not willing to accept alternative employment during the strike and were thus disqualified from receiving welfare assistance. The plaintiff's claim, however, was based on inference rather than on direct evidence. The plaintiff merely asserted that since the strikers were likely to return to work at the struck employer at the conclusion of the strike, they had "in effect refused to accept any other employment."[93] But the Court of Appeals said, "The short answer to the plaintiff's argument is that applicants for assistance in the present case have—and this is conceded—registered for other employment . . . and there is no evidence whatever in the record that they have either failed to attend job 'interviews' or refused 'referrals' or that they have refused to accept an offer of such employment."[94]

The issue of striker eligibility for welfare benefits reached the federal courts for the first time in *ITT Lamp Division v. Minter* in 1970.[95] The principal question the court had to decide in this case was whether paying strikers welfare benefits amounted to state interference with the employer's right under federal labor law to engage freely in collective bargaining and was therefore barred under the doctrine of federal preemption. Recall that we analyzed the question of federal preemption in our discussion of the *New York Telephone* case. At this point we deal only with ITT's claim that granting AFDC-U to strikers violated the provisions of the Social Security Act that prohibit the payment of benefits to persons who "without good cause . . . refused a bona fide offer of employment."[96]

The *Minter* case arose out of a strike by a teamsters local against ITT's lamp division plant in Lynn, Massachusetts. Some of the striking workers applied for and received both AFDC-U and general assistance.[97] ITT sought a temporary restraining order in the district court to stop the payment of benefits to its striking employees. The district court denied ITT's motion and the corporation appealed. The first circuit affirmed the lower court's denial of injunctive relief.[98]

Although ITT's principal argument was based on the preemption doctrine, it also maintained that strikers should not be eligible for welfare benefits because by striking they had voluntarily left their jobs and hence were persons who "without good cause" had refused a "bona fide offer of employment." The district court rejected the corporation's argument, pointing out that the strikers were engaged in a "rightful activity" that was protected by federal labor statutes. Moreover, the court said, "the possible consequences to a union member of returning to work as a strike breaker may well constitute good cause for failing to return to work."[99]

In its consideration of the same point of law, the first circuit court declared that equating a refusal to work at a struck establishment with a refusal to accept a *bona fide* offer of employment "is no less circular or more persuasive than the contrary assumption," namely that exercising one's federally protected right to strike always constitutes "good cause" to refuse employment.[100] The correct approach, in the first circuit court's view, was to allow the state, without deciding the merits of a particular dispute, "to make the determination of what is covered by 'good cause' and what constitutes a 'bona fide' offer of employment."[101] Since the strikers in the ITT case had registered for employment and (presumably) would be required to accept suitable alternative employment if it became available, the court held that the state welfare commissioner's determination that the strikers were eligible for benefits had not been precluded by either federal or state statutes.[102]

In summary, efforts to prohibit or restrict the payment of welfare benefits to strikers through the courts were generally unsuccessful in the 1960s and 1970s. Those who sought to restrict striker eligibility for welfare benefits won only one major court victory, and that came in the Supreme Court's decision in *Batterton v. Francis.* The Court upheld the prerogative of a state participating in the AFDC-U program to deny benefits to strikers, but its ruling in no way disturbed the opposite choice that had been made by the majority of states in the program.

Otherwise federal and state courts did not accept the argument that the payment of welfare benefits to strikers violated the public policy principle of state neutrality in labor relations. Most courts simply did not believe that the payment of welfare benefits to strikers had a demonstrable effect on collective bargaining. The first circuit court in *Minter,* however, maintained that a court should engage in a balancing test, weighing "the impact on the state of declaring needy strikers and their families ineligible for welfare against the extent to which making them eligible stripped state government of its neutrality in a labor-management dispute."[103] The impact on collective bargaining, the *Minter* court said, was in effect an empirical matter, depending in part on "whether or not strikes tend to be of longer duration where welfare is received."[104] Such empirical evidence was lacking in *Minter,* but even if a court had evidence suggesting that welfare payments did have a discernible effect on collective bargaining, it was still necessary, according to the *Minter* court, to weigh that impact against the state's legitimate interest in "minimizing hardships to families of strikers who have no other resources than the weekly pay check."[105] Clearly, the court believed that it would be difficult, if not impossible, to muster enough evidence on the impact of welfare payments on collective bargaining to overcome the presumption that needy strikers deserved state support.

The courts also refused to accept the proposition that strikers should be ineligible for welfare because, by striking, they had without good cause refused to accept suitable or "bona fide" employment. In *Strat-O-Seal, Lascaris I* and *II,* and *Minter,* the courts recognized that adopting such a view would, in the words of *Strat-O-Seal,* place "a hangman's noose" over the right to strike.[106] On the other hand, the courts have held that to be eligible for welfare strikers had to register for employment, accept referrals to jobs, and accept alternative employment, if suitable work was available. In *Minter* the court said it would be interested in knowing whether strikers actually did accept alternative employment,[107] but direct knowledge on this factual matter was absent in *Minter* and in other cases as well. It is possible that some courts would have denied welfare benefits to strikers if they had had direct evidence that otherwise eligible strikers had been offered suitable, *bona fide* jobs by other employers and had refused to accept them. But to date no court has been offered such evidence.[108]

Courts have typically heard cases in which there was no explicit statutory ban on the payment of welfare to strikers and the state had a long history of paying benefits to strikers.[109] Under these circumstances courts have been unwilling to prohibit the payment of benefits to strikers and their families. As the court said in *Lascaris II,* "In light of this State's long-standing administrative policy sanctioning assistance payments to strikers, the Legislature, if it considers such a policy impermissible, should manifest its design in clear and unmistakable terms.''[110] The *Minter* court expressed essentially the same view with respect to the payment of AFDC-U to strikers, declaring that Congress was ''the preferable forum'' for resolving the issue.[111] Of course, in 1981, Congress did speak clearly on this issue, eliminating striker eligibility for both AFDC-U benefits and food stamps.[112]

Although the issue of striker eligibility for AFDC-U generated intense political controversy and a substantial amount of litigation, it is not likely that program benefits played a major role in the vast majority of labor disputes in the 1960s and 1970s. It must be remembered that only a subset of states participate in the AFDC-U program and, before 1981, not all of the participating states granted benefits to strikers. Moreover, program rules effectively limited eligibility to the most impoverished strikers with dependent children. Furthermore, although some strikers might have qualified for emergency assistance, most strikers had to wait 30 days before they could attain eligibility—and, of course, the majority of strikes are settled well within 30 days.[113] Finally, applicants for AFDC-U only become eligible for benefits when they have exhausted their eligibility for unemployment compensation; strikers receiving unemployment benefits, therefore, would not also receive AFDC-U.[114]

Given these restrictions, it is not surprising that relatively few strikers ever received AFDC-U benefits, despite claims to the contrary. Thieblot and Cowin, in their 1972 book, tried to estimate the annual cost of paying eligible strikers AFDC-U. The case studies they had conducted suggested to them that 15 percent of all strikers would receive AFDC-U benefits in a ''normal'' year. Using this assumption, Thieblot and Cowin estimated that paying AFDC-U to strikers carried an annual price tag of $62.6 million.[115] There is reason to believe, however, that Thieblot and Cowin's figure is grossly exaggerated. In its consideration of the Omnibus Budget Reconciliation bill in 1981, the Senate Budget Committee received a staff report suggesting that the elimination of AFDC-U for strikers would save about $5 million in a year.[116] If credence is given to the Senate estimate, then only .6 of 1 percent of total AFDC-U payments went to strikers in 1980.[117]

The Senate cost estimate can also be used to generate an estimate of the number of strikers who received assistance in 1980. Suppose we assume, for the sake of argument, that every striker received just one month of AFDC-U benefits. Since the average AFDC-U payment per family was about $400 a month in 1980, then *at most* 12,500 strikers received assistance during that year.[118] This is obviously an upper-bound estimate, since eligible strikers would have received two or more months of benefits if they were involved in strikes lasting longer than 60 days. (In the next chapter we present data showing that 14 percent of all strikes last longer than 56 days.) Nevertheless, our estimate suggests that in 1980 less than .7 of 1 percent of AFDC-U families included a striker and less than 1 percent of all strikers received benefits.[119]

These estimates present a very different picture from the one painted by Thieblot and Cowin.[120] The estimates are not intended, of course, to refute evidence that in some long strikes the AFDC-U program was a major source of support for strikers' families.[121] But they cast doubt on the perception, certainly widespread in the business community, that welfare benefits were commonly available to strikers. This perception was fostered by media coverage of some of the court cases discussed here as well as the extensive publicity given certain protracted strikes (such as the coal strikes of 1978 and 1981) in which large numbers of workers were reported to have received welfare and food stamps.[122]

For more than a decade employers and their allies waged a campaign against the use of welfare assistance in labor disputes. As we have seen, their efforts to achieve their objective in the courts were largely unavailing. Similarly, until 1981 efforts to ban payment of AFDC-U to strikers through Congressional action were also unsuccessful. But when President Reagan came into office and control of the Senate passed to the Republicans in 1981, the stage was set for major alterations in the nation's social legislation. One of the principal targets of the Reagan administration was the AFDC program. Under the leadership of Budget Director David Stockman, the administration sought amendments to the Social Security Act designed to cut $1.2 billion from federal expenditures for AFDC (and therefore the same amount from State expenditures). All of the changes proposed by the administration were incorporated into the Omnibus Budget Reconciliation Act, which was enacted into law on August 13, 1981.[123] Included in OBRA was an amendment to the Social Security Act that prohibited the payment of AFDC-U benefits to strikers and their families.[124]

Food Stamps

The food stamp program has several features that distinguish it from other welfare programs. Most obvious is the fact that instead of providing cash to needy recipients, the program provides coupons or "stamps" that can only be used to purchase food. Less obvious, but perhaps substantially more important, the program operates under uniform federal rules. Unlike the AFDC program, the rules governing food stamp eligibility and benefit determination are the same throughout the United States. Moreover, the federal government pays the full cost of the stamps and half of the administrative costs. Although the states are responsible for the day-to-day administration of the program and the other half of the administrative costs, they have no control over policy. Essentially the states implement rules that are written in Washington.[125] By contrast, eligibility and benefit determination under the AFDC program are substantially in the hands of the states.

In addition, the food stamp program covers a broader population than the AFDC program. Whereas the AFDC-U program is restricted to families with dependent children, the food stamp population encompasses AFDC-U eligibles, single individuals, couples with children, and even communes.[126] Thus, in 1981, at the time OBRA was passed, there were 23 million food stamp recipients but only 2 million families receiving AFDC-U.[127]

To be eligible for food stamp assistance, a household must qualify under a federal standard of need, below which a household's resources must fall for it to be eligible for benefits. The standard of need under the food stamp program has generally been more liberal than the standard of need established by most states under the AFDC-U program. For example, in 1975 most four-person families would qualify for assistance if the household's liquid assets did not exceed $1,500 and its annualized net income did not exceed $6,480.[128] Essentially, a household qualified for assistance if its net income was at or below the federal poverty line.

In 1981, however, OBRA changed the eligibility test from one based on net income to one based on gross income. Households without an elderly or disabled member were required to have gross income, before any deductions for expenses, below 130 percent of the federal poverty level of income. Net income was to be used only to determine benefits. For example, a working family of four with a monthly income of $1,191 (30 percent more than the poverty level of $916) became ineligible for benefits. The shift to a gross-income eligibility test was designed to remove from the program nearly one million recipients who were on the high end of the low-income population.[129]

Whereas in the case of the AFDC-U program, an unemployed spouse must wait 30 days before becoming eligible for benefits, food stamp assistance is provided without a waiting period. This feature of the food stamp program was particularly significant for strikers, who until 1981 could potentially become eligible for food stamp assistance on the first day of a strike. In addition, a household's receipt of food stamps did not decrease the welfare grants that may have been available to it under other federal and state laws. Thus, until 1981 strikers could potentially qualify for both food stamps and state general assistance on the first day of a strike, and for both food stamps and AFDC-U if the strike lasted longer than 30 days.[130]

The food stamp program also contains a work requirement not unlike the one contained in the AFDC-U program. A "physically and mentally fit" adult loses eligibility for food stamps if he refuses to register for employment, voluntarily quits his job without good cause, or refuses to accept a suitable offer of employment. Before 1981 the Food Stamp Act specifically allowed an applicant to refuse employment at a plant or site because of a strike or lockout. OBRA, however, altered this proviso so that now an applicant can refuse employment at a struck plant only if the household does not contain a member on strike.[131]

When a household is deemed to be eligible for food stamps, it receives a monthly allotment of free stamps. A benefit schedule, which varies according to the size and net income of the household, is used to determine the allotment. A Thrifty Food Plan, which is based on recommended daily allowances of nutrients for persons in various age/sex categories, is used to calculate the maximum food stamp benefit payable to a household of a particular size. A household's monthly allotment is the Thrifty Food Plan amount, reduced by 30 percent of a household's net income. Historically, the allotment for a family of four has generally been about 25 percent of its net income.[132]

The origins of the food stamp program date to the Great Depression of the 1930s. At a time when farmers produced food they could not sell while thousands of unemployed workers stood in bread lines, the federal government began to distribute surplus food to the hungry. The first food stamp program was established in 1939. Needy households purchased stamps at their face value and also received free stamps as well. The stamps could be used to buy surplus food available at retail stores. The plan, however, was discontinued in 1943, at a time when the booming wartime economy had virtually eliminated both the unemployment and surplus food problems.[133]

There were sporadic experiments with surplus commodity programs throughout the postwar period. In 1961 President Kennedy launched the immediate predecessor of the current program when he issued an executive order establishing pilot food stamp programs in seven states. The number of participating states had grown to 43 by 1964 when Congress passed the Food Stamp Act, which remains the statutory framework for the current program.[134]

The initial program under the Food Stamp Act was modest in scale. Much like the AFDC-U program, a state could choose not to participate in the program, and states that did choose to participate exercised substantial control over eligibility criteria and allotment levels. In 1965 the program provided benefits to only 632,000 people at a cost of $32.5 million to the federal government.[135] In the late 1960s several public interest groups focused national attention on the problem of hunger in America.[136] This attention caused Congress to increase substantially federal outlays for the food stamp program. In 1971 Congress established uniform national income and resource eligibility standards and again increased benefits available under the program. Then in 1973 Congress required that all counties in the nation offer food stamps by July 1974. By 1975 the food stamp program provided benefits to 19.2 million people at a cost of $4.4 billion.[137]

The Food Stamp Act of 1964 did not speak to the issue of whether strikers should receive food stamps. Rather the issue arose only when reports began to surface that strikers were receiving stamps. Carney reports that in the fall of 1965, "lumberers in the Northwest became the first group of strikers to find in the Act a source of public subsidy."[138] In 1967 strikers used food stamps during the UAW's strike against Ford, and later that year striking copper workers also received food stamps. These strikes generated considerable publicity over the issue of food stamps for strikers, leading representatives of the business community to voice opposition to the practice.[139]

In 1968 the House of Representatives passed a food stamp bill prohibiting strikers from receiving assistance. Senate opposition to the House measure resulted in the striker disqualification being removed from the final legislation. In 1970 Congress again confronted the issue. A motion in the House to prohibit strikers from receiving food stamps was defeated. Instead, Congress included language in the Act that explicitly permitted strikers to receive food stamps: "Refusal to work at a plant or site subject to a strike or a lockout for the duration of such strike or lockout shall not be deemed refusal to accept employment."[140] The House Agricultural Committee's report on the 1970 amendments to the Food Stamp Act noted that it had adopted the striker provision because it did "not wish to take sides in labor disputes and does not believe this bill is the proper place to solve labor-management problems."[141]

The controversy, however, raged on. Throughout the 1970s repeated attempts were made in Congress to curtail striker participation in the food stamp program, but all such efforts failed. In 1971, for example, the House Agricultural Committee voted to eliminate striker eligibility for food stamps but the committee's bill never reached the House floor for debate. The following year, the committee reversed its position, voting to allow strikers to continue to receive food stamps.[142] In 1974, the Ford administration attempted to overturn the existing policy, but the Senate voted against an administration-backed proposal.[143]

Congress again considered the issue in 1977. This time new language was added to the Food Stamp Act that reflected the political pressure on Congressional supporters of food stamps for strikers:

> No household that contains a person involved in a labor-management dispute shall be eligible to participate in the food stamp program unless the household meets the income guidelines, asset requirements, and work registration requirements of this Act.[144]

By emphasizing that only strikers who were otherwise eligible could receive food stamps, the supporters hoped to eliminate the perception that strikers were somehow treated differently from other food stamp recipients. In discussing this provision, the House Agricultural Committee said in 1979:

> [We] have constantly grappled with the issue of providing food stamp benefits to strikers. In the 1977 Act, we refused to eliminate them and the members of their households from consideration for participation simply because they were on strike, since such an automatic exclusion seemed unfair and inequitable and would have involved the government in the non-neutral act of pressuring the worker to abandon the strike. . . .
>
> The Committee wishes to reiterate its intention that the food stamp program be limited to the truly needy as defined by the existing eligibility criteria. . . . Accordingly, the Committee has determined to add an amendment that makes crystal clear that it does not countenance making any striker or the striker's household eligible for food stamps by virtue solely of the existence of the strike and that [it] in no way condones strikers viewing being on strike as the sole qualifying criterion enabling them to receive food stamps. That is not the way the program works now. That is not the way the program ought to work ever.[145]

But the committee then acknowledged that the amendment had not in any way changed existing policy; it had merely altered the emphasis.[146]

The effort made by congressional supporters in 1977 to deflect criticism of the policy did not succeed. Congressional opponents and their business allies continued to press their efforts to remove the striker qualification provision from the Food Stamp Act. Their efforts were fueled by reports that thousands of miners collected food stamps during the 111-day coal strike of 1977-78. When coal miners again went on strike in March 1981, the press reported that food stamp administrators in the coal states were preparing for an onslaught of applications from the striking miners. Later reports suggest that the administrators overestimated the number of strikers who would qualify for assistance.[147]

Shortly after Congress convened in January 1981, Senator Strom Thurmond introduced legislation to bar food stamps for strikers. Thurmond cited the coal strike of 1977-78 as evidence of the need for the legislation. In offering the bill, Senator Thurmond said that the federal government, by providing food stamps to strikers, was ''injecting itself into the dispute.'' He maintained that providing food stamps in such a situation merely prolonged a strike and worsened the damage to the economy.[148] By June, the Senate had voted to adopt the Thurmond bill as part of legislation reauthorizing the food stamp program for four years. In the meantime, the House Agricultural Committee approved a comparable prohibition as part of a broad farm bill.[149]

It was at this point that most of the pending 1981 social legislation was incorporated into the OBRA. In its final form, the OBRA contained the ban on food stamps for strikers that Senator Thurmond and his conservative allies had long sought.[150] Actually, the new legislation did not ban *all* strikers from receiving food stamps. One proviso permits strikers to continue to receive food stamps *if* the strikers' household had been eligible for assistance immediately prior to the commencement of the strike. (Another proviso allows a household that does not contain a member on strike to maintain its eligibility for food stamps when any of its members refuses to accept employment at a struck plant or site.) Thus, even if a strike causes household income to fall to the point where the household satisfies the food stamp program's income and asset requirements, if the household had not been eligible for stamps prior to the beginning of a strike the household does not become eligible for stamps during the strike. In any event, it is clear that the 1981 legislation makes the great majority of strikers ineligible for food stamp assistance.[151]

How much did this prohibition save the federal treasury? In February 1981 Senators Helms and Thurmond, joined by Congressmen E. Thomas Coleman and William L. Dickinson, asked the General Accounting Office to gather "available data on participation in the Food Stamp Program by households with members involved in labor-management disputes."[152] In a report submitted in March 1981, the GAO examined the food stamp caseload in five separate one-month periods during the interval 1976-79. The GAO review revealed the following:

> ". . . The percentage of food stamp households containing a striker ranged from 0.29 percent to 2.1 percent of total food stamp households.
>
> ". . . Of all persons on strike, the percentage of strikers who participated in the Food Stamp Program ranged from 3.6 percent to 36.4 percent.
>
> ". . . Food Stamp benefits provided to strikers' households may have amounted to $37 million in fiscal year 1980."[153]

The $37 million figure implies that less than .5 of 1 percent of fiscal 1980 food stamp expenditures took the form of benefits to strikers. Moreover, the percentage of food stamp households containing a striker reached an abnormally high level of 2.1 percent and the percentage of strikers participating in the food stamp program reached an equally abnormal level of 36.5 percent only in February 1978, in the middle of the 1977-78 coal strike. In each of the four other months examined by the GAO, the percent of food stamp households containing a striker never exceeded .4 of 1 percent of the total number of households receiving assistance and the number of strikers receiving food stamps never exceeded 11 percent of the number of workers on strike.[154]

The Congressional Budget Office estimated that eliminating food stamps for strikers would result in savings of $50 million in 1982, $55 million in 1983, and $60 million in 1984.[155] Note that these estimates mesh with the estimate of $37 million produced by the GAO for 1980.[156]

Again, it is important to contrast the GAO and CBO numbers with those contained in Thieblot and Cowin. Their influential 1972 book claimed that in a typical year (which they called "1973") 60 percent of all strikers "would be expected to receive food stamps."[157] Recall that in 1972 many counties did not even have a food stamp program. Contrast their claim with the GAO finding that for the period 1976-79 between 3.6 and 36.4 percent of all strikers received food stamps. Thieblot and Cowin also maintained that providing food stamps to strikers would cost $239 million a year in 1973.[158] The Thieblot and Cowin estimates were widely cited, especially by those seeking a ban on food stamps for strikers, but the estimates produced 10 years later by the GAO and the CBO demonstrate that Thieblot and Cowin's numbers were again grossly exaggerated.[159]

In contrast to unemployment compensation, AFDC-U, and general assistance, there was very little litigation over the issue of food stamps for strikers prior to the 1981 legislation. Most of the issues that were subjected to judicial scrutiny in cases dealing with the payment of benefits to strikers under other government transfer programs had little or no relevance to the food stamp program. For example, because the program operates under a federal statute and uniform federal standards, and states lacked the discretion—and apparently never attempted—to set their own rules, the doctrine of federal preemption clearly had no relevance to the policy. In Congressional debates, as we have seen, both proponents and opponents of the policy claimed that the principle of government neutrality in labor disputes required the adoption of the position they advocated. Whether government neutrality was or was not violated by the payment of food stamps to strikers was, however, an issue that was never tested in the courts.

On the other hand, one federal district court had occasion to consider, in *Jaramillo v. County of Santa Clara,* whether a regulation issued by the Department of Agriculture was in conflict with the plain language of the Food Stamp Act.[160] The Department had issued a regulation that prohibited the payments of food stamps to applicants who were participating in a strike "which has pursuant to a court decision currently in force been determined to be unlawful."[161] When employees of Santa

Clara County, California, planned to go on strike in 1975, the county obtained a temporary restraining order which enjoined the strike. Nevertheless, the employees did strike and, subsequently, some of them applied for food stamps. The county, which had the responsibility of administering the food stamp program, denied food stamps to the strikers on the grounds that they were participating in an unlawful strike.[162]

Plaintiffs in *Jaramillo* contended that the denial of food stamps to strikers because they were participating in an unlawful strike violated the Food Stamp Act, which, plaintiffs argued, made food stamps available to strikers regardless of whether a strike was lawful or unlawful. The court agreed with the plaintiffs. "By adopting regulations which in effect rule that food stamps shall be denied to participants in strikes judicially determined to be unlawful, the Department of Agriculture presumes to make a distinction not made by Congress and is engaging in legislation beyond its powers," the court said.[163] The court therefore held that the Department's regulation was void.[164] Apart from this case, however, the courts have had very few opportunities to rule on the payment of stamps to strikers.[165]

In 1986, however, the UAW challenged the constitutionality of the 1981 amendment banning food stamps for strikers in *UAW v. Lyng*.[166] The UAW argued that the 1981 amendment "impairs the constitutional rights of the individual plaintiffs to associate with their families and unions in violation of the First Amendment" and "impairs these rights without rationally furthering a legitimate governmental purpose in violation of the Due Process clause of the Fifth Amendment."[167] Judge Oberdorfer of the District Court for the District of Columbia agreed with the UAW. He argued that the statute infringes upon individuals' First Amendment rights to free speech and free association, since it forces strikers experiencing economic hardship either to quit their jobs, cross the picket line and return to work, leave their families so that they may qualify for food stamps, or put pressure on their union to end the strike. Furthermore, the Court found that it violates the equal protection clause of the Fifth Amendment, by singling out striking employees for punitive treatment, treating them worse than individuals who voluntarily quit their jobs, and by directing "the 'onus' of the striker's exercise of his associational rights'' as much ''on the innocent members of the family as . . . on the striker himself.''[168]

The district court's view in *UAW v. Lyng* differs from the second circuit court's view in *Russo v. Kirby,* decided 15 years earlier. In the earlier case, Judge Hays said the argument that denying welfare benefits and food stamps to strikers infringes their first amendment rights ''borders on the frivolous.''[169] He added, ''The equal protection claim is almost as insubstantial since the basis of classification is clearly not unreasonable.''[170] In 1987 two federal courts specifically rejected the conclusions reached by the UAW court. In *Eaton v. Lyng,* the constitutionality of the 1981 amendment was challenged by two strikers and members of their households.[171] In this case, a federal district court in Iowa ruled that the amendment did not interfere with plaintiffs' First Amendment rights, since it did not create a ''genuine incentive to choose any of the alternatives which would require a waiver of a constitutional right'' outlined by the UAW court.[172] The incentive ''is created by the strike, and Congress has simply refused to use the food stamp program to solve the problem.''[173] Rejecting the UAW court's argument that a ''heightened level of scrutiny'' should be applied to the law since it affected a group which has historically been discriminated against, the Court held that it was rationally related to legitimate government objectives and did not violate the equal protection clause of the Fifth Amendment.[174]

Similar issues were addressed by the U.S. Court of Appeals in *Ledesma v. Block.*[175] As in the *Eaton* case, the Court rejected the heightened scrutiny test and instead used a rational basis test to determine whether the statutory classification of strikers violates the equal protection clause. The Court held that the amendments ''were rationally related to goals of government neutrality in labor disputes and concentrating benefits on people who are unable to work, and thus do not violate equal protection.''[176]

The courtroom battle over food stamps for strikers was ended in March, 1988, when the Supreme Court reversed the district court's *UAW* decision.[177] The Supreme Court ruled that the 1981 amendment does not ''directly and substantially'' interfere with strikers' rights to freely associate with their families and their unions.[178] Delivering the opinion of the majority, Justice Byron White wrote: ''Exercising the right to strike inevitably risks economic hardship, but we are not inclined to hold that the right of association requires the government to minimize that result by qualifying the striker for food stamps.''[179] For similar reasons, the Court held that the amendment does not infringe upon the right to freedom of expression: ''it does not 'coerce' belief; and it does not require appellees to participate in political activities or support political views with which they disagree.''[180] Finally, the Supreme Court ruled that, since the statute ''has no substantial impact on any fundamental interest and does not 'affect with particularity any protected class,''' the proper level of scrutiny under the equal protection clause is the rational basis test.[181] Relying on the findings in the *Hodory* case, the Court ruled that the 1981 Amendment does not violate the Fifth Amendment since it is rationally related to legitimate legislative objectives of neutrality in labor disputes and protecting the government's fiscal integrity.

General Assistance

The General Assistance program is the nation's oldest assistance program. Its roots stretch back to the nineteenth century. The program provides cash and in-kind benefits to impoverished people that fall outside the federal-state public assistance programs (e.g., Aid to Families with Dependent Children and Supplemental Security Income). For example, it might provide emergency assistance to an able bodied single male who is without money and is unable to find work. It is distinguished from both AFDC-U and food stamps by the absence of a federal role. General Assistance is a state and local program. In some states, e.g., Georgia, it is funded and administered by counties, with county level administrators having substantial say over who receives benefits and how much they receive.

Since the federal government does not play a role in this program, *General Assistance benefits are still available to strikers.* The 1981 OBRA legislation, which effectively cut off AFDC-U and Food Stamp benefits to strikers, did not touch the General Assistance program.

Of course, whether a striker is eligible for GA benefits and the level of benefits received depends upon where the striker lives. Another implication of the absence of a federal role is incredible diversity in GA programs across states. New York State runs a GA program that in August, 1974 provided an average monthly benefit of $98.85 to 164,000 recipients. The corresponding numbers for Alabama's GA program were a benefit of $12.50 to 42 recipients.[182] In general, GA programs are much less generous and exhibit greater interstate variation than federal-state programs like AFDC.

Since GA eligibility rules are written by either states or counties, it is not surprising that there have been several instances where strikers received GA benefits. Indeed, the earliest U.S. litigation over strikes and transfers occurred in 1904 when striking coal miners in Illinois obtained General Assistance benefits.[183] As noted above, the 1940s and 1950s saw strikers receive GA benefits in several important labor disputes including the 1945 UAW strike against General Motors, and the 1946 and 1959 steel strikes. Furthermore, as indicated by the litigation over AFDC-U, we know that many strikes involving receipt of AFDC-U also involved receipt of GA. Unfortunately, however, our knowledge in this area is largely anecdotal. We cannot answer such basic questions as, what fraction of strikers receive GA? or what fraction of GA benefits go to strikers? Moreover, we cannot answer these questions for the current year, for any earlier year, for the nation, or for any state.

Litigation over GA has largely followed the same paths as that over AFDC-U. Two themes are central. First, does payment of GA benefits to strikers violate federal labor law in that it compromises the principle of state neutrality in labor disputes? Second, in the absence of an explicit legislative prohibition against striker receipt of GA, do other seemingly applicable provisions in the state's statutes *imply* a prohibition? The cases addressing these questions are largely the same as those for AFDC-U.[184] Moreover, the answers are basically the same for the two programs.

With regard to the first question, the courts have not viewed payment of GA to strikers as inconsistent with the public policy standard of neutrality. As for the second question, a state may choose to prohibit strikers from receiving GA. Like AFDC-U, however, the state's legislation must be explicit on the matter.

The major difference between GA and AFDC-U litigation lies in its relevance to the present. Given the 1981 OBRA legislation, past litigation over AFDC-U is legally irrelevant. That is not true for GA. Since strikers can still receive GA, past litigation influences the interpretation of laws governing that receipt.

Before proceeding to the next chapter, the reader may find it useful to refer to exhibits 4.1 and 4.2 for summaries of the legislative history and judicial decisions pertaining to the provision of public assistance to strikers.

Conclusion

Because welfare is quite distinct from unemployment insurance, the issues raised in this chapter are in some ways quite distinct from those raised in the previous two chapters. Welfare assistance is targeted on families with very low incomes; families with greater need (more dependents and lower incomes) generally receive larger welfare benefits. Unemployment insurance is paid to eligibles irrespective of family income. Here the level of benefits primarily depends on the individual's past earnings record rather than on current needs. Whereas welfare assistance is targeted on the poor, unemployment insurance is targeted on the middle class.[185]

This difference in the nature of the programs creates a subtle difference in the nature of the controversy surrounding payment of transfers to strikers. It is one thing to say that a striker with a private home and a working spouse should be denied unemployment insurance. It is quite another to say that a striker with no assets and children on the edge of starvation should be denied public assistance. The latter raises a tension between the government's role in labor disputes and its role in alleviating poverty—a role that governments have played since the middle ages. While that tension may also arise in unemployment insurance,

Exhibit 4.1
Legislative History of AFDC and Food Stamp Regulations Pertaining to Strikers

Date	Program	Provisions	Prevalence
1935	AFDC	The Social Security Act established the program to provide assistance to children in need because of the death, incapacity, or continued absence of a parent. In most states, a family was disqualified from receiving benefits if an able-bodied man was living in the house. The Act did not prohibit the payment of AFDC to needy strikers; the matter was left to the states to decide.	All jurisdictions
1961	AFDC-U	Congress amended the program to provide assistance to the needy children of unemployed parents. Provisions in the Act state that an individual is ineligible for AFDC-U if he is out of work "without good cause" or if he has refused a "bona fide offer of suitable employment." States electing to participate in the program had the option of deciding whether strikers did or did not fall within the definition of an unemployed parent. Applicants must be unemployed 30 days before becoming eligible.	Approximately 25 states
1964	Food Stamps	The Food Stamp Act established the program to provide needy individuals with coupons that could be used solely for the purchase of food. Uniform federal rules govern eligibility in all states. A work requirement provides that an employable recipient loses eligibility if he refuses to register for employment, voluntarily quits his job without good cause or refuses to accept a suitable offer of employment. The issue of striker eligibility was not specifically addressed. There is no waiting period.	All jurisdictions

Date	Program	Provisions	Prevalence
1968	AFDC-U	Congress amended the Social Security Act, withdrawing some of the States' authority to define an unemployed parent. Participating states were required to provide AFDC-U where a needy child "has been deprived of parental support or care by reason of the unemployment (as determined in accordance with standards prescribed by the Secretary) of his father." The definition of unemployment subsequently issued by the Secretary of Health, Education, and Welfare did not address the issue of strikers.	Approximately 25 states
1970	Food Stamps	Congress included language in the Act that explicitly permitted strikers to receive food stamps.	All jurisdictions
1973	AFDC-U	The Secretary of Health, Education, and Welfare issued a new regulation that explicitly gave states the option to deny benefits where the parent's unemployment resulted from participation in a labor dispute.	Eight states denied benefits to strikers prior to 1981
1973	Food Stamps	Congress required all counties in the country to offer food stamps by July 1974.	All jurisdictions
1981	Food Stamps & AFDC-U	Omnibus Budget Reconciliation Act prohibited the provision of AFDC-U and Food Stamp benefits to strikers and their families. Those strikers who had been eligible for food stamps just prior to the commencement of the strike may continue to receive them, however the allotment cannot be adjusted to compensate for the striker's lost income.	All jurisdictions

Exhibit 4.2
Principal Judicial Decisions Pertaining to the Provision of Public Assistance to Strikers

Case	Issue	Findings
Strat-O-Seal Mfg. Co. v. Scott 72 Ill. App. 2d 480 (1966)	Whether the payment of welfare benefits to strikers violates the principle of state neutrality in labor disputes.	The Circuit Court of Illinois upheld the State's long-standing policy of paying welfare benefits to strikers who were otherwise qualified. The Court held that need arising out of an employee's participation in a bona fide strike and his refusal to return to his employer is not a bar to public assistance.
Lascaris v. Wyman 305 N.Y.S. 2d 212 (1969)	Whether the payment of welfare benefits to strikers violates the principle of state neutrality in labor disputes.	The New York Supreme Court held that striking GE employees who refused available work from their employer were not barred from receiving welfare assistance if they were otherwise qualified.
ITT Lamp Division v. Minter 318 F.Supp. 364 (1970), 435 F.2d 989 (1970), cert. denied, 402 U.S. 933 (1971)	Whether paying strikers welfare benefits violates federal law by compromising the principle of state neutrality in labor disputes.	The First Circuit Court held that payment of welfare benefits to teamsters on strike against ITT was not preempted by either federal or state law.
	Whether granting AFDC-U to strikers violates provisions of the Social Security Act.	Provisions of the Social Security Act that prohibit the payment of benefits to persons who "without good cause...refused a bona fide offer of employment" do not necessarily apply to strikers. States should be allowed "to make the determination of what is covered by 'good cause' and what constitutes a 'bona fide' offer of employment."
Russo v. Kirby 453 F.2d 548 (1971)	Whether the denial of welfare benefits to strikers infringed upon rights guaranteed by the First and Fifth Amendments.	The U.S. Court of Appeals reversed a lower court decision requiring payment of welfare benefits to all strikers. The court held that federal courts did not have jurisdiction.

Case	Issue	Findings
Francis v. Davidson 340 F.Supp. 351 (1972), summarily aff'd 409 U.S. 904 (1972)	Whether a Maryland rule denying AFDC-U benefits to families in which the father was unemployed as a result of participation in a labor dispute was in conflict with federal regulations.	The federal District Court held that the Maryland rule was invalid. The Court found that a man out of work because of a labor dispute was "unemployed," as defined by HEW regulations, and therefore eligible for benefits as prescribed by the Social Security Act.
Lascaris v. Wyman 340 N.Y.S. 2d 397 (1972)	Whether striking employees were precluded from receiving public assistance under a New York statute that disqualified employable persons who have refused to accept employment. Whether payment of welfare benefits to strikers violates the State's policy of neutrality in labor disputes.	The New York Court of Appeals held that strikers were eligible to receive general assistance, provided they registered with the state employment office and did not refuse suitable employment. Going out on strike does not, by itself, constitute refusing employment. The Court held that payment of benefits does not violate the State's policy of neutrality.
Francis v. Davidson 379 F.Supp. 78 (D.Md. 1974)	Whether a Maryland rule denying AFDC-U benefits to children whose fathers are unemployed because of labor disputes, and the 1973 HEW regulation that expressly permits the rule, are valid.	The District Court held that the HEW regulation is incompatible with the federal AFDC-U statute, and is thus invalid. Accordingly, the Maryland regulation is also invalid.
Jaramillo v. County of Santa Clara 91 LRRM 2755 (1976)	Whether a Department of Agriculture regulation prohibiting payment of food stamps to applicants who were participating in an unlawful strike violated the Food Stamp Act.	The federal District Court held that the regulation was void since Congress in passing the Food Stamp Act had not intended to make a distinction between lawful and unlawful strikes.

Case	Issue	Findings
Batterton v. Francis 432 U.S. 426 (1977)	Whether states participating in the AFDC-U program could be given the option of denying benefits to strikers' families.	The Supreme Court overturned the lower court ruling that states did not have the authority to deny AFDC-U benefit to strikers. The Court held that a regulation issued by HEW in 1973 explicitly giving states the option of disqualifying AFDC-U fathers whose unemployment resulted from participation in a labor dispute was valid.
UAW v. Lyng 648 F.Supp. 1234 (1986)	Constitutionality of the 1981 amendment to the Food Stamp Act banning the provision of benefits to strikers and their families.	The District Court held that the amendment is unconstitutional, since it interferes with individuals' First Amendment rights to free speech and free association, and violates the equal protection clause of the Fifth Amendment.
Eaton v. Lyng 669 F.Supp. 266 (N.D. Iowa 1987)	Constitutionality of the 1981 amendment to the Food Stamp Act banning the provision of benefits to strikers and their families.	The District Court held that the 1981 amendment violates neither the First nor the Fifth Amendment, and is rationally related to a legitimate government objective of neutrality in labor disputes.
Ledesma v. Block 825 F.2d 1046 (6th Cir. 1987)	Constitutionality of the 1981 amendment to the Food Stamp Act banning the provision of benefits to strikers and their families.	The U.S. Court of Appeals held that the striker amendment is rationally related to government goals of neutrality in labor disputes and concentrating benefits on individuals who are unable to work and therefore does not violate the equal protection clause.
Lyng v. UAW 108 S.Ct. 1184 (1988)	Constitutionality of the 1981 amendment to the Food Stamp Act banning the provision of benefits to strikers and their families.	The Supreme Court reversed the the District Court's ruling that the striker amendment is unconstitutional. The Court held that the statute does not interfere with strikers' rights to freely associate with their families and their unions, nor with their right to freely express themselves about union matters. The Court also held that the amendment does not violate the equal protection clause, since it is rationally related to the legitimate government objective of neutrality in labor disputes. The decision essentially ended the legal battle over the constitutionality of the OBRA.

it is attenuated by the fact that alleviation of poverty is not the primary purpose of the unemployment insurance program.

Despite this difference, however, the issues raised in this chapter are in some ways quite similar to those raised in chapters 2 and 3. In particular, like unemployment insurance, there is significant diversity in welfare assistance to strikers over time and space. With regard to time, the introduction of AFDC-U and food stamps in the 1960s increased the availability of welfare aid to strikers, while the 1981 OBRA legislation sharply restricted that availability. With regard to space, some states provided AFDC-U to strikers and some did not. This diversity has been a major issue in the litigation over strikes and transfers. An anomaly in the pattern should, however, be noted. The FERA program of the 1930s and the food stamp program of the 1970s are instances of a uniform national policy under which strikers receive government transfers. Both policies were controversial and short-lived.

Another common theme of this and previous chapters is the issue of state neutrality in labor disputes. State neutrality lies at the center of federal labor law, and any government policy that aids or hinders strikers must address it. The courts have generally found that neither a policy of providing nor denying transfers to strikers infringes on state neutrality to the extent that it must be prohibited. This is true for both welfare and unemployment insurance.

A final common theme of the chapters is the question of the *effect* of government transfers on strike behavior. That question has been raised by legislators and judges in the most "practical" of settings. It was raised in reference to unemployment insurance during the New York Telephone strike. It was raised in *ITT v. Minter* when the court ruled that "there is no evidence to show that the payment of AFDC-U and General Assistance benefits to eligible strikers in any way prolonged the strike." It is a question with implications that extend well beyond the "academic." The next several chapters seek to answer that question.

NOTES

1. James T. Carney, "The Forgotten Man on the Welfare Roll: A Study of Public Subsidies for Strikers," *Washington University Law Quarterly,* Vol. 1973, No. 3 (Summer 1973), p. 471.

2. Arthur Schlesinger, *The Coming of the New Deal* (Boston: Houghton Mifflin, 1958), p. 264.

3. Ibid., pp. 266-269. See also, Carney, p. 471.

4. Federal Emergency Relief Administration, *Monthly Report* 7 (July 1933), quoted in Carney, pp. 471-472; Armand J. Thieblot, Jr. and Ronald M. Cowin, *Welfare and Strikes: The Use of Public Funds to Support Strikers* (Philadelphia, Pa.: University of Pennsylvania Press, 1972), p. 34.

5. Carney, p. 472.

6. Carney, p. 472; Thieblot and Cowin, p. 34. See also, *Super Tire Engineering Co. v. McCorkle,* 412 F. Supp. 192 at 195 (1976).

7. Cletus E. Daniel, *Bitter Harvest: A History of California Farmworkers, 1870-1941* (Ithaca and London: Cornell University Press, 1981), pp. 167-221. Quote is on pp. 220-221. Three strikers were killed and dozens more were wounded or beaten during the strike.

8. Daniel, pp. 202-213.

9. Daniel, p. 213.

10. Daniel, pp. 214-216.

11. Daniel, p. 216. See also Irving Bernstein, *Turbulent Years: A History of the American Worker 1933-1941* (Boston: Houghton Mifflin, 1969), pp. 156-60.

12. Bernstein, p. 158.

13. Carney, p. 473.

14. Quoted in Bernstein, p. 308.

15. Thieblot and Cowin, p. 35; see also, Bernstein, p. 312; Carney, p. 472-473.

16. Josephine Chaplin Brown, *Public Relief: 1929-39* (New York: Henry Holt, 1940), p. 270, as cited in Thieblot and Cowin, p. 34. See also Bernstein, pp. 156-160; Carney, pp. 272-274; Thieblot and Cowin, 34-36.

17. Bernstein, pp. 307-308; Carney, p. 473; Thieblot and Cowin, pp. 34-36.

18. Brown, p. 270, as cited in Thieblot and Cowin, p. 36.

19. George E. Rejda, *Social Insurance and Economic Security* (Englewood Cliffs, New Jersey: Prentice-Hall, 1984), p. 400.

20. U.S. Department of Health and Human Services, Social Security Administration, *Characteristics of State Plans for Aid to Families with Dependent Children,* 1984 ed., pp. 77-78.

21. *Batterton v. Francis,* 432 U.S. 416 at 418 (1976); see also, *Burns v. Alcala,* 420 U.S. 575 at 581-582 (1975).

22. Sar A. Levitan, Garth L. Mangum, and Ray Marshall, *Human Resources and Labor Markets* (New York: Harper and Row, 1981), p. 327.

23. *Batterton v. Francis.* 432 U.S. 416 at 418 (1977).

24. Thieblot and Cowin, p. 36.

25. Thieblot and Cowin, p. 36.

26. Thieblot and Cowin, p. 36; see also, Bernstein, p. 434. It is not clear, however, that this union official was referring to AFDC or, more likely, to general assistance. In any event, the contemplated strike was averted when Myron C. Taylor, chairman of U.S. Steel's board of directors, agreed to recognize and enter into collective bargaining with S.W.O.C. See, e.g., Joseph G. Rayback, *A History of American Labor* (New York: The Free Press, 1966). p. 351.

27. Thieblot and Cowin, pp. 37-38; Carney, pp. 474-475.

28. Neil W. Chamberlain and James W. Kuhn, *Collective Bargaining,* 2nd ed. (New York: McGraw-Hill, 1965), p. 174.

29. *U.S. News and World Report,* October 3, 1960, pp. 101-103. In addition, Abel reported, the U.S.W. paid the strikers $20 million in strike benefits.

30. Thieblot and Cowin, pp. 42-43. In New York, Thieblot and Cowin report, 35,000 striking steelworkers received $9 million in unemployment compensation.

31. Carney, pp. 476-477.

32. Thieblot and Cowin, p. 38.

33. Thieblot and Cowin, p. 40.

34. Robert J. Myers, *Social Insurance and Allied Government Programs* (Homewood, Ill.: Richard D. Irwin, 1965). pp. 20-22.

35. Levitan et al., p. 327.

36. Carney, p. 476.

37. Levitan et al., pp. 328-329.

38. See Tom Joe and Cheryl Rogers, *By the Few, For the Few: The Reagan Welfare Legacy* (Lexington, Mass.: Lexington Books, 1985), pp. 19-21.

39. Pub. L. 87.31, 1, 75 Stat. 75. The program was originally set to expire on June 30, 1962. It was extended, however, first for five years, 76 Stat. 193 (1962) and then for one year, 81 Stat. 94 (1967). In 1968, the program was made permanent, 81 Stat. 882 (1968).

40. In the debate preceding passage of the program, Congressman Wilbur Mills noted that states would be able to use AFDC-U to subsidize strikers. 107 *Cong. Rec.* 3766 (1961).

41. Carney, p. 477.

42. Eligibility requirements for the AFDC-U program are described in U.S. Department of Health and Human Services, Social Security Administration, *Characteristics of State Plans for Aid to Families with Dependent Children, 1982* ed. (Washington, D.C.: Government Printing Office, 1982), pp. xi, xvi.

43. *Francis v. Davidson,* 340 F. Supp. 351 (1972), summarily aff'd. 409 U.S. 904 (1972); *Francis v. Davidson,* 379 F. Supp. 78 (D.Md. 1974); *Batterton v. Francis,* 432 U.S. 416 (1977).

44. The AFDC-U program was added to Title IV of the Social Security Act in 1961 as §407. Section 407 (a) referred to "unemployment (as defined by the State)." 75 Stat. 75 (1961).

45. 432 U.S. 416 at 419.

46. 42 U.S.C. §607(a).

47. Specifically, the HEW regulation said that the definition of an unemployed father was "any father who is employed less than 30 hours a week." 45C.F.R. Sec.233.100(a). 45C.F.R. Sec.233.100(a). The regulation was silent on other possible disqualifying conditions, including the father's participation in a labor dispute.

48. 340 F.Supp. 351 (D.Md.1972), summarily aff'd. 409 US 904(1972).

49. Ibid. at 366. The court reasoned identically in considering workers disqualified because of their participation in a labor dispute.

50. The 1973 regulation required that a person would be considered unemployed for AFDC-U purposes if he worked less than 100 hours a month (except for intermittent employment), "except that, at the option of the state, such definition need not include a father whose unemployment results from participation in a labor dispute or who is unemployed by reason of conduct or circumstances which result or would result in disqualification for unemployment compensation under the State's unemployment compensation law." 45 C.F.R. §233.100 (a)(l) (1976).

51. Frank S. Bloch, "Cooperative Federalism and the Role of Litigation in the Development of Federal AFDC Eligibility Policy," *Wisconsin Law Review*, Vol. 1979, No. 1 (1979), pp. 48- 50.

52. The book prompted much commentary in the popular and business press. See, for example, "How Your Tax Dollars Support Strikes," *Nation's Business*, Vol. 61, No. 3 (March 1973); "Should Strikers Get Public Aid?" *Business Week* (March 24, 1973).

53. Bloch, p. 50.

54. *Francis v. Davidson*, 379 F.Supp. 78(D.Md.1974), especially at 81-82.

55. The case was consolidated with *Bethea v. Mason*, 384 F.Supp. 1274(D.Md.1974), a case that dealt with the denial of benefits to fathers who had voluntarily quit their previous jobs. The district court decisions in the two cases were affirmed by the fourth circuit in 1975. 529 F.2d514(1975).

56. *Batterton v. Francis*, 432 U.S. 416 at 428.

57. Ibid.

58. Ibid. at 428-429.

59. Ibid. at 431.

60. Ibid. at 432.

61. Unpublished information on the number and identity of the states participating in the AFDC-U program, and the number and identity of those participating in the program that granted or denied benefits to strikers' families from 1962 through 1981 was supplied by the Office of Family Assistance, Social Security Administration, U.S. Department of Health, Education and Welfare.

It should be noted that, before *Batterton*, the court had issued a series of decisions dealing with conflicting federal and state eligibility criteria for AFDC. In general the court had prohibited states from imposing eligibility criteria that excluded recipients who would otherwise be eligible under federal standards. The three leading cases in this line (sometimes referred to as the trilogy) are *King v. Smith*, 392 U.S. 309(1968) (invalidating an Alabama provision that denied AFDC benefits to mothers cohabiting on a regular basis with an able-bodied man); *Townsend v. Swank*, 404 U.S.282(1971) (invalidating an Illinois provision that disqualified children between the ages of 18 and 20 who were attending a college or university but not those attending high school or vocational training); and *Carleson v. Remillard*, 46 U.S. 598(1972) (invalidating a California statute that defined "continued absence" in such a way as to exclude fathers in the military). In view of these decisions and others, one commentator stated, "The Supreme Court's holding in *Batterton* could be viewed as something of a surprise in that it was contrary to the obvious legislative intent and possibly in conflict with previous decisions in the field of AFDC eligibility." Note, "Social Welfare Law: the AFDC-UF Program and State Eligibility Discretion .. *Batterton v. Francis*," *New York Law School Review*, Vol. 23, No. 4 (1978), p. 756.

62. For a discussion of the policy of state neutrality in labor disputes dating to 1940, see Herbert A. Fierst and Marjorie Spector, "Unemployment Compensation in Labor Disputes," *The Yale Law Journal*, Vol. 49, No. 461 (January 1940), especially pp. 463-465.

63. U.S., Congress, Senate, *Congressional Record*, 80th Cong., 1st sess., 1947, 93, 3951.

64. The Supreme Court has spoken of the aims of federal policy in labor relations in a number of cases. See, for example, *Teamsters Union v. Oliver*, 358 U.S. 283 (1959) and *NLRB v. American National Insurance Co.*, 343 U.S. 395 (1952).

65. U.S. Congress, Senate, *Congressional Record*, 92d Cong., 2nd sess., 1972, 118, p. 26: 33992.

66. Ibid. at 33992-33993. This attempt to eliminate striker eligibility for AFDC-U came in the wake of the decision in *Francis I*, discussed above. In the debate over the proposed amendment, Senator Fannin (Rep., Ariz.) relied heavily on the recently published study by Thieblot and Cowin

to support his view that the amendment should be passed. Ibid. at 33995. The attempt to eliminate striker eligibility failed when a motion to table the proposed amendment was passed by a vote of 68 to 5. Ibid. at 33995.

67. 72 111. App. 2d 480 (1966).

68. Ibid. at 482.

69. Actually, Strat-O-Seal's contention that Illinois had consistently refused to pay unemployment compensation to strikers was incorrect. Illinois had (and still has) a stoppage-of-work provision in its unemployment insurance statute. Ibid. at 482.

70. Ibid. at 484.

71. Ibid. at 485-486.

72. *Lascaris v. Wyman*. 305 N.Y.S.2d 212 (N.Y. Sup. Ct. 1969).

73. Ibid. at 216-217.

74. The amendment is described in *Lascaris v. Wyman*, 340 N.Y.S.2d 397 at 399 (1972). The amendment said that a person would be considered employable unless he was unable to work because of illness, mental or physical incapacitation, advanced age, full-time attendance at school in the case of a minor, or "full-time, satisfactory participation in an approved program of vocational training or rehabilitation." The amendment is contained in Law of May 24, 1971, ch. 298. §5, N.Y. Laws 942, amending N.Y. Social Services Law §131 (4) (McKinney 1966).

75. See our discussion of the *New York Telephone* case in chapter 3, pp. 3-14 to 3-16.

76. 68 Misc. 2d 523 (1971).

77. 38 A.D.2d 163 (1972).

78. 340 N.Y.S. 2d 397 (1972).

79. Ibid. at 401.

80. Ibid. at 402.

81. Ibid. at 402-403.

82. Ibid. at 403, quoting *ITT Lamp Division of Int. Tel. & Tel. Corp v. Minter*, 435 F.2d 989 at 994-995 (1970). The major argument in *ITT v. Minter* was that payment of welfare benefits to strikers violates the preemption doctrine.

83. Another case that had its genesis in the 1971 telephone workers strike was *Russo v. Kirby*, 453 F.2d 548 (1971). After the welfare commissioner of New York's Suffolk County refused to accept new welfare applications from striking telephone workers and terminated the benefits of those already receiving them, the telephone workers brought a class action suit alleging that their federal rights had been infringed in several respects. A federal district court granted injunctive relief and ordered the Suffolk County commissioner to make retroactive and future payments to all strikers without regard to whether their unemployment was caused by a strike. The commissioner refused to comply with the order and appealed to the circuit court, which held that the district court did not have jurisdiction because there was no basis for concluding that the strikers' federal rights had been infringed by the denial of state welfare benefits. The court said, "No colorable constitutional claim is presented to justify taking jurisdiction . . . the argument that denying welfare benefits to strikers infringes their first amendment rights borders on the frivolous. The equal protection claim is almost as insubstantial since the basis of classification is clearly not unreasonable." Ibid. at 551. Moreover, the court pointed out, the issue of striker eligibility for state welfare benefits was being litigated in the New York courts (in *Lascaris v. Wyman*), which was another reason for the federal courts to abstain from intervening. Ibid. at 552.

84. Carney, p. 522.

85. 340 N.Y.S. 2d 397 at 404. The lack of empirical evidence on the effect of welfare payments on the system of collective bargaining, and particularly on strike activity, was also a factor

considered by the circuit court in *ITT Lamp Division v. Minter.* 435 F. 2d 989 (1970). We quote the *Minter* case on this point in chapter 1, pp. 1-12.

86. Ill. Rev. Stats. C23, §401 (1963), quoted in *Strat-O-Seal Mfg. Co. v. Scott.* 72 Ill. App. 2d 480 at 481.

87. Ibid. at 486-487.

88. Ibid. at 487.

89. Ibid.

90. *Lascaris v. Wyman,* 305 N.Y.S. 2d 212 at 217 (1969).

91. *Lascaris v. Wyman,* 325 N.Y.S. 2d 289 at 292-293 (1972).

92. The court simply said that, under the provisions of the Social Services Law, "It is obvious that a striker is an 'employable individual' at least for the duration of the strike. Of course, if a striking worker refuses to accept employment [that is, at another employer], then public assistance should be denied." Ibid. at 292. But the court made no finding on whether any strikers had refused alternative employment.

93. The plaintiff's argument is quoted in *Lascaris v. Wyman,* 340 N.Y.S. 2d 397 at 403 (1972).

94. Ibid. at 403.

95. *ITT Lamp Division v. Minter,* 318 F. Supp. 364 (1970), 435 F. 2d 989 (1970), cert. denied. 402 U.S. 933 (1971).

96. 42 U.S.C. §601.07 (1970).

97. More than 25 percent of the 660 strikers applied for welfare benefits. 435 F.2d 989 at 991. The strike lasted more than two months (from August 24, to October 27, 1970). Note, "Welfare for Strikers: *ITT v. Minter*" by (Robert W. Clark III), *The University of Chicago Law Review,* Vol. 39, No. 1 (Fall 1971), pp. 81-82. Although the AFDC-U program normally requires a 30-day waiting period of unemployment before applicants become eligible for assistance, states have the option of providing immediate emergency relief under the Social Security Act. 42 U.S.C. §602 (1970). Neither the district court nor the court of appeals indicated how many strikers received General Assistance and how many received AFDC-U.

98. 318 F. Supp. 364 (1970). 435 F.2d 989 (1970).

99. 318 F. Supp. 364 at 366.

100. 435 F. 2d 989 at 994.

101. Ibid.

102. Ibid. at 995. As in *Lascaris II* and other cases, there apparently was no direct evidence on whether any of the recipients actually had been offered alternative jobs and had refused to accept them.

103. *ITT Lamp Division v. Minter.* 435 F. 2d 989 at 993 (1970).

104. Ibid.

105. Ibid.

106. 72 Ill. App. 2d 480 at 487.

107. 435 F.2d 989 at 993.

108. In *Super Tire Engineering v. McCorkle,* 412 F. Supp. 192 (1976), a case that arose out of a strike by a Teamsters local against two affiliated New Jersey corporations in 1971, the district court also considered the question of whether strikers should be denied public assistance because, by striking, they had refused a *bona fide* offer of employment without good cause. The court echoed the opinion expressed in previous decisions, saying, "Nothing In the New Jersey regulations relieves a striker of any of the eligibility requirements which must be met by others. A striker

must register for work and accept an offer of employment other than the job at issue in the strike . . . The New Jersey regulation . . . simply removes any presumption of ineligibility of an individual due to the exercise of his federally protected right to strike.'' Ibid. at 196. Once again, however, the court merely presumed that the strikers had met the requirements included in the regulation.

Super Tire had a long history in the federal courts. After the strike began, the plaintiffs sought injunctive relief against the New Jersey welfare administrators making welfare benefits available to strikers. But before the case was heard, the strike was settled. When the district court first heard the case in 1971 it nonetheless proceeded to consider the merits of the controversy and dismissed the complaint. On appeal, however, the third circuit did not reach the merits but remanded the case, holding that the appeal was rendered moot by virtue of the fact that the labor dispute had ended before the district court had dismissed the complaint. The Supreme Court then accepted *certiorari.* On appeal, the Supreme Court, 416 U.S. 115 (1974), reversed the judgment of the court of appeals and remanded the case for further proceedings on the merits of the controversy. The court held that the case was not moot because the issues it presented were ''capable of repetition, yet evading review,'' so that the petitioners might be adversely affected by government action ''without a chance of redress.'' Ibid. at 122, quoting the standard enunciated in *Southern Pacific v. ICC.* 219 U.S. 498 (1911). When the district court heard the case again in 1976 it considered the issue of whether strikers were ineligible for welfare benefits because they were unwilling to accept suitable employment. Super Tire once again appealed the district court's decision, but the third circuit agreed with the lower court's ''careful analysis'' and affirmed the judgment. 550 F. 2d 903 (1976). (The quote is from Ibid. at 909.)

109. Of course, *Francis I* and *II* as well as *Batterton v. Francis* did not fit this fact pattern. See citations in footnote 43. Another case that differed from the typical pattern was *State of Montana v. Department of Public Welfare,* 136 Mont. 283 (1959). In this case, striking copper workers applied for public assistance with the State Department of Public Welfare. The Department paid otherwise eligible strikers welfare benefits, but set the level of benefits at a percentage of amounts granted other welfare recipients in the same class. The State of Montana, acting in behalf of members of the Mine, Mill and Smelter Workers Union, sought a writ of mandate to compel the Department of Public Welfare to treat union members on strike and in need of assistance the same as other similarly situated applicants for assistance. The Supreme Court held that the Department had to provide ''equal consideration for persons equally situated'' and could not discriminate against welfare recipients because of the source of their unemployment or the reason for their need.

110. *Lascaris v. Wyman,* 340 N.Y.S. 2d 397 at 403 (1972).

111. *ITT Lamp Division v. Minter,* 435 F2d 989 at 994 (1970).

112. But as we shall see, one district court rules in 1986 that the congressional ban on striker eligibility for food stamps is unconstitutional. *UAW v. Lyng.* 648 F. Supp. 1234 (D.D.C., 1986).

113. AFDC Emergency Assistance payments usually constitute less than 1 percent of total AFDC payments. See U.S. Department of Health and Human Services, Social Security Administration, *Public Assistance Statistics,* various issues. In November 1980, for example, AFDC (including AFDC-U) payments were $1.1 billion; AFDC Emergency Assistance payments were $8.5 million, about .8 of 1 percent of the total. *Public Assistance Statistics, November 1980* (September 1981), table 1, p. 5. Since strikers are likely to have more resources than the general AFDC population, the proportion of strikers receiving Emergency Assistance was probably very close to zero.

114. Before the Supreme Court's decision in *Philbrook v. Glodgett,* 421 U.A. 707 (1975), states could deny AFDC-U benefits if the applicant was merely *eligible* for unemployment compensation. In *Philbrook,* the Court ruled that families could be excluded from AFDC-U assistance only with respect to any week for which the applicant actually received unemployment compensation.

Thus, under the Court's decision, an unemployed father of dependent children who was eligible for both AFDC-U and unemployment compensation had to be given the option of receiving either. The following year, however, Congress nullified the Court's decision by amending the Social Security Act to require those eligible for both AFDC-U and unemployment compensation to collect any unemployment compensation to which they are entitled before they receive AFDC-U benefits for which they might qualify. Under the amendment, an applicant can be denied AFDC-U benefits if he is eligible for unemployment compensation but refuses to apply for it. Act of October 20, 1976, P.L. 94-566, 90 Stat. 2681 at 2688 (1976). See also Bloch, pp. 47-48 and Note, "Social Welfare .. Effect of Eligibility for Unemployment Compensation on AFDC Benefits," *West Virginia Law Review,* Vol. 78, No. 2 (February 1976), pp. 268-277.

115. Thieblot and Cowin, pp. 190-193.

116. *Daily Labor Report,* No. 131, July 9, 1981, pp. A.9 to A.11. Unfortunately we have not been able to obtain a copy of the Senate staff report and therefore do not know the basis for its estimate. However, the Department of Health and Human Services also conducted a study of the effect of the 1981 changes in the AFDC program. The Department's statistical estimates were based on an examination of a sample of 23,000 AFDC cases nationwide. The study concluded, as did the Senate Budget Committee, that eliminating AFDC-U aid for strikers would save $5 million a year. See *New York Times,* September 8, 1981, p. B15 (reporting the results of the Department's study). Arguably, part of the difference between Thieblot and Cowin's estimate and the Senate's estimate might be the result of the decline in strike activity between the early 1970s and 1981. There were 5,010 strikes and 1.7 million workers involved in strikes in 1972. Over the course of the decade, strike activity markedly declined: by 1981 there were 2,568 strikes and 1.1 million workers involved in strikes. See U.S. Department of Labor, *Handbook of Labor Statistics* (Washington, D.C, 1983), p. 380. It is evident, however, that the decline in strike activity can account for only a fraction of the difference in the two estimates.

117. Total AFDC-U payments were about $800 million in 1980. See U.S. Department of Health and Human Services, Social Security Administration, *Public Assistance Statistics, December 1980* (November 1981), table 2, p. 9.

118. In January 1980, the average AFDC-U payment per family was $405.83. See *Public Assistance Statistics, January 1980* (September 1980), p. 2. There is no reason to believe that, on average, strikers received either a higher or a lower payment than AFDC-U families in general.

119. Almost 2 million families received AFDC-U assistance in 1980. See *Public Assistance Statistics, December 1980* (November 1981), table 3, p. 10. In the same year about 1.3 million workers were involved in work stoppages. See *Handbook of Labor Statistics,* (1983), p. 380.

120. Thieblot and Cowin, pp. 190-193.

121. For example, it is estimated that during the 71-day strike by the United Auto Workers against General Motors in 1970, 13 percent of the strikers in Michigan received AFDC-U assistance. On the other hand, it is also estimated that only 2 percent of the strikers in Illinois received AFDC-U benefits during the same strike. One reason for the difference was that in 1970 an applicant for AFDC-U in Illinois could not have assets exceeding $300, while in Michigan the asset limit was $1,500. See Thieblot and Cowin, pp. 102-142, and "Welfare for Strikers: *ITT v. Minter.*" p. 92. See also our previous discussion of the *Minter* case, especially footnote 97, where it is indicated that more than 25 percent of the strikers at ITT received either AFDC-U or general assistance.

122. The authors have in their possession a large number of newspaper and magazine articles published between 1971 and 1981 that deal with the payment of welfare benefits to strikers. Many editorials were printed, and almost all of them criticized the practice. The business press paid

close attention to the issue throughout the decade. *The Wall Street Journal,* for example, ran several feature articles and editorials on the topic. We also have in our files an abundance of material produced by special interest groups. Employer groups, such as the Chamber of Commerce, the Labor Policy Association, and the Public Service Research Council, distributed newsletters, reprints of speeches, and other publications denouncing the use of welfare in labor disputes. The labor movement, of course, defended the practice in its own publications. The use of welfare and food stamps by striking coal miners was widely reported by the press in 1978 and 1981.

123. P.L. 97-35 (August 13, 1981). For an account of the 1981 budget reconciliation process that focuses on the AFDC proposals, see Joe and Rogers, especially pp. 33-57. OBRA cut the federal budget by $35 billion. According to Joe and Rogers, "The AFDC changes included in OBRA were part of a budget package that was unprecedented both in its level of spending cuts and in its lack of attention to particular provisions. As a result, the budgets of many social programs were slashed, reducing benefits and protections to the most vulnerable and least powerful groups in society. AFDC was one such program." Joe and Rogers, p. 56.

124. Specifically, Section 402(a) of the Social Security Act was amended by the addition of the following paragraph:

"(21) provide ..

"(A) that for purposes of this part, participation in a strike shall not constitute good cause to leave, or to refuse to seek or accept employment; and

"(B) (i) that aid to families with dependent children is not payable to a family for any month in which any caretaker relative with whom the child is living is, on the last day of such month, participating in a strike, and (ii) that no individual's needs shall be included in determining the amount of aid payable for any month to a family under the plan if, on the last day of such month, such individual is participating in a strike." P.L. 97-35, 42 USC 602 (1981).

125. 7 U.S.C. 2011-2029(1982). The present program was established by the Food Stamp Act of 1964, P.L. 88-525, 78 Stat. 703. It was significantly amended on several occasions, particularly in 1971 (P.L. 91-671), 1977 (P.L. 9S-113), 1980 (P.L. 96-249) and 1981 (through the Omnibus Budget Reconciliation Act, P.L. 97-35). For an account of the development of the Food Stamp program through 1977, see Maurice MacDonald, *Food, Stamps, and Income Maintenance* (New York, Academic Press, 1977), particularly pp. 1-48.

126. 7 U.S.C. 2014 (1982). See also *U.S. Department of Agriculture v. Moreno.* 413 U.S. 528 (1978). In *Moreno,* the Supreme Court held the exclusion of households of "unrelated" persons from food stamp eligibility to be unconstitutional. The Court explained that the exclusion of communes had nothing to do with the purpose of the Food Stamp Act, which is to meet food needs, and that the goal of discriminating against "hippies" was not a legitimate government objective.

127. "Review of Food Program Developments in 1981." *Clearinghouse Review* (January, 1982), p. 776; *Public Assistance Statistics, December 1980* (November 1981), table 3, p. 10.

128. MacDonald, pp. 24-27. Included as liquid assets were cash, bank accounts, stocks and bonds, nonrecurring lump-sum payments, extra cars, and recreational vehicles. The family's home, one car, household and personal goods, insurance policies, pension funds, and any property essential to self-support were excluded from the asset test. As MacDonald points out, in 1975 "the countable net income definition [was] quite complicated, since many deductions from total household income [were] permitted." MacDonald, p. 25.

129. 7 U.S.C. 2014(c)(1982); "Review of Food Program Developments in 1981," p. 777; *Federal Register,* Vol. 46, No. 172 (September 4, 1981), p. 44712. The Food Stamp amendments in the Budget Reconciliation Act of 1982, however, restored the use of a net income standard of eligibility. Since 1982, households without an elderly or disabled member are required to have net monthly

incomes (after various deductions) below 100 percent of the federal poverty line and gross monthly incomes below 130 percent of the poverty line in order to be eligible for food stamps. P.L. 97-253(1982), amending 7 U.S.C. 2014(C).

130. 7 U.S.C. 2019(d). The 1981 OBRA, however, gave states the option of counting food stamps as income in determining AFDC benefits. See "Review of Food Program Developments in 1981," p. 779.

131. 7 U.S.C. 2015(d)(1982). An applicant must register for employment at least once every 12 months. Suitable employment is defined as "an offer of employment at a wage not less than the higher of either the applicable State or Federal minimum wage, or 80 per centum of the wage that would have governed had the minimum hourly rate under the Fair Labor Standards Act of 1938, as amended, been applicable to the offer of employment." 7 U.S.C. 2015(d)(l). Before 1981, an applicant who had quit his job without good cause was ineligible for assistance for 60 days following the quit. OBRA applied the sanction for voluntarily quitting a job to both *applicants* and *recipients*. In 1982 the period of disqualification was extended to 90 days. 7 U.S.C. 2015(d)(l)(iii)(1982). See also, "Legislative History, P.L. 97.253," *Congressional and Administrative News*. Vol. 3, 1982, pp. 1676-1677.

132. MacDonald, pp. 27-34; *Federal Register*, Vol. 46, No. 172 (September 4, 1981), p. 44719.

133. MacDonald, pp. 1-3.

134. MacDonald, pp. 5-8. See also, Gilbert Y. Steiner, *The State of Welfare* (Washington, D.C.: The Brookings Institution, 1971), pp. 198-213.

135. MacDonald, pp. 8-12.

136. Noteworthy were the efforts of the Citizens Crusade Against Poverty, the Citizens' Board of Inquiry into Hunger and Malnutrition in the United States (which produced the influential report, *Hunger, U.S.A.* in 1968), and various national women's organizations (which combined to produce a report called *Their Daily Bread*). See Steiner, pp. 229-232.

137. MacDonald, pp. 10-12; Steiner, pp. 232-236.

138. Carney, p. 514.

139. This history is recounted in Carney, pp. 514-515.

140. 7 U.S.C. 2014(c)(Supp.V 1975). See also, Thieblot and Cowin, p. 46; Carney, pp. 516-517.

141. The committee report is quoted in Comment. "Strikers' Eligibility for Public Assistance: The Standard Based on Need," *Journal of Urban Law*, Vol. 52, No. 1, 1974, p. 125. The committee report on the House bill appeared in the Fall of 1970. (H.R. Rept. No. 91-1402, 91st Cong., 2d Sess. 10-11 (1970).) The bill became law in January 1971. (Act of Jan. 11, 1971, Pub. L. No. 91-671, §4, 84 Stat. 2048.)

142. *New York Times*, June 7, 1972, p. 30.

143. *New York Times*, May 25, 1974, p. 58.

144. 7 U.S.C. 2015 (1977).

145. "Legislative History, P.L. 96-249," *Congressional and Administrative News*, Vol. 1, 1979, p. 964.

146. "Legislative History, P.L. 96-249," pp. 964-965.

147. We have in our files a large collection of newspaper articles that deal with striker use of food stamps during the 1977-78 and 1981 coal strikes. During the former strike, President Carter's Secretary of Agriculture, Bob Bergland, threatened to cut off food stamp assistance to striking miners, but the strike ended before he could carry out his threat. It is doubtful that Secretary Bergland had authority under the Food Stamp Act to terminate the strikers' assistance. See *New*

York Times, March 11, 1978, p. 12. In 1981, the United Mine Workers began their strike on March 27. In Illinois, for example, 17,500 miners went on strike and several newspapers reported that the Illinois Public Aid Department expected 12,000 to apply for food stamps. The Department opened temporary field offices in the Southern Illinois coalfields to handle the anticipated influx of applicants. But in May the Department acknowledged that only 1,717 Illinois miners had applied for assistance; of those applying, 277 had been denied aid. See *The Lexington Leader,* April 9, 1981, p. A-16 and the *St. Louis Post-Dispatch,* May 12, 1981, p. 1OA. United Press International reported that West Virginia expected 30,000 miners to apply for food stamps; by the end of April 1981, 18,000 had done so. UPI wire service, April 25, 1981.

148. *Daily Labor Report,* No. 18, January 28, 1981, p. A.2.

149. *Daily Labor Report,* No. 114, June 15, 1981, p. 2.

150. Senator Jesse Helms co-sponsored the striker ban with Senator Thurmond. On the Senate floor in July 1981, Senator Helms said, ''I am pleased that both the Senate reconciliation bill and the House Republican substitute contained identical language which I offered to make . . . strikers ineligible to participate in the food stamp program. . . . The public has been demanding this change for many years. I am pleased that the reconciliation process has brought this desire to fruition.'' *Congressional Record-Senate,* July 31, 1981, p. 59137. The Reagan administration also supported the ban on striker participation in the food stamp program. The union movement, of course, voiced strong opposition. For example, during the 1980 presidential campaign the UAW said Reagan ''showed [his] true colors on the food stamps for strikers issue. Reagan only a few days ago spoke out against food stamps for worker families on strike. . . . To show you what kind of 'labor leader' he is, Reagan called food stamps for strikers a form of subsidy for a strike. American workers . . . are not fooled by Reagan's conservative kick-the-worker-in-the-teeth doctrine.'' *UAW Washington Report,* Vol. 20, No. 36. September 26, 1980, p. 1.

151. The ban on strikers receiving food stamps is contained in Section 2015 (d)(4) of the Food Stamp Act. It reads as follows: ''Not withstanding any other provision of law, a household shall not participate in the food stamp program at any time that any member of such household, not exempt from the work registration requirements . . . , is on strike . . . *Provided,* that a household shall not lose its eligibility to participate in the food stamp program as a result of one of its members going on strike if the household was eligible for food stamps immediately prior to such strike, however, such household shall not receive an increased allotment as the result of a decrease in the income of the striking member or members of the household: *Provided further,* that such ineligibility shall not apply to any household that does not contain a member on strike, if any of its members refuses to accept employment at a plant or site because of a strike or lockout.'' 7 U.S.C. 2015(d)(4).

152. Letter to Senators Helms and Thurmond and Congressmen Coleman and Dickinson from Henry Eschwege, Director, GAO, March 26, 1981, p. 1.

153. Letter from Eschwege, pp. 1-2.

154. Letter from Eschwege, pp. 4-5. According to the GAO, the House Agriculture Committee, using other sources, computed similar estimates for 1975. Letter from Eschwege, p. 4.

155. ''Legislative History—Omnibus Budget Reconciliation Act, P.L. 97-35,'' *Congressional and Administrative News,* Vol. 2, 1981, p. 453.

156. Most press accounts in 1981 reported that elimination of striker eligibility for food stamps would save the treasury $30 million a year. Apparently this was an estimate produced by the Department of Agriculture for the Senate Agriculture Committee. See, for example, *Daily Labor Report,* No. 114, June 15, 1981, p. A-1.

157. Thieblot and Cowin, p. 191.

158. Thieblot and Cowin, p. 193.

159. Thieblot and Cowin's estimates have been cited by almost every article written on this topic since their book appeared in 1972. See, for example, Carney, p. 527 ("It has been estimated that in 1973 strikers will receive approximately $238,826,000 in food stamps . . ."); Note, "Strikers, Eligibility for Public Assistance: The Standard Based on Need," p. 126 ("The estimated rate of participation in the Food Stamp Program in 1973 for all strikers in all labor disputes is sixty percent . . ."); Note, "Federal Preemption of State Welfare and Unemployment Benefits for Strikers," *Harvard Civil Rights and Civil Liberties Law Review*, Vol. 12, No. 2 (1977), p. 453 ("One study estimated that only 15 percent of all strikers would receive AFDC-UF benefits in 1973, as compared to 60 percent for food stamps."). Thieblot and Cowin's numbers were also used by groups lobbying against the use of welfare benefits in labor disputes, such as the Chamber of Commerce, the Labor Policy Association, and the Public Service Research Council.

160. *Jaramillo v. County of Santa Clara*, 91 LRRM 2755 (1976).

161. 7 CFR 271.3(d)(5) quoted in 91 LRRM 2755 at 2756.

162. 91 LRRM 2755 at 2756.

163. Ibid. at 2757.

164. After the air traffic controllers went on strike and were fired by President Reagan in 1981, an unknown number received food stamp assistance. Even though the controllers' strike occurred after the passage of the 1981 OBRA, those controllers who were otherwise eligible received food stamps because following their termination they were no longer considered to be "strikers." In 1982 Senator Helms, prompted by the case of the air traffic controllers, sponsored an amendment to the Food Stamp Act that would have prohibited the participation in the food stamp program of public employee strikers who had been terminated from their jobs for participation in an unlawful strike for a period of 90 days following termination. The Helms amendment was approved by the Senate but was never passed by the House. See, "Legislative History-Budget Reconciliation Act (P.L. 97-253)," *Congressional and Administrative News*, Vol. 3, 1982, pp. 1677-1678.

165. Another case involving the provision of food stamps to strikers is *Russo v. Kirby*, 453 F.2d 548 (1971), which we discuss in note 83.

166. *UAW v. Lyng*, 648 F. Supp. 1234 (D.D.C. 1986). The UAW was joined in the suit by the United Mine Workers and several individual union members.

167. Ibid. at 1237-1238.

168. Ibid. at 1240.

169. 453 F.2d 548 at 551.

170. 453 F.2d 548 at 551.

171. *Eaton v. Lyng*, 669 F. Supp. 266 (N.D. Iowa 1987).

172. Ibid. at 271.

173. Ibid.

174. Ibid. at 272.

175. *Ledesma v. Block*, 825 F.2d 1046 (6th Cir. 1987).

176. Ibid. at 1046.

177. *Lyng v. UAW*, 108 S. Ct. 1184 (1988).

178. Ibid. at 1186.

179. Ibid. at 1191.

180. Ibid.

181. Ibid. at 1191-1192, quoting *Hodory v. Ohio Bureau of Employment Services*, 431 U.S. 471 at 489 (1977).

182. Congress of the United States, Joint Economic Committee, *Handbook of Public Income Transfer Programs: 1975,* Paper No. 20, Studies in Public Welfare, 1974, p. 354.

183. *City of Spring Valley v. County of Bureau,* 115 Ill. App. 545 (1904).

184. For a fine treatment of this subject see 57 ALR 3d p. 1303, 23 ALR FED 232, p. 263, and Kenneth Neiman, "General Assistance: A Preliminary Legal Analysis," *Clearinghouse Review,* Vol. 13, No. 3, July 1979, pp. 179-181.

185. In 1970 only 11 percent of all UI payments went to families with incomes below the poverty line. For further details see Ronald Ehrenberg, Robert Hutchens, and Robert Smith, "The Distribution of Unemployment Insurance Benefits and Costs," U.S. Department of Labor, Technical Analysis Paper No. 58, 1978.

5

Government Transfer Programs and Strike Theories

Designing an Empirical Test

The task of this chapter is to develop a theory and set of hypotheses that explain the effect of government transfer policies on strike activity. We begin the chapter with a brief review of previous strike research, noting the disparate theories and models that researchers have used. We then propose a formulation that we believe serves as a useful basis for understanding the link between transfer policies and strikes. Using this formulation, we are able to generate a set of hypotheses that can be tested in econometric models. The chapter concludes with a discussion of the principal dependent, policy, and control variables that we used in our statistical tests.

The long history of research on strike activity[1] contains analysis of strikes over time[2] and across industries,[3] economies,[4] bargaining relationships,[5] and other units of analysis.[6] But to our knowledge no researcher has ever used the state as the unit of analysis, partly because bargaining relationships are not ordinarily based on state-level units. For purposes of analyzing the effects of transfer policies, however, the state is an appropriate unit of analysis. This is because transfer policies affecting strikers (with the exception of food stamps) vary across states but not within states. If transfer policies affect strike behavior, then that should be revealed through differences in strike behavior across states. In discussing the specification of our model, we consider the problem of reconciling the inconsistency between the level of the problem we wanted to address and the level at which previous theory and research on strikes exists.

Models of Strike Activity

Distinct analytical models of industrial conflict have been developed from two perspectives. The dominant school of thought originates in economic models and their explanations of strikes. The alternative perspective, while acknowledging the importance of economic factors, concentrates on the influence of political, social, and organizational conditions.

Hicks introduced the earliest economic model in his discussion of wage determination.[7] In this model employers choose between granting higher wages or accepting the costs of a strike, and workers choose between continuing a strike or taking lower wages. He argues that rational actors can always avoid a strike if each actor knows the tradeoffs for each side. Knowing the tradeoffs allows the actors to reach a settlement, the cost of which each side prefers to the cost of a strike. Strikes, according to Hicks, occur only when one actor has imperfect information about the other side's preferences or when the union wishes to maintain the credibility of its strike threat. In the latter case, Hicks acknowledges that the union may wish to keep its "weapon" from getting "rusty." Under this scenario, most strikes are accidental, based on ignorance, and might be viewed as mistakes. The implication is that environmental conditions should not affect strike activity except to the extent that they block the free flow of information.

Mauro begins with Hicks's formulation in his analysis of strikes and imperfect information.[8] He argues that misinformation producing strikes may arise from the use by each side of different variables to assess its own position. The source of misinformation is the assumption by one party that its opponent actually uses the same variables it does. Examining strike frequency only, he finds that a strike at the expiration of the previous contract decreases the probability of a current strike, as do recent increases in productivity and high unemployment rates. He concludes that strikes are a means of transmitting information that corrects the parties' misperceptions about one another. His data also suggest that relative wage changes have a more important influence on strike frequency than do absolute wage levels. Work in this tradition by Singh et al.[9] and Gartner[10] examines the predictors of real wages in an attempt to explain the concession and strike costs that face unions and management.

Although the Mauro analysis moves research in Hicks' tradition toward a recognition of the role of environmental forces on strike decisions, such research still gives little emphasis to their systematic nature. Yet empirical evidence consistently demonstrates that the assumption that there is no systematic environmental effect is incorrect.

A second class of economic models is based on the assumption that bargaining involves three parties, rather than two. Ashenfelter and Johnson changed the direction of much succeeding strike research by developing a model based on certain assumptions about "union politics."[11] In this model, Ashenfelter and Johnson assume that union leaders and rank-and-file members have different interests and goals. Union leaders want to stay in office, while the rank and file want high-wage settlements. Union leaders and company representatives have perfect information about the market and the firm's financial condition, but the rank and file do not. Rank-and-file myopia often causes them to have unrealistic expectations about wage settlements, given market and firm conditions. Strikes occur because union leaders stay in office by managing the level of expectations of their members. When union members raise the level of their wage demands, leaders permit strikes to take place to lower their members' expectations. Thus, it is argued, a growing economy, inflation, low unemployment, high profits, and other economic factors should increase strikes because worker wage expectations are raised.

Research based in the Ashenfelter-Johnson tradition is plentiful. Both Flaherty[12] and Kaufman[13] support the general findings of the model, but suggest that it applies to strikes over contract renegotiation and not over intracontractual disputes. They find that changes in the consumer price index are associated with increased strike frequency while real wage changes are associated with lower frequencies. However, another longitudinal study, which also takes a cross-national perspective, finds that, over time periods similar to those examined by Flaherty and Kaufman, the negative coefficients for unemployment and wage changes are only stable in the U.S.[14] Another qualification is offered by Moore and Pearce, who find that wage and cost expectations are most likely to influence strikes only during periods of rapid inflation.[15] Researchers in this tradition often examine profit rates as an indicator of worker expectations. Results have been inconsistent, with the weight of evidence suggesting that firm or industry profit rates have no effect on strike activity.[16] Firm inventories have also failed to show significant relationships with strikes in these studies.[17]

The recent work that uses the Ashenfelter-Johnson frame of reference is ordinarily done at the economic-system and interindustry level. Unfortunately, such levels of analysis restrict the range of variables available to test the theory, and movement to a more appropriate unit of analysis, such as firms or bargaining units, always suggests the importance of other variables that change the analysis considerably. The theories developed both by Hicks and by Ashenfelter and Johnson were originally presented at the level of the bargaining relationship, but they have always been tested at a substantially more abstract level. A further problem is that the Ashenfelter-Johnson model places the entire blame for strikes on workers or more precisely on union leaders who manipulate worker expectations. Aside from the problem of ignoring the role of management in instigating strikes, the model assumes that union leaders have control over their members and can actually manipulate their expectations very well.

Yet a third class of models is based on a bargaining-power theory of strikes. Factors that give resources or opportunity to one side or the other, it is maintained, alter the frequency, size (number of participants), and duration of strikes. Such models have tried to integrate the economic, sociological, and organizational analysis of strikes. Empirical research in this tradition spans the range of units of analysis from the economywide[18] to interindustry level.[19]

Power models also use economic variables in predicting strike activity. For example, bargaining-power theory suggests that unemployment rates should affect strikes. Low unemployment gives an advantage to workers because a tight labor market limits the ability of employers to easily replace them and increases the availability of alternative job income; high unemployment gives advantage to management by making the replacement of strikers relatively easy. These models, however, also give prominence to noneconomic factors, particularly the size and strength of the unionized sector in an industry. Also, attention is given to the legal structure, which affects the strength of parties in collective bargaining relationships.

Much of the work on strikes by Kaufman is exemplary.[20] Kaufman tries to show that in some periods, particularly 1945-77, economic explanations of strike activity are sufficient because of the enormous stability of the U.S. economy and of the institutional framework of collective bargaining. In earlier periods, when union organization and the legal structure of bargaining were less settled, political and organizational elements were more influential. A number of researchers would interpret such results as reflecting the joint determination of both strikes and the strength of unions as a function of similar economic conditions in the post-World War II period.[21] Before World War II, the effect of union density and union size on strikes seems to have been more important than the influence of economic factors. This issue is particularly important in designing research on strikes because underspecified models have often led to conflicting interpretations of the importance of the degree of unionization.[22]

When the bargaining-power model is applied at the firm or industry level, the predominance of organizational and bargaining relationship factors over purely economic explanations of strikes emerges. Edwards, for example, emphasizes the importance of plant size and union density in explaining strike activity;[23] Leigh adds workers' risk preference as a factor predicting strikes;[24] Siebert *et al.*, add the size of union fund balances.[25]

The bargaining-power approach to strike analysis has its basis in what is currently referred to as the "resource mobilization theory of collective behavior."[26] Whether labor unions are social-movement organizations or institutionalized parts of the economic system does not matter, according to this theory. The critical factor in explaining the power of labor and management is the ability of each to mobilize people, money, political power, sentiment, and other resources in its behalf. Strikes and management countermovements against strikes require organization and resources. An elaboration of this perspective leads to models that include elements of the legal structure presumed to affect bargaining and strikes, firm characteristics that affect the ability of each side to mobilize participants, i.e., ease of communication and coordination, characteristics of the labor force that inhibit or enhance the chances that someone will join in opposition to or support of a strike, and environmental forces.[27] Less developed forms of this type of analysis appear in early works on strikes such as the classic argument by Kerr and Siegel that isolated living arrangements and physically demanding work combine to make some industries strike prone. Under such conditions, workers develop common lifestyles and close communication with one another. Close living arrangements and difficult work are capable of increasing the salience of an issue and allowing workers to more easily coordinate their activities against an employer.[28] These factors increase the union's mobilization potential. Though the analysis of mobilization on the employer side has been absent from research using the resource perspective, Griffith *et al.*, have demonstrated the importance of employer resistance to labor militancy.[29]

Modified Model

Some economists and collective bargaining researchers have proposed a number of modifications of the economic and bargaining-power models. Of particular concern in these modifications is the inability of previous theory to specify the manner in which each side estimates the other's intentions or chooses its own criteria for strike decisions. One such variation is termed a joint-choice model and posits that strike activity is a function of the joint (union and management) cost of strikes relative to other mechanisms for reaching a settlement.[30] The most elaborated version of this perspective was developed by Reder and Neumann.[31]

Reder and Neumann argue that bargainers usually become involved in continuing relationships. When continuing relationships are established, the frequency and duration of strikes is a decreasing function of the combined (union plus management) cost of strikes. They propose that as combined strike costs rise, bargainers develop protocols that make reaching an agreement easier. Protocols specify the procedures for negotiations, what topics will be covered, how to know when a settlement is reached, what tactics are expected, and how each side will behave in the face of given variable states and constraints. Protocols are "the rules or conventions governing the procedure for negotiating collective-bargaining agreements."[32]

A protocol might specify that in a particular bargaining relationship each side will submit a written proposal to the other before face-to-face negotiations begin, or that meetings will always be held away from the work location. More important, however, are portions of protocols that govern the actual basis of settling wage and benefit differences. For example, the parties might develop the practice of "imitating" the settlement of another firm in the industry—pattern bargaining. It is well known that the wage pattern established by the United Auto Workers and the major automobile producers is closely followed by the UAW and employers in other UAW jurisdictions (such as auto supplies, aerospace, and agricultural implements). Acceptance of the auto pattern in these other industries serves as a protocol that facilitates settlements. Similarly, many municipal fire departments and firefighter unions abide by the protocol that their salary settlements should exactly equal the salary settlements reached by the municipalities and their police unions. The "wage parity" protocol clearly makes it easier for cities to reach agreement with their firefighters, although the agreements may be quite costly.

Reder and Neumann argue that such protocols will cover as many contingencies as are effective in making settlement costs lower than they would be given a strike. However, exceptional circumstances will arise that are not covered by the protocol and will increase conflict. They suggest that such a circumstance might be one in which product price is falling at the same time that living costs rise.

Bargainers are thought to choose among alternative protocols, with each protocol associated with a different expected cost of strike activity. The objective of the parties is to minimize the expected costs of negotiating contracts. The costs consist of two parts. One part is the actual cost of strikes, and the other is the cost of making more and more elaborate specification of negotiating procedures. That is, protocols may reduce the probability of strikes but there is a cost attached to specifying the protocol. The more contingencies and procedures that are figured into the protocol, the more costly is its specification. "In selecting a protocol, bargainers balance the cost reduction from reduced strike activity against the increased cost of specifying a more detailed protocol. . . ."[33]

Bargainers who face higher costs per strike will then "choose more comprehensive protocols that are associated with a smaller expected quantity of strike activity, and larger costs of protocol specification than those pairs which are faced with lower unit costs of strike activity."[34] Thus, factors that increase the combined cost of striking should lead to more elaborate procedural protocols and a reduction in strike activity. Likewise, factors in the bargaining environment that reduce the combined cost will lead to increases in strike activity. In the Reder-Neumann model, neither side is necessarily responsible for strike activity. Allowing both sides to determine the decision to strike or avoid a strike, we submit, provides a more realistic model for estimating the effects of factors such as the payment of unemployment insurance to strikers on strike activity.

There is an interesting connection between the ideas of Reder and Neumann and the work of Ronald Coase. Coase argued that even in the absence of well-defined property rights, voluntary bargaining can lead to efficient outcomes.[35] He illustrated his analysis with a discussion of a problem confronting two neighbors: a rancher and a farmer. On occasion, the rancher's cattle stray onto the farmer's property and destroy some of his crops. According to Coase, even if property rights are ill-defined (i.e., even if it is not clear who is liable), the two can reach an efficient solution through voluntary bargaining. For example, if the straying cattle cost the farmer $25 in lost crops, and if it costs either the rancher or the farmer $20 to build a fence, then it would be efficient to spend the $20.

Coase argued that voluntary bargaining will tend to yield this efficient outcome irrespective of how the parties share the costs. If the rancher is liable for the lost crops then he will build a $20.00 fence to avoid $25.00 in damages. If the rancher is not liable, then the farmer will build the fence. If the cost of lost crops is shared, then the two parties will bargain their way to building a fence. Thus, according to

Coase the two parties reach an efficient outcome—building a fence—irrespective of how the costs are shared. Moreover, one might expect that the greater the cost of crop damage, the more resources will be devoted to building fences.

It is but a small leap from the Coase Theorem to the ideas of Reder and Neumann. Much like straying cattle, strikes use up resources. Protocols can reduce the frequency and duration of strikes, but, like building fences, protocols are costly to implement. The Coase Theorem would suggest that irrespective of the division of strike and protocol costs between union and management, the parties will arrive at an efficient level of protocols and strikes. Moreover, the more costly the damage of the strike to the two parties combined, the more resources will be devoted to establishing protocols that prevent or attenuate strikes.[36]

Interpreting Transfer Payment Effects on Strikes

The ideas of Reder and Neumann are particularly attractive from our perspective. Not only does their theory encompass both parties in the bargaining relationship, it also yields interesting hypotheses on the link between transfer payments and strike behavior. We hesitate to embrace their theory with too much fervor; it has many worthy competitors and it is largely untested. We use it here, not because we think it is the dominant theory, but, rather, because it yields intellectually interesting hypotheses that are helpful in organizing our analysis.

Transfer payments such as unemployment insurance, food stamps, or AFDC can alter the combined (employer/employee) costs of strikes. These payments can obviously reduce the cost of strikes to strikers. If there is not an offsetting effect on employer costs, then they unambiguously reduce the combined cost of strikes. By the logic of Reder and Neumann, that implies increased strike activity. If, however, the transfer payments are wholly financed out of taxes on the struck employer, then they will not alter the combined costs of strikes. In this case, although transfer payments reduce the cost of strikes to strikers, they increase the cost of strikes to the employer by an equal amount. Since the combined cost of strikes is not altered, by the logic of Reder and Neumann, strike activity remains unchanged.

Once again, note the links to the Coase Theorem. In Coase's example the fence was built irrespective of whether the farmer or the rancher bore the cost of the crop damage. "The rule of liability does not affect efficiency."[37] In the present case, a rule of law that requires employers to finance strike benefits for their employees (e.g., through the unemployment insurance payroll tax) should similarly not affect efficiency; it should not affect the amount of resources devoted to establishing protocols that prevent or attenuate strikes. The probability of a strike occurring, however, increases to the extent that the cost of the strike benefits are not borne by the parties themselves—that is, to the extent that the grant of benefits represents a pure subsidy to the parties provided by the government.

The key to understanding the effect of transfer payments on strike behavior then lies in understanding how the transfers are financed. Welfare benefits are financed out of general revenues. A struck employer does not have to bear the cost of welfare benefits received by the strikers. In this case, the ideas of Reder and Neumann lead to an unambiguous conclusion: when welfare benefits are paid to strikers, strike activity (both frequency and duration) should increase. Unemployment insurance benefits pose a different problem in that they are financed out of taxes on employers. Employers pay "experience rated" taxes; when a worker receives $1.00 in unemployment insurance benefits, the employer is supposed to pay $1.00 in taxes. Yet experience rating is not perfect. In all states there are firms that pay taxes that are not commensurate with benefits received by their workers. Moreover, it was once the case that unemployment insurance benefits were not subject to the federal income tax. Such "tax preferences" are a form of subsidy to the recipient from the rest of society. Although experience rating usually insures that the struck employer will bear some of the cost of unemployment insurance benefits to strikers, imperfect experience rating and tax preferences insure that the employer will generally not pay the full cost. Under these conditions Reder and Neumann's model implies that when unemployment insurance benefits are paid to strikers, strike activity will increase.

State unemployment insurance law is directly interpretable in these terms. Our discussion in chapters 2 and 3 makes it clear that a majority of states permit strikers to collect unemployment insurance during a strike if their employer continues to operate. These states, termed "work-stoppage" states, are identified in table 5.1, and changes in such provisions during the period covered by this study are shown in table 5.2. The tables show that 34 states had this provision in 1961 and that 6 states dropped the provision during the next 13 years. New Jersey dropped, then reinstated the provision during this time. Let us consider the effect of this provision on strike activity.

Table 5.1
Existence of Work-Stoppage and Innocent Bystander Provisions of State Unemployment Insurance Laws Regarding Strikers, 1961

	Yes	No
Work-stoppage provision	AK, CO, DE, GA, HA, ID, IL, IN, IW, KN, ME, MD, MA, MI, MS, MO, MT, NE, NH, NJ, NM, NC, ND, OH, OK, PA, SD, TX, UT, VT, VA, WA, WV, WY	AL, AZ, AR, CA, CT, DC, FL, KT, LA, MN, NV, NY, OR, RI, SC, TN, WI
Innocent bystander provision	AK, AZ, AR, CO, CT, DC, FL, GA, HA, ID, IL, IN, IA, KN, LA, ME, MD, MA, MI, MS, MO, MT, NE, NV, NH, NJ, NM, NC, ND, OH, OK, OR, PA, RI, SC, SD, TN, TX, VT, VA, WA, WV, WY	AL, CA, DE, KT, MN, NY, UT, WI

If payments to strikers under this provision are not fully financed out of taxes on the struck employer, then the provision reduces the expected total cost of strike activity. As such, the model would predict less comprehensive protocols and more strike activity. *We hypothesize then that states with a work-stoppage provision should have higher rates of strike activity than states without such a provision. Such increases should occur for strike frequency and duration, but not for strike size (number of workers involved).* Unemployment insurance provisions should not affect the size of units on strike, but will permit strikers to maintain a strike over a longer period. This effect should be ever greater as unemployment benefits increase because the cost of striking, given imperfect experience rating, is further reduced. *Thus, we hypothesize that in states with a work-stoppage provision, strike frequency and duration will increase as the level of unemployment benefits increase, ceteris paribus.* The importance of such increases lies in their interaction with the work-stoppage provision.

Table 5.2
Changes in Unemployment Disqualification of Strikers, 1961–1974

Year	Start work-stoppage	Stop work-stoppage	Start innocent bystanders	Stop innocent bystanders
1961				
1962		NC		NC
1963		MI, OH		OH
1964		CO		
1965				
1966		ID		
1967		NJ		NJ
1968	NJ		NJ	
1969				
1970				
1971		VA		
1972				
1973				
1974	MN			

Similar logic applies to other unemployment insurance rules that allow strikers to collect benefits. *Thus, we hypothesize that a lockout rule, an interim employment rule, or a rule whereby strikers receive benefits after a period of disqualification (as in New York or Rhode Island) will increase the frequency and duration of strikes.* Once again, there should be an interaction with benefit levels.

The "innocent bystander" provision raises a more complex problem. As discussed in chapter 3, the innocent bystander provision permits workers who are not strikers but who are out of work because of a strike to collect unemployment benefits. The effects of such a provision on the total cost of strikes is difficult to predict. On the one hand, it could be argued that strikers get nothing from this provision and the firm pays for it through higher experience rated taxes. The result would be an increase in the total cost of strikes and a reduction in strike activity. On the other hand, one could argue that firms benefit from this provision because even in its absence firms would have to compensate innocent bystanders.

To elaborate the last point, note that in the absence of the innocent bystander provision, individuals may hesitate to accept jobs in a strike-prone firm. Given a choice between two jobs at the same wage, one with a strike-prone firm and the other not, a rational individual would presumably prefer to avoid the strike-prone firm. In consequence to draw a workforce a strike-prone firm would have to compensate potential "innocent bystanders" through compensating wage differentials. (The situation is the same as that which produces such differentials for individuals in layoff-prone firms.)[38] Alternatively, innocent bystanders may be compensated through prestrike inventory buildup or poststrike catch-up. In either case, the innocent bystander provision could lead to lower employer cost resulting from a strike. Without the provision, employers bear the full cost of compensating innocent bystanders. With the provision, employers bear only part of this cost. The remainder is financed by the rest of society through imperfect experience rating and less-than-comprehensive taxation. *The logic leads to the hypothesis that states that have an innocent bystander provision will haved higher strike frequencies and strikes of longer duration, ceteris paribus. As before, there should be an interaction with benefit levels.*

Welfare benefits in the form of food stamps, general assistance, or AFDC-U (Aid to Families with Dependent Children-Unemployed

Parent) are similarly interpretable in terms of the Reder-Neumann model. Both of these programs reduce the cost of striking for those strikers who are sufficiently poor to be eligible. Since they are not financed out of taxes on a struck employer, they should decrease the total cost of strikes. *Our last hypothesis, therefore, states that an increase in the amount of welfare benefits available to strikers in a given state will lead to increased strike frequency and duration, ceteris paribus.* Note, however, a key caveat to this hypothesis: welfare will only have this effect if strikers are sufficiently poor to be eligible for the benefits. One would be surprised, for example, if strikes by skilled craftsmen, e.g., printers, were affected by welfare programs. Since organized workers are usually skilled workers, organized workers are often not sufficiently poor to be eligible for welfare payments.

It is important to note that our hypotheses focus on the probability of reaching agreements, and not on the terms of the agreements. For example, the prospective grant of unemployment benefits to employees, which are entirely financed by the parties themselves, may not affect the probability of a strike occurring, but may affect the parties' wage agreement. Wage agreements may be higher, lower, or unchanged compared to what they would have been in the absence of strike benefits. Once again, note the link to the Coase Theorem. The Coase Theorem deals only with the efficiency of agreements, and not with the distribution of rewards available to the parties through bargaining. Similarly, our hypotheses deal only with the level of strike activity, and not with the rewards that arise out of bargaining.

Empirical Implementation

Our approach to testing these hypotheses is a standard one. We specify a model of the form:

$$(1) \quad y = a_0 + \sum_{i=1}^{n} b_i X_i + \sum_{j=1}^{m} c_j T_j + u$$

We estimate the effect of transfer policies on strike activity by using Ordinary Least Squares (OLS) regressions, supplementing traditional models of strike activity with measures of transfer program characteristics. In this model y represents a measure of strike activity, the X_i's are a set of n control variables, the T_j's are a set of m transfer policy variables, and u is the error term; also a_0 is the constant term, the b_i's are the coefficients of the control variables, and the c_j's, of course, provide an estimate of the effect of the transfer policies on strike activity.

As noted above, we used the state as the unit of analysis. In particular, we obtained data on the y, X , and T variables for 50 states and the District of Columbia over the period 1960-1974. We restrict our analysis to this period for several reasons. First, prior to 1960 (and the 1960 census), it is difficult to obtain measures of some of our control variables. Second, the government stopped collecting comprehensive strike data in 1981, making it impossible to extend our analysis to the present. Third, during the period 1960–1974 one observes across-state variation in all of the programs we analyze. In particular, prior to 1974 there was substantial interstate variation in the food stamp program, and afterwards the program was the same in all states.

It is eminently reasonable to use state-level data for purposes of examining links between transfer policy and strike activity. This is because unemployment insurance and AFDC policies vary across but not within states. If transfer policies affect strike activity, then, holding other factors constant, one should observe predictable patterns of strike activity across states and over time. Yet, while it makes sense to use state-level data, as discussed below, these data are not without complications.

Dependent Variables

Comprehensive time series data on work stoppages are available in the Work Stoppage Historical File, which we obtained from the U.S. Department of Labor. This data base provides information on all work stoppages in the U.S., between 1953 and 1974, involving six workers or more for one day or more. Table 5.3 lists the variables available for each strike observation.

Table 5.3
Work-Stoppage Historical Files, 1953-1974
Variables Available for Each Strike Observation

Duration of strike	Contract status
Workers involved	Beginning date
State	Ending date
SIC code	Major issue
Total work days lost	

A variety of measures of three basic dimensions of strike activity—frequency (number of work stoppages), size (number of workers involved), and duration (average length of strikes)—were derived for each state from the basic data. For example, with these data we were able to compute the measures of strike frequency in table 5.4 for each state and year.

Table 5.4
Measures of Strike Frequency

No. of strikes over the negotiation of new contracts
No. of strikes during negotiation of a new contract over economic issues
No. of strikes during negotiations that are single state-single industry strikes
No. of strikes over the negotiation of economic issues
No. of strikes in manufacturing
No. of strikes in nonmanufacturing
No. of strikes in construction
No. of strikes which are single state-single issue strikes
No. of strikes with duration under 30 days
No. of strikes with duration over 30 days
No. of strikes with duration under 56 days
No. of strikes with duration over 56 days
No. of strikes with duration over 80 days

In using states as the unit of analysis, it is necessary to standardize for population size. One would, for example, expect to observe a greater number of strikes in New York than in Nevada simply because of population differences. Even if other determinants of strike activity were the same in the two states, New York would have the greater number of strikes. Ideally, the table 5.4 frequency measures would be standardized for the number of bargaining units with the given characteristic. For example, an ideal dependent variable would be the number of strikes over the negotiation of new contracts divided by the number of bargaining units that were negotiating new contracts. Unfortunately, there do not exist state-level data on numbers of bargaining units. As such, we had to develop alternative ways to standardize measures of strike frequency. In particular, we used number of labor force participants, number of union members, and number of establishments in the state.

The result is a plethora of measures of the dependent variable. Table 5.4 contains 13 measures of strike frequency, and each measure can be standardized with three variables: labor force participants, union members, and establishments. That means 39 measures of strike frequency! And which of these is the "correct" measure for our purposes? Our theory does not really speak to that issue.

In order to deal with the plethora of measures, we used 1970 data as a laboratory. We regressed different measures of the dependent variable on the same vectors of X and T variables. We did this to assess whether results were sensitive to choice of dependent variable. As detailed in chapter 6, in general the results were not sensitive to this change in specification. This is because the different measures of the dependent variable are highly correlated. Of course, that simplifies the analysis; in that case the analysis can simply focus on a small subset of the many measures.

Our approach to measuring the average duration and average size of strikes was similar to our treatment of strike frequency. The average duration of strikes within a state in a given year is computed by adding up the duration of strikes for the state and year and dividing by the corresponding number of strikes. The average size of strikes is similarly computed by adding up the number of workers involved in strikes for the state and year and dividing by the corresponding number of strikes.

Once again the Work Stoppage Historical File yields a long list of possible measures. The average duration and average size of strikes can be computed for all strikes, for strikes concerned with the negotiation of new contracts, for strikes concerned with economic issues, and so forth. Indeed, one could construct tables for duration and size that are every bit as lengthy as table 5.4.[39] Once again, to deal with this plethora of measures, we used 1970 data as a laboratory for assessing whether results are sensitive to choice of dependent variable. As discussed in chapter 6, in general results were not sensitive to this change in specification.

Several alternative measures were created using combinations of the frequency, breadth and duration measures because combined measures such as "work days idle" appear in the literature. However, these composite measures were dropped from the analysis because they are products of other dependent variables, and because our theoretical framework yields no direct predictions on how transfer programs will affect such variables. The fundamental variables have straight forward interpretations.

Table 5.5 presents descriptive data on a subset of our dependent variables. The data include state-level observations across all years from 1960 through 1974. (Since there are 51 jurisdictions and 15 years in our data base, the sample size is 765.) The data in table 5.5, therefore, provide a profile of the nature of strike activity in the United States during the period 1960-74.

A few aspects of this profile are worth noting. For example, about 51 percent of all strikes were strikes over economic issues. (This proportion can be derived by dividing FREQLAB2 by FREQLAF.) FREQUM implies that there was one strike for every 3,000 union members during this period. FREQEST shows that there was only one strike for every 1000 establishments. This number would be substantially higher, of course, if we had data on the number of unionized establishments.

The average duration (AVDUR) of all strikes during this period was 26 days. Strikes over economic issues were slightly longer (AVDUR2=30 days). The 30-day cutoff is significant because needy strikers in two-parent families only became eligible for AFDC-U benefits after a 30-day waiting period. Only about one-quarter of all strikes that occurred during the 1960-74 period exceeded the 30 day limit. Of course, we know from other evidence that only a small proportion of the workers involved in such strikes would have qualified for benefits.

About 14 percent of all strikes lasted longer than 56 days. The 56-day cutoff is significant because of the New York law, which qualifies strikers to collect benefits after eight weeks. As we noted in chapter 3, the New York State Department of Labor estimated that about 13 percent of all strikers in the state were involved in strikes lasting longer than eight weeks during the period 1947-78.

The average strike during the 1960-74 period involved 356 workers (WORKSTRK). This statistic reflects the fact that unions are concentrated in larger plants and establishments. WORKLAB implies that there was a little more than a 2 percent probability that a member of the labor force would be involved in a strike in a given year. But WORKUM suggests the probability that a union member would go on strike in any given year in this period was close to 12 percent.

The standard deviations listed in table 5.5 show that there was considerable variation in these strike measures across years and across states. It is, of course, this variation that we seek to analyze in our regression analysis.

Measures of Transfer Program Characteristics

The initial problem of data collection was the identification of the important dimensions of the three public policy areas. Food stamps, AFDC-U, general assistance, and unemployment compensation are complex programs that use multiple criteria for eligibility and have a variety of benefit levels. Translating complex programs into variables suitable for testing was no easy task.

For the unemployment insurance program, our initial approach was to use a series of dummy variables to indicate whether a state allowed workers involved in a labor dispute to collect unemployment benefits under one of the several provisions previously discussed. For example, the unique approach taken by New York and Rhode Island made it

Table 5.5
Means and Standard Deviations of Strike Measures Over All States and All Years, 1960-74
(n=765)

Strike measure	Symbol	Mean	Standard deviation
Number of strikes/labor force (X1000)	FREQLAF	.068	.074
Number of strikes over economic issues/labor force (X1000)	FREQLAB2	.035	.022
Number of strikes/union members (X1000)	FREQUM	.337	.221
Number of strikes over economic issues/union members (X1000)	FREQUM2	.175	.088
Number of strikes/ establishments	FREQEST	.001	.002
Average duration in days	AVDUR	26.235	9.676
Average duration of strikes over economic issues in days	AVDUR2	30.401	12.616
Number of workers involved in strikes/strikes	WORKSTRK	355.866	204.399
Number of workers involved in strikes over economic issues/strikes	WORKSTRK2	221.056	171.597
Number of workers involved in strikes/ labor force (X1000)	WORKLAB	24.444	29.121
Number of workers involved in strikes over economic issues/labor force (X1000)	WORKLAB2	14.277	14.645

Table 5.5 (continued)

Strike measure	Symbol	Mean	Standard deviation
Number of workers involved in strikes/union members (X1000)	WORKUM	115.863	95.466
Number of workers involved in strikes over economic issues/union members (X1000)	WORKUM2	68.624	59.059
Percentage of strikes lasting longer than 30 days	FDUR30	.249	.010
Percentage of strikes lasting longer than 56 days	FDUR56	.136	.078
Percentage of strikes lasting longer than 84 days	FDUR84	.079	.060

obvious that a dummy variable representing those two states should be included in the analysis. Our legal and institutional research on the operation of the unemployment insurance system made it apparent that we also needed to specify variables for four other "UI Rules:" stoppage-of-work, innocent bystander, interim employment, and lockout. We therefore constructed dummy variables for each of these rules; in each case, the dummy variable indicates whether the state used the rule in a particular year.

Our theory and hypotheses suggested that the effect of these rules on strike activity would depend on (1) the "generosity" of the state's unemployment insurance system, and (2) the tax and experience rating practices used by a state to finance benefits. We measured the generosity of the state's system by using various measures of a state's benefit levels (e.g., the maximum benefit in the state, benefits as a percentage of weekly covered earnings, the average weekly benefit in the state), and also by the maximum weeks of benefit eligibility for claimants in a state.

The exceptional complexity of state practices regarding the financing of unemployment benefits made it particularly difficult to capture this dimension of the unemployment insurance system in a parsimonious manner. We included five variables in our data base that we hoped would adequately describe a state's financing arrangements: the taxable wage base for employers in the state, the minimum tax rate in the state, the ratio of the taxable wage base to average yearly earnings in the state, and an experience rating index for the state (developed in work by Becker).[40] We also included a variable denoting the percent of workers in a state covered by the state's unemployment insurance law. Table 5.6 lists the principal policy variables that we included in our analysis.

For welfare programs, we collected data, first, on whether a state had the AFDC-U program in a particular year and, second, on whether the state allowed strikers to collect AFDC-U benefits. These were coded as dummy variables. We also collected data on the maximum weekly benefit that a state paid to a family of four under its AFDC-U program, and we interacted the maximum benefit with the AFDC-U dummies.

Specifying variables for the food stamp program presented another set of difficulties. Since food stamps are provided under federal law, program characteristics (eligibility, benefit levels, etc.) are uniform across all states. Obviously, the invariance of these program characteristics made it impossible to test the effect of food stamps on strike activity in a given year. Prior to 1974 there was substantial variation in the availability of food stamps within states. Some counties had food stamp programs and some did not. Thus, we constructed a measure of the percent of the poverty population in the state residing in counties that operated a food stamp program, for each state and every year in our data base. Although this variable is an imperfect proxy, it was the only recourse open to us.

Finally, we constructed a dummy variable indicating whether strikers were eligible for general assistance in a particular state in a given year. Eligibility criteria and benefit levels under general assistance programs vary greatly from state to state, and even from county to county within a state, and comprehensive data on the characteristics of these programs are not available. We were able to collect enough information on state practices to use the variable in our analysis, but we acknowledge that the variable is subject to considerable measurement error.

Our interviews with individuals in the Unemployment Insurance Service and other agencies helped us to identify the precise policy variables we needed to include in our analysis. Our surveys of state employment security agencies also helped. In these surveys, for example, we were alerted to the importance of the stoppage-of-work provision. We were also told by several of these respondents that unemployment insurance provisions that require payment of benefits to strikers when their employer has violated either the collective bargaining agreement or one of the labor laws were trivial and we should ignore them. Our reading of the case law confirmed this belief, and we followed this advice.

There is an interesting statistical problem associated with these variables. The specification in equation (1) implies that the vector of policy variables (T) is exogenous to strike activity. That means that the policies affect strike activity, but strike activity does not affect the existence of the policies. Is this a defensible position? On the one hand, it can be argued that the policies we are dealing with were put in place, in the vast majority of states, in the 1930s and 1940s and were not changed thereafter. It is unlikely that such longstanding policies are somehow endogenous. On the other hand, table 5.2 shows that eight states changed their policies regarding the work-stoppage and innocent bystander rules during the 1961-74 period, and we have anecdotal evidence suggesting that, in at least a few of these cases, the policies were changed because of increased use by strikers. In that sense, the change in the policy was a function of the state's (recent) strike activity. Moreover, there is no question that Congress' decision to change the AFDC-U and food stamp policies in 1981 was motivated, at least in part, by the perception that the availability of these benefits had increased strike activity. Thus, endogeneity is conceivable.

Note, however, the form of that endogeneity. Increased strike activity is associated with a decreased propensity for states to provide transfers to strikers. That is a negative relationship. Our principal hypothesis concerns a positive relationship, i.e., increased government transfers to strikers are associated with increased strike activity. That

Table 5.6
Variables Measuring Characteristics of Transfer Programs
(Data Sources Appear in Appendix B)

Variable		Definition
Unemployment Insurance Program Variables:		
UI RULE 1	=	1 if strikers receive benefits when employer continues to operate; else = 0
UI RULE 2	=	1 if New York and Rhode Island; else = 0
UI RULE 3	=	1 if "innocent bystanders" receive benefits; else = 0
UI RULE 4	=	1 if strikers laid off from "interim employment" job receive benefits; else = 0
UI RULE 5	=	1 if workers receive benefits during a lockout; else = 0
UIMAX	=	maximum weekly UI benefit in state
UIMETH1	=	benefits as a percent of weekly covered earnings for benefits below the maximum in state
AVEBEN1	=	UIMETH1 * AHEMAN (see table 5.7 for AHEMAN)
UITAX	=	taxable wage base for employers in state
TAXEMAN	=	UITAX / (AHEMAN * 2000)
UIMAXRAT	=	maximum UI tax rate in state
UIMINRAT	=	minimum UI tax rate in state
UIPIST	=	Experience Rating Index from Becker (see footnote 41)
COVPC	=	percent of workers in state covered by state UI laws
DURAT	=	maximum number of weeks of benefits in state
Welfare Program Variables:		
PCTPOOR	=	percent of state's poverty population residing in counties that participate in food stamp program
AFDCAID	=	1 if state allows strikers to receive AFDC-U payments; else = 0
AFDCPROG	=	1 if state has an AFDC-U program; else = 0
AFDCMAX	=	AFDC maximum weekly payment for a family of four in state
ADCBEN	=	AFDCMAX * AFDCAID
GENAID	=	1 if state provides general assistance to strikers; else = 0

means that the form of endogeneity described above will impart a negative bias to a coefficient on a transfer policy variable. Alternatively stated, if transfer policy exhibits this kind of endogeneity, then we are less likely to find a positive relationship between transfer policy and strike activity. We will return to this issue in chapter 6.

The Control Variables

Finally, to test our hypotheses we needed a vector of control variables, X. All of our hypotheses posit a relationship between transfers and strikes holding other factors constant. That raises the vexing problem of what should be held constant. The standard social science approach to this problem is to let the theory dictate the vector of control variables. Yet, available theories of strike activity, including that of Reder and Neumann, focus on the bargaining unit. For good reason, the present work takes the state as the unit of analysis. Clearly, variables that are appropriate controls for an analysis of bargaining unit strike activity may not be appropriate (or, if appropriate, may not be available) for an analysis of state-level strike activity.

As an illustration of this point, consider the empirical specification employed by Reder and Neumann.[41] They argue that two key determinants of strike activity are the within-year coefficient of variation of finished good inventories and the within-year coefficient of variation of shipments. Other things equal, a larger coefficient of variation of inventories reveals firms that can buffer output streams from shocks to the flow of inputs, and "the greater the extent to which a firm engages in such buffering, the lower is the incremental cost of a unit of strike activity."[42] Thus a larger coefficient of variation of finished good inventories should be negatively associated with strike activity. A parallel argument yields the prediction that a larger coefficient of variation in shipments should be positively associated with strike activity. Since our research assesses hypotheses linked to the Reder and Neumann theory, one could argue that these coefficients of variation should be included as control variables in our specification. But that does not make sense when the state is the unit of observation. Even if data were available on within-year variation in finished good inventories by state (and they are not), the variable would be of doubtful value. If a state has large inventory variation, that does not necessarily imply that unionized firms within the state have large inventory variation. And for purposes of understanding strike activity, it is the unionized firms that are important.

Moreover, there is a philosophical problem here. As indicated above, we do not view the Reder and Neumann theory as the dominant theory of strike activity. We rely upon it because it yields intellectually interesting hypotheses that are helpful in organizing our analysis. Given that, we hesitate to formulate a vector of control variables from their theory alone. Previous research, which was motivated by other theories, yields important insights into potential control variables.

Of course, previous research does not solve our problem. For example, previous research suggests that the unemployment rate influences the propensity to strike. But is it true that state-level unemployment rates influence state-level strike activity? When strike activity is aggregated to the state level, it encompasses many different types of bargaining relationships. Some of them are plant-level relationships, others are multiplant, multistate, industrywide, or national relationships. Conceptually, one might expect the state unemployment rate to be the relevant measure for some of the relationships, particularly those at the plant or establishment level. But it is hardly likely that the state unemployment rate is the relevant measure for industrywide or national relationships. This illustrates our quandary: when the state is the unit of analysis, it is difficult to formulate a vector of conceptually "correct" control variables.

We resolved our quandary by collecting data on a long list of control variables. Table 5.7 presents the list.

Previous strikes research had shown that these variables influence strike activity. Since we did not have a clear basis for claiming that one control variable was preferable to another, we sought to examine whether results on the transfer policy variables (T) were robust to different vectors of control variables. After all, our goal was to obtain meaningful estimates of the influence of transfer policies on strikes—we were not concerned about the robustness or reliability of the results for the control variables. Thus, we constructed a series of tests in which combinations of the table 5.7 variables were substituted for one another. Robust findings occur when the relationships between transfer policy measures and strike measures are maintained regardless of the control variables employed. It should, perhaps, be noted that our approach is not a new one. It is in part derived from the ideas of Leamer.[43]

Data were coded by a group of students who were trained and supervised by the authors. We collected data for all states and the District of Columbia for all dependent and policy variables from 1960 through 1974. We begin with 1960 because, with minor exceptions, our data for these variables are complete. We end with 1974 because that is the last year of the *Work Stoppage Historical File.* Data for our control variables, however, are complete only for the two census years, 1960 and 1970. There are complete data for most of the other control variables (including several of particular interest, such as the unemployment rate in the state, the number of union members in the state, average hourly earnings in the state for production workers, etc.), but there are missing values for certain others (particularly those denoting the composition of the labor force in the state). Where there were missing data for certain key variables, we estimated the values by means of interpolation, using the closest years for which we did have data.

Conclusion

This chapter began with a discussion of models other researchers have used to analyze strike activity. On the basis of this discussion, it is clear that there is no general consensus in the literature on the "right" theory of strikes. Rather, there are competing, and often contradictory, theories. Fortunately, we did not require a general theory of strike activity in this study. What we required was a theory that would specifically link transfer policies with strike activity. That theory was found in the work of Reder and Neumann, who used a joint-cost model of strike activity. The fundamental proposition in this theory is that strike activity is a decreasing function of the combined (union plus management) cost of strikes. As the potential cost of a strike increases, according to Reder and Neumann, the parties have a greater incentive to develop protocols that allow them to reach peaceful settlements. On the basis of the

Table 5.7
Control Variables Employed in the Analysis
(Data Sources Appear in Appendix B)

Variable		Definition
UNMEMLAB	=	No. of union members / LFTOT[a]
MINELAB	=	No. of workers in mining / LFTOT
CONSTLAB	=	No. of workers in construction / LFTOT
MANULAB	=	No. of workers in manufacturing / LFTOT
TRANLAB	=	No. of workers in transportation / LFTOT
TRADELAB	=	No. of workers in trade / LFTOT
FINLAB	=	No. of workers in finance / LFTOT
SERVLAB	=	No. of workers in services / LFTOT
PCTURB	=	LFTOT in urban areas / LFTOT
PCTPHMALE	=	males between age 25 and 55 / LFTOT
PCTFEM	=	No. females in labor force / LFTOT
AFLMEMLAB	=	No. AFL-CIO members / LFTOT
PCTMIG	=	net civilian migration 1960-1970 / civilian resident population 1970
SOUTH	=	1 if state is in South Census Division; else = 0
RTTOWORK	=	1 if state has right to work law; else = 0
VALADPC	=	value added by manufacturing / total no. of employees in manufacturing
ESIZE100	=	No. establishments with 100+ employees / no. establishments
ESIZE 20	=	No. establishments with 20+ employees / no. establishments
AVESIZE	=	No. employees in state / no. establishments
AHEMAN	=	average hourly earnings of production workers on manufacturing payrolls in state
WCH6970	=	percent change in AHEMAN between 1969 and 1970
WCH6870	=	percent change in AHEMAN between 1968 and 1970
MEDINC	=	median income of families in state in 1969
POVRTY	=	percent of families with money income below poverty line in state
URAT	=	unemployment rate in state
INDUST	=	State Industrialization Index
AFFLUENC	=	Affluence Index

a. LFTOT = number of people in state's labor force.

Reder-Neumann model, we argue that transfer payments will increase strike activity only if they reduce the total cost of a strike to the parties. Since the cost of transfer payments are not fully borne by the parties to the dispute, we argue that transfer policies generally reduce the joint cost of strikes to the parties and therefore increase strike activity. On the basis of this premise, we then developed a set of specific hypotheses linking transfer policies to strike activity.

The policy variables of principal interest in this study are well defined for the unemployment insurance and AFDC-U programs. We acknowledge, however, that the policy variables are less well-defined for the food stamp and general assistance programs and may suffer from measurement error. We therefore have more confidence in our results for the two former programs than we do for the two latter programs.

The next chapter discusses the results of our econometric tests.

NOTES

1. For one of the earliest studies of strikes in the U.S., see Alvin Hansen, "Cycles of Strikes," Vol. 11 (December 1921), pp. 616-621. For a review of empirical research through 1980, see P.K. Edwards, *Strikes in the United States, 1881-1974* (New York: St. Martin's Press, 1981).

2. For example, Orley Ashenfelter and George Johnson, "Bargaining Theory, Trade Unions, and Industrial Conflict," *American Economic Review*, Vol. 59, No. 1 (March 1969), pp. 35-49.

3. For example, Edwards, especially pp. 189-212; Clark Kerr and Abraham Siegel, "The Interindustry Propensity to Strike: An International Comparison," in Arthur Kornhouser, Robert Dubin, and Arthur Ross, eds., *Industrial Conflict* (New York: McGraw-Hill, 1954), pp. 189-212.

4. For example, M. Paldum and P.J. Pederson, "The Macro-Economic Strike Model: A Study of Seventeen Countries, 1948-1975," *Industrial and Labor Relations Review*, Vol. 35, No. 4 (July 1982), pp. 504-521; Kenneth Walsh, *Strikes in Europe and the United States* (New York: St. Martin's Press, 1983).

5. For example, Cynthia Gramm, "The Determinants of Strike Incidence and Severity: A Micro-Level Study," *Industrial and Labor Relations Review*, Vol. 39, No. 3 (April 1986), pp. 361-376.

6. For a study using the metropolitan area as the unit of analysis, see Robert N. Stern, "Intermetropolitan Patterns of Strike Activity," *Industrial and Labor Relations Review*, Vol. 29, No. 2 (January 1976), pp. 218-235.

7. John R. Hicks, *The Theory of Wages* (London: MacMillan, 1932), pp.136-158.

8. Martin J. Mauro, "Strikes as a Result of Imperfect Information," *Industrial and Labor Relations Review*, Vol. 35, No. 4 (July 1982), pp. 522-538.

9. Davinder Singh, Glyn Williams, and Ronald Wilder, "Wage Determination in U.S. Manufacturing 1958-1976: A Collective Bargaining Approach," *Journal of Labor Research*, Vol. 3 (Spring 1982), pp. 223-337.

10. Manfred Gartner, "Strikes and the Real Wage-Employment Nexus: A Hicksian Analysis of Industrial Disputes and Pay," *Journal of Labor Research*, Vol. 6 (Fall 1985), pp. 323-336.

11. Ashenfelter and Johnson. The Ashenfelter and Johnson model is based on the work of Arthur Ross, *Trade Union Wage Policy* (Berkeley, Calif.: University of California Press, 1948).

12. Sean Flaherty, "Contract Status and the Economic Determinants of Strike Activity," *Industrial Relations*, Vol. 22 (Winter 1983), pp. 20-33.

13. Bruce Kaufman, "The Determinants of Strikes in the United States, 1900-1977," *Industrial and Labor Relations Review*, Vol. 35 (July 1982), pp. 473-490.

14. Paldum and Pederson (1982).

15. William Moore and Douglas Pearce, "Comparative Analysis of Strike Models During Periods of Rapid Inflation, 1967-1977," *Journal of Labor Research*, Vol. 3 (Winter 1982), pp. 39-53.

16. Stanley Siebert, Phillip Bertrand and John Addison, "The Political Model of Strikes: A New Twist," *Southern Economic Journal*, Vol. 52 (Summer 1985), pp. 23-33.

17. David Sapsford, "The Theory of Bargaining and Strike Activity," *International Journal of Social Economics*, Vol. 9 (February 1982), pp. 3-31.

18. Andrew Buck, "A Reexamination of British Strike Activity," *Atlantic Economic Journal*, Vol. 10 (September 1982), pp. 38-39.

19. Bruce Kaufman, "Interindustry Trends in Strike Activity," *Industrial Relations*, Vol. 22 (January 1983), pp. 45-57; David Britt and Omer Galle, "Industrial Conflict and Unionization," *American Sociological Review*, Vol. 37 (February 1972), pp. 46-57.

20. Kaufman, 1982; Kaufman, 1983.

21. Jack Skeels, "The Economic and Organizational Basis of Early United States Strikes, 1900-1948," *Industrial and Labor Relations Review*, Vol. 35 (July 1982), pp. 491-503.

22. David Britt and Omer Galle, "Structural Antecedents of the Shape of Strikes: A Comparative Analysis," *American Sociological Review*, Vol. 39 (October 1974), pp. 642-651.

23. P.K. Edwards, "The Strike-Proneness of British Manufacturing Establishments," *British Journal of Industrial Relations*, Vol. 19 (July 1981), pp. 135-148.

24. J. Paul Leigh, "Risk Preference and the Interindustry Propensity to Strike," *Industrial and Labor Relations Review*, Vol. 36, No. 2 (January 1983), pp. 271-285.

25. Siebert *et al.* (1985).

26. John D. McCarthy and Mayer N. Zald, "Resource Mobilization and Social Movements: A Partial Theory," *American Journal of Sociology*, Vol. 82 (May 1977), pp. 1212-1242.

27. Charles Tilly, *From Mobilization to Revolution* (Reading, MA: Addison-Wesley, 1978).

28. Kerr and Siegel (1954).

29. Larry J. Griffith, Michael E. Wallace and Beth A. Rubin, "Capitalist Resistance to the Organization of Labor Before and After the New Deal: Why? How? Success?" *American Sociological Review*, Vol. 51 (April 1986), pp. 147-167.

30. Gramm (1986).

31. Melvin Reder and George R. Neumann. "Conflict and Contract: The Case of Strikes," *Journal of Political Economy*, Vol. 88 (October 1980), pp. 867-886.

32. Ibid., p. 870.

33. Ibid., p. 871.

34. Ibid., p. 871.

35. Ronald H. Coase, "The Problem of Social Cost," *Journal of Law and Economics*, Vol. 3 (October 1960), pp. 1-44.

36. Another important antecedent is the work of Kennan. Like Reder and Neumann, Kennan focuses on the combined (employer and employee) costs of a strike. He hypothesizes that as the marginal cost of a strike (the combined cost of another day of striking) increases, the probability that the strike continues will fall. Reder and Neumann differ from Kennan in that instead of focusing on a single strike, they relate the cost of strike activity over several negotiations to the incidence of strike activity. Moreover, they specify a mechanism—protocols—through which strike costs alter strike activity.

37. Robert Cooter, "The Cost of Coase," *Journal of Legal Studies*, Vol. XI (January 1982), p. 15. Cooter discusses several variants of the Coase Theorem and we have picked a formulation that captures the core of the Theorem.

38. John Abowd and Orley Ashenfelter, "Anticipated Unemployment, Temporary Layoffs and Compensating Wage Differentials," in Sherwin Rosen, ed., *Studies in Labor Markets* (Chicago: University of Chicago Press, 1981), pp. 141-170; Robert M. Hutchens, "Layoffs and Labor Supply," *International Economic Review*, Vol. 24 (February 1983), pp. 37-55.

39. Unlike frequency, strike duration and strike size do not require standardization for population. The fact that New York has more bargaining units than Nevada does not imply anything about average strike duration or average strike size in New York versus Nevada.

40. Joseph M. Becker, *Experience Rating in Unemployment Insurance: Virtue or Vice* (Kalamazoo, Mich.: The W.E. Upjohn Institute, 1972), pp. 22-23.

41. Their empirical work uses time series data on a small set of manufacturing industries.

42. Reder and Neumann, p. 875.

43. Edward E. Leamer, "Let's Take the Con Out of Econometrics," *American Economic Review*, (March 1983), pp. 31-43.

6
An Empirical Analysis of the Effect of Government Transfer Programs on Strike Activity

As detailed in the previous chapter, we approached the empirical work with a small set of hypotheses linking government transfer programs to strike behavior. Because the proper specification of a model estimated with state-level data was in doubt, we used 1970 data as a "laboratory" for developing a model. Thus, our strategy was first to estimate the model with 1970 data and then to examine whether the 1970 results were robust to alternative model specifications and alternative years of data. We used 1970 for this purpose because the 1970 Census provides a wealth of state-level data for control variables.

The organization of this chapter reflects that strategy. The chapter begins with our findings on the relationship between unemployment insurance and strike behavior. That work can be broken into three phases. In the first we sought to test whether state labor dispute disqualification policies were related to strike behavior. The second phase examined whether disqualification policies affected strike behavior through an interaction with other unemployment insurance program characteristics. Finally, we sought to test whether the 1970 results could be replicated in other years. Most of this chapter focuses on these three phases of our unemployment insurance research. It ends with a brief discussion of our findings on the effects of AFDC, food stamps, and general assistance on strike activity.

Labor Dispute Disqualification Policies and Strike Behavior

As indicated previously, we had reason to expect several types of state labor dispute disqualification policies to affect strike behavior. With 51 observations in 1970, we could not include all of the table 5.6 UI variables in one model. To resolve this, we focused on the three UI rules that unemployment insurance administrators had viewed as potentially important. These were the "stoppage-of-work" rule (UI Rule 1), the "New York-Rhode Island" rule (UI Rule 2), and the "innocent bystander" rule (UI Rule 3).[1] We hypothesized that these rules would tend to increase activity along several dimensions. As argued in chapter 5, such rules tend to decrease the total cost of strikes, thereby leading to less comprehensive protocols and increased strike activity. The first phase of the unemployment insurance research sought to test these hypotheses with 1970 data. Although some of the regression coefficients for these rules proved to be statistically significant, in general the data did not support the hypotheses.

Table 1 illustrates the point. The dependent variables in the three regressions are the natural logarithm of strike frequency (number of strikes per labor force participant), average duration of strikes, and average size of strikes (number of workers involved per strike).[2] One can, of course, claim that these are imperfect measures of the theoretically appropriate dependent variables (e.g., one can argue that the analysis should focus only on strikes dealing with economic issues rather than on all strikes). As indicated in chapter 5, to address this argument we ran the same regressions for several alternative measures of strike frequency, duration, and size. In addition, we estimated the model for specific industries, e.g., construction and manufacturing. Our results were remarkably insensitive to redefinitions of the dependent variable.

The key results in table 6.1 concern UI Rules 1, 2, and 3. Our hypotheses led us to expect statistically significant positive coefficients. The results for strike frequency in the first column, for example, show that UI Rules 1 and 2 have positive coefficients, but neither coefficient is statistically different from zero at conventional significance levels. The other two models are thoroughly inconsistent with our hypotheses. To our surprise, for example, UI Rules 1 and 2 have significantly *negative* effects on strike duration. That is, New York and Rhode Island as well as states with the work-stoppage rule appear to have experienced significantly shorter strikes than other states in 1970. Later we will examine whether the negative effects of these rules on strike duration are found in other years and when other specifications are tested.

Table 6.1
Regressions on the Frequency, Duration, and Size of Strikes
(*t*-statistics in parentheses)

Independent variable	Frequency	Duration	Size
UI Rule 1 = 1	.251	.230	-.174
	(1.8)	(2.6)	(1.4)
UI Rule 2 = 1	.454	-.066	.031
	(1.4)	(3.3)	(0.1)
UI Rule 3 = 1	.000	.058	-.080
	(0.0)	(.6)	(0.5)
Unemployment Rate	-.036	.039	-.067
	(.8)	(1.3)	(1.5)
% establishments with 100+ employees	17.729	-4.171	20.724
	(1.3)	(0.5)	(1.6)
% of labor force in unions	4.052	-.400	.813
	(5.2)	(0.8)	(1.1)
% females in labor force	-11.098	4.760	-9.563
	(3.1)	(2.1)	(2.8)
% urban in labor force	-.998	-.730	1.112
	(1.8)	(2.0)	(2.1)
% of population in poverty	.001	-.007	1.014
	(0.0)	(0.8)	(1.1)
Intercept	.988	2.154	8.525
	(0.8)	(2.7)	(7.4)
N	50	50	50
R Square	.559	.300	.392
F	5.638	1.908	2.670

Definition of variables:

Frequency = ln [# strikes in a state in 1970/labor force size in state in 1970]
Duration = ln [average duration of strikes in the state in 1970]
Size = ln [# workers involved in strikes in the state in 1970/# strikes in the state in 1970]
—UI Rule 1 = 1 if strikers collect benefits when employers continue to operate during the strike.
—UI Rule 2 = 1 in New York and Rhode Island, otherwise zero.
—UI Rule 3 = 1 if "innocent bystanders" are permitted to collect benefits.

Of course, such results in part depend upon the other independent variables in the model. The table 6.1 models include six control variables. They are intended as proxies for the complex web of social and economic forces that shape strike activity within a geographic unit. As noted in chapter 5, a review of past theoretical and empirical work on strike behavior yields a wealth of additional possible control variables. We therefore estimated the table 6.1 models with several different combinations of control variables; all of the control variables we tested are listed in table 5.7. None of the alternative specifications yielded meaningful results for the various labor dispute disqualification policies.

It is tempting to seek "explanations" for the coefficients on the control variables in table 6.1. Such temptation should, however, be resisted. Consider, for example, the results on the variable, "Percent Establishments with 100+ Employees." None of the table 6.1 coefficients on this variable are statistically significant at conventional levels. Does one then conclude that establishment size has little effect on strike activity? Probably not. An assessment of the relationship between establishment size and strike activity should ideally use plant or bargaining unit data.[3] State-level data are inappropriate for this purpose. The state is, however, an appropriate unit of observation in an analysis of the relationship between strike activity and the characteristics of state unemployment insurance programs. Moreover, in such an analysis it is appropriate to control for the complex web of forces outside the unemployment insurance program that influence strike activity in a state. The establishment size variable simply plays this role, as do the other control variables in table 6.1.

In summary, the first phase of our research indicated no statistically significant relationship between labor dispute qualification policies and strike frequency and size; the results for strike duration were contrary to our expectations. It appeared that either our hypotheses were incorrect or that "noise" in the data made it impossible to discern the effects of the disqualification policies. We could not, however, draw a firm conclusion without examining whether the disqualification policies interact with other program characteristics to influence strike behavior. The second phase of the research focused on this interaction.

The Interaction of Labor Dispute Disqualification Policies and Program Generosity

As argued in chapter 5, the strike effects of UI Rules 1, 2, and 3 may in part depend upon program generosity. Given imperfect experience rating and the tax treatment of unemployment benefits, a more generous program in states with these UI rules should lead to lower total strike costs, less comprehensive protocols, and increased strike activity. We therefore tested several models that interact measures of program generosity with two of the disqualification rules, UI Rule 1 and UI Rule 3. (UI Rule 2 was not included in this work because only two states—New York and Rhode Island used the rule, and the estimated coefficient would in consequence be meaningless.)[4] Here we found an interesting relationship between strike frequency and interactions involving a state's maximum unemployment benefit. Table 6.2 presents the evidence.

For purposes of comparison, the first regression in table 6.2 is the strike frequency regression from table 6.1. The second regression indicates the effect of interacting the maximum unemployment benefit with UI Rule 1. Since the coefficient on this interaction is positive and statistically significant, the results indicate that a higher maximum benefit in states with UI Rule 1 is associated with higher strike frequency. Although similar results obtain when UI Rule 3 is interacted with the maximum benefit, if both the UI Rule 1 interaction and UI Rule 3 interaction are included in the same regression, neither is statistically significant. (See column 3.) Of course the reason for this is that the two interaction terms are highly correlated. Accordingly, this evidence indicates that *either* the UI Rule 1 interaction *or* the UI Rule 3 interaction is associated with higher strike frequencies. It provides, however, no basis for claiming that one of the interactions is the principal source of the association. Thus, we ran a fourth regression with an interaction between the maximum UI benefit and a variable indicating states that use either UI Rule 1 or UI Rule 3. The coefficient on this interaction term was positive and statistically significant. We believe this is a plausible result. It indicates that for states with UI Rule 1 or UI Rule 3, an increase in program generosity, as proxied by the maximum benefit, is associated with more strikes.[5]

Table 6.2
Strike Frequency Regressions That Include Interaction Variables
(*t*-statistics in parentheses)

Independent variable	1	2	3	4
UI Rule 1 = 1	.251	-.651	-.190	.192
	(1.8)	(1.6)	(.4)	(1.5)
UI Rule 2 = 1	.454	.522	.494	.508
	(1.4)	(1.7)	(1.7)	(1.7)
UI Rule 3 = 1	.000	-.034	-.668	-.470
	(0.0)	(.2)	(1.6)	(1.9)
[UI Rule 1] x max. UI benefit		.015	.008	
		(2.3)	(1.0)	
[UI Rule 3] x max. UI benefit			.010	
			(1.6)	
[Either UI Rule 1 = 1 *or* UI Rule 3 = 1] x max. UI benefit				.010
				(2.4)
Unemployment rate	-.036	-.064	-.079	-.074
	(.8)	(1.4)	(1.7)	(1.6)
% establishment with 100+ employees	17.729	5.261	2.488	10.502
	(1.3)	(.4)	(.2)	(.8)
% of labor force in unions	4.052	4.363	4.355	4.349
	(5.2)	(5.9)	(6.0)	(5.8)
% females in labor force	-11.098	-11.150	-11.589	-11.940
	(3.1)	(3.3)	(3.5)	(3.5)
% urban in labor force	-.998	-1.240	-1.254	-1.287
	(1.8)	(2.5)	(2.5)	(2.4)
% of population in poverty	.001	.009	.017	.014
	(0.0)	(.6)	(1.2)	(1.0)
Intercept	.988	1.453	1.655	1.540
	(.8)	(1.2)	(1.4)	(1.3)
N	50	51	51	50
R Square	.559	.6161	.6411	.6178
F	5.638	6.420	6.332	6.303

See bottom of table 6.1 for variable definitions.

This result led us to test models that included not only an interaction with the maximum benefit but other interactions as well. For example, we tested models with measures of unemployment insurance taxes interacted with UI Rule 1 and UI Rule 3 (see table 5.6 for the full list). In general, either this type of interaction variable had no effect on the regression or it was so highly correlated with the maximum benefit interaction variable that both coefficients had low *t*-statistics. Evidently, 50 observations are insufficient to distinguish the effect of a state's maximum benefit from other characteristics of the state program (e.g., the minimum tax rate, the maximum tax rate, maximum duration of benefit receipt, coverage, etc.). Thus, we chose to represent program generosity with a single proxy—the maximum benefit.

If one must choose a single proxy for unemployment insurance generosity, the maximum benefit is an attractive choice. For purposes of this work, a proxy for program generosity should reflect the workers' and firms' perceptions of generosity at the time they decide to initiate or continue a strike. Given their comparatively high earnings, union members are likely to receive unemployment benefits that are at or near the maximum. This is one reason why the maximum benefit is a better proxy for program generosity than the average benefit. Moreover, a good proxy for program generosity should not be affected by factors that have nothing to do with legislative decisions regarding generosity. A proxy like the average benefit level depends not only on state policy but also on demographic factors (e.g., the average wage in the state or the state's ratio of part-time to full-time workers), while the maximum benefit is an instrument of and depends only on state policy. Thus, for purposes of analyzing interactions between UI Rules 1 and 3 and program generosity, we focused on their interaction with the maximum benefit.

Our next step was to examine whether results on the interaction variable were sensitive to the set of independent variables included in the model. As in the first phase of the research, we tested a long list of alternative independent variables (see table 5.7 for the list). The result obtained on the interaction variable was remarkably insensitive to such changes in specification. Table 6.3 illustrates this point. The first model in table 6.3 includes measures of industry composition, and the second includes two dummy variables standing for states with right-to-work laws and southern states—variables that may reflect community attitudes toward strikes. Although neither of these dummy variables has a significant effect on the dependent variable, the proportion of a state's labor force employed in the construction industry is associated with a significantly higher level of strike frequency.[6] Nevertheless, the inclusion or exclusion of such variables has little effect on the magnitude or statistical significance of the interaction variable.

Table 6.3
Strike Frequency Regressions with Alternative Control Variables
(*t*-statistics in parentheses)

Independent variable	1	2
UI Rule 1 = 1	.2215	.2045
	(1.6)	(1.4)
UI Rule 2 = 1	.6628	.5869
	(2.1)	(1.7)
UI Rule 3 = 1	-.4941	-.4613
	(2.0)	(1.8)
[Either UI Rule 1=1 *or* UI Rule 3=1] x max. UI benefit	.0088	.0101
	(2.1)	(2.4)
Unemployment rate	-.1310	-.0900
	(2.1)	(1.5)
% establishment with 100+ employees	-1.0784	10.5060
	(1.1)	(.6)
% of labor force in unions	5.0981	3.8847
	(4.4)	(3.3)
% females in labor force	-11.1873	-11.9525
	(2.4)	(3.4)
% urban in labor force	-.4457	-1.3087
	(.6)	(2.3)
% population in poverty	.0103	.0150
	(.7)	(.6)
South = 1		.0871
		(.4)
Right-to-work law = 1		-.0626
		(.4)
Average hourly earnings		.1292
		(.4)
% of labor force in mining	.1407	
	(.0)	
% of labor force in construction	16.2212	
	(2.0)	
% of labor force in transportation	-1.4436	
	(.2)	

Table 6.3 (continued)

Independent variable	1	2
% of labor force in trade	-5.9277	
	(.9)	
% of labor force in finance	-11.4634	
	(1.1)	
% of labor force in services	.8072	
	(.5)	
Intercept	1.9141	1.2701
	(1.0)	(.8)
N	50	50
R Square	.7026	.6241
F	4.872	4.597

See bottom of table 6.1 for variable definition.

The last step in this phase of the work was to include the interaction variable in regressions that use the size of strikes (average number of workers involved per strike) and average duration of strikes as dependent variables. Although we had no hypothesis on strike size, given our theoretical framework and the strike frequency results, we anticipated a positive relationship between the interaction and strike duration. But that is not what we found. In models using strike size as the dependent variable, the coefficient on the interaction variable was usually negative but not statistically significant. In models using strike duration as the dependent variable, however, the coefficient on the interaction variable was usually both negative and statistically significant at conventional levels. Thus, it appears that states with a high maximum unemployment benefit and either an innocent bystander or work-stoppage rule had shorter strikes than other states. Once again, this result contradicted our expectations.

Thus, our results at the end of the second phase of the research were rather confusing. We had found a statistically significant relationship between strike frequency and an interaction variable, and that relationship was insensitive to changes in model specification. Although the positive sign accorded with our theoretical framework and hypotheses, the result was suspect for two reasons. First, the interaction variable took an opposite sign in the strike duration model—a result that did not accord with our theory. That was a surprise, but perhaps not indicative of a serious problem; it could simply mean, for example, that our theoretical framework was wrong. Moreover, as developed below, there was reason to believe the duration regression suffered a selection bias and that, in consequence, the model provided an inadequate test of the theoretical hypotheses. Second, and perhaps more important, the interaction result was based on 1970 data, and we had already tested numerous models with these data. The more models one tests on a given data set, the greater the probability of finding a statistically significant coefficient. We thus had good reason to suspect that the interaction result would not hold in a different data set. That possibility led to the third phase of the work, in which we used data from different years to test the models developed in the first two phases of our testing procedures.

Replicating the Results

Accordingly, in the third phase we sought to replicate the frequency and duration results using cross-section data from different years. As indicated in tables 6.4 and 6.5, we took the table 6.2, column 4 model and applied it to 1960, 1966, and 1974 data.[7] The results were an unqualified surprise. In table 6.4, the relationship between the interaction variable and strike frequency is thoroughly robust across the different samples.[8] These results led us to believe that the 1970 frequency result was not a statistical artifact. States that have a high maximum unemployment benefit and either the innocent bystander or work-stoppage rule consistently have significantly more strikes than other states. On the other hand, the results shown in table 6.5, where strike duration is used as the dependent variable, are not nearly so impressive. They show that the coefficients for the interaction variable are negative but statistically insignificant in all years except 1970. Thus it appears that the negative relation between the interaction variable and strike duration in 1970 is merely a statistical artifact.

Table 6.4
Strike Frequency Regressions for Different Years
(*t*-statistics in parentheses)

Independent variable	1960	1966	1970	1974
UI Rule 1 = 1	.247	.018	.192	.008
	(1.2)	(.1)	(1.5)	(.1)
UI Rule 2 = 1	.106	.390	.508	−.074
	(.2)	(1.4)	(1.7)	(.2)
UI Rule 3 = 1	−.790	−.350	−.470	−.583
	(2.3)	(1.5)	(1.9)	(2.3)
[Either UI Rule 1=1 *or* UI Rule 3=1] x max. UI benefit	.019	.017	.010	.008
	(2.3)	(2.4)	(2.4)	(2.6)
Unemployment rate	.112	.056	−.074	−.014
	(1.8)	(1.1)	(1.6)	(.3)
% establishment with 100+ employees	−32.509	19.187	10.502	−.909
	(1.4)	(1.4)	(.8)	(.1)
% of labor force in unions	1.977	2.576	4.349	5.711
	(1.7)	(3.7)	(5.8)	(7.2)
% females in labor force	−2.262	−10.832	−11.940	−14.298
	(.6)	(3.9)	(3.5)	(4.3)
% urban in labor force	.550	−.606	−1.287	−.586
	(.6)	(1.2)	(2.4)	(1.1)
% of population in poverty	−.003	.002	.014	.037
	(.2)	(.2)	(1.0)	(2.5)
Intercept	−3.359	.114	1.540	1.434
	(2.5)	(.1)	(1.3)	(1.3)
N	50	50	50	50
R Square	.4753	.5840	.6178	.6899
F	3.533	5.471	6.303	8.678

See bottom of table 6.1 for variable definitions.

Table 6.5
Strike Duration Regressions for Different Years
(*t*-statistics in parentheses)

Independent variable	1960	1966	1970	1974
UI Rule 1 = 1	-.136	-.156	-.1991	-.065
	(1.0)	(1.7)	(2.3)	(.5)
UI Rule 2 = 1	-.131	-.466	-.0939	-.137
	(.5)	(2.2)	(.5)	(.5)
UI Rule 3 = 1	.297	.187	.3028	.214
	(1.4)	(1.1)	(1.9)	(.9)
[Either UI Rule 1=1 *or* UI Rule 3=1] x max. UI benefit	-.006	-.001	-.0052	-.004
	(1.1)	(.4)	(1.9)	(1.3)
Unemployment rate	.051	-.056	.0589	.018
	(1.2)	(1.5)	(1.9)	(.4)
% establishment with 100+ employees	-10.706	4.780	-.4169	-5.230
	(.7)	(.5)	(.0)	(.4)
% of labor force in unions	-.303	.685	-.5540	-1.232
	(.4)	(1.3)	(1.1)	(1.7)
% females in labor force	-1.569	-.547	5.1973	1.652
	(.7)	(.3)	(2.3)	(.6)
% urban in labor force	.478	.462	-.5799	1.125
	(.8)	(1.2)	(1.6)	(2.2)
% of population in poverty	-.009	.001	-.0135	.002
	(.9)	(.1)	(1.5)	(.2)
Intercept	3.511	2.894	1.8667	2.282
	(4.0)	(4.2)	(2.4)	(2.2)
N	50	50	50	50
R Square	.1436	.3461	.3615	.2111
F	.654	2.064	2.207	1.044

See bottom of table 6.1 for variable definitions.

Although the table 6.4 results are more persuasive than those for 1970 alone, there are still legitimate reasons to question them. In particular, one could argue that there exist unobserved determinants of strike frequency in different states and that these unobserved variables are correlated with the interaction variable. The argument implies that the table 6.4 results do not address the issue of whether the unemployment insurance system actually leads to more strikes; the results may simply reveal that the interaction variable is correlated with some unobserved state-specific determinant of strike frequency that persists over time.

In order to examine this possibility, we ran a fixed-effects version of the model.[9] In essence we pooled together 15 years of data on the 51 jurisdictions and estimated the table 6.2, column 4 model with a separate intercept for each jurisdiction.[10] Since separate intercepts control for time-invariant (fixed) unobserved state characteristics, the fixed-effects model allows us to test whether the interaction result in table 6.4 is due to state-specific fixed effects that have nothing to do with the unemployment insurance system.

Before discussing our results, two data issues should be noted. First, state-specific time-invariant *observed* variables must be excluded from a fixed-effects model. For this reason the New York and Rhode Island dummy variable (UI Rule 2) was excluded from the model. The variable equals "1" in New York and Rhode Island and zero in all other states for the entire 15-year sample period. As such, it is perfectly correlated with the state-specific intercepts and must be excluded to avoid collinearity. The second data issue concerns the measurement of the independent variables. Although we had data on strike frequency and duration for all states and all years, that was not the case for the independent variables. For example, data on UI Rules 1 and 3 are not available for 1961, 1963, 1965, and 1969. In such cases we used interpolation to impute the missing data.[11]

As indicated in table 6.6, the fixed-effect results were quite similar to the tables 6.4 and 6.5 cross-section results. The interaction variable ([Either UI Rule 1 or 3 = 1] x max. UI benefit) is positive and statistically significant in the frequency model and negative and not statistically significant in the duration model. These findings imply that the results for the interaction variable are not attributable to unobserved state-specific fixed effects. Moreover, since we only tested one model with this pooled data set, the table 6.6 results are statistically meaningful in the sense that they are not a consequence of testing numerous models in the same data set.[12]

Table 6.6
Fixed-Effects Regressions on the Frequency and Duration of Strikes, 1960-1974
(*t*-statistics in parentheses)

Independent variable	Frequency	Duration
UI Rule 1 = 1	–.055	.225
	(0.6)	(2.2)
UI Rule 3 = 1	–.653	–.069
	(3.3)	(0.3)
[Either UI Rule 1 *or* UI Rule 3=1] x max. UI benefit	.010	–.003
	(4.3)	(1.2)
Unemployment rate	–.072	.061
	(6.7)	(5.2)
% establishments with 100+ employees	15.210	2.852
	(1.8)	(0.3)
% labor force in unions	1.410	.364
	(1.8)	(0.4)
% females in labor force	–4.742	.900
	(3.3)	(0.6)
% urban in labor force	1.514	2.502
	(1.4)	(2.2)
% of population in poverty	–.019	–.008
	(3.7)	(1.3)
Intercept	–2.586	.201
	(2.8)	(0.2)
N	763	763
R Square	.782	.3037
F	42.781	5.197

See bottom of table 6.1 for variable definitions.

In summary, all three phases of the empirical work point to the same conclusion: the interaction variable is positively associated with strike frequency. That result is robust to changes in control variables and data sets. Moreover, it holds in a fixed-effects model. Given these findings, there remains a question that our statistical tools cannot answer directly: why does this association exist? In our best judgment, the most plausible explanation is causation running from the unemployment insurance system to strike frequency. The empirical results are thoroughly consistent with the hypothesis that a more generous unemployment insurance system causes a higher strike frequency in states that use the "stoppage-of-work" and "innocent bystander" labor dispute disqualification rules. Moreover, the hypothesis flows logically from a plausible theory of strike behavior, i.e., in states with these disqualification rules, a more generous unemployment insurance system leads to less comprehensive protocols and thereby to greater strike frequency.

This interpretation raises two additional questions that need to be addressed. First, even if certain features of the unemployment insurance system cause higher strike frequencies, are the effects so small as to be of little social relevance? Second, if a theory of protocols is applicable, why is the interaction variable not positively related to strike duration?

With regard to the first question, the coefficient of .010 on the interaction variable in table 6.6 implies that a $10 increase in the maximum unemployment benefit (measured in 1967 dollars) is associated with a 10 percent increase in strike frequency in states with either UI Rule 1 or 3. Since the sample mean for the maximum benefit was $50, that implies an elasticity of .5, i.e., a 1 percent increase in the maximum benefit in states with either rule was associated with about a .5 percent increase in strike frequency. Alternatively stated, an increase in the maximum unemployment benefit from $50 to $55 (measured in 1967 dollars) is associated with an increase in strike frequency from 6.8 strikes per 100,000 labor force participants (the sample mean) to 7.5 strikes per 100,000 labor force participants (6.8 x 1.1 = 7.5). This sentence could, however, be seriously misinterpreted if an important caveat is not noted. The maximum benefit is being used as a proxy for program generosity. It is not the maximum *per se* but the level of generosity proxied by the maximum that has this effect. The point remains, however, that the coefficient in table 6.6 implies that the unemployment insurance system can have rather large effects on strike frequency.

With regard to the second question, throughout this work we found a negative and in most cases statistically insignificant relationship between the interaction variable and strike duration. Such findings may cause one to question whether the relationship between the unemployment insurance system and strike frequency can be explained with a protocol theory. After all, the protocol theory predicts that the interaction variable will not only be positively related to strike frequency but also to strike duration.

The inconsistent results obtained for strike duration may, however, simply reflect a data problem. The coefficients in our duration models probably suffer from a selection bias. This is because our data on duration come from a sample of bargaining units that actually experienced a strike. Since strikes are not generated by a random process, this is not a random sample.[13] As a consequence, coefficients estimated in this sample may be biased. Moreover, since our data are aggregate data, standard "Heckit" techniques for solving the problem are not applicable.[14] Our duration models, therefore, do not provide a meaningful test of the protocol theory. They neither confirm nor contradict the strike frequency result.

Figure 6.1

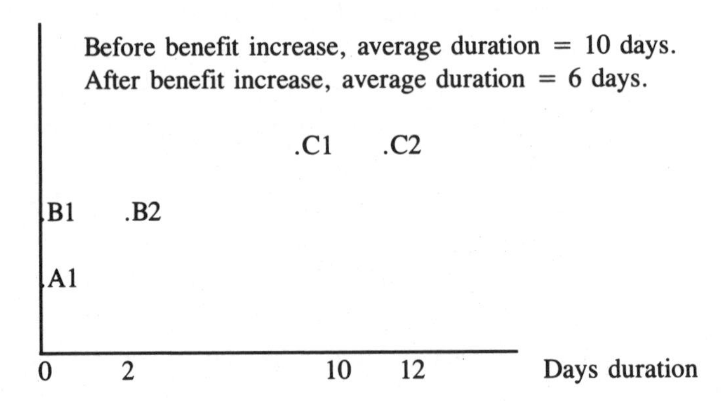

Figure 6.1 helps to illustrate this point. Consider a sample of three bargaining units denoted as A, B, and C. Whereas units A and B reach settlements without a strike, unit C has a strike of 10 days. This initial position is denoted as A1, B1, and C1 in the diagram. Since we only

measure strike duration when a strike occurs, our measure of average strike duration in this sample would be 10 days. Now suppose that the state government increases unemployment insurance payments to strikers, and that the strike duration for unit C increases from 10 days to 12 days, the strike duration for unit B increases from 0 to 2 days, and unit A again settles without a strike. This new position is denoted as A1, B2, and C2 on the diagram. Since we only measure strike duration when a strike occurs, our measure of strike duration in this new position would be 6 days ([10 + 2]/2). Thus, *although no unit experienced a decrease in strike duration (indeed, B and C experienced an increase), our measure indicates that average duration dropped from 10 days to 6 days.* The problem is that our measure of strike duration does not include bargaining units that do not go to strike and that thereby have durations of zero. Only by including those in the sample (or by adjusting for the statistical effect of their exclusion) can one obtain a meaningful test of the strike duration effects predicted by protocol theory.

The Effect of the AFDC, Food Stamp, and General Assistance Programs on Strike Behavior

As noted in chapter 5, although a theory of protocols predicts a relationship between welfare benefits for strikers and strike behavior, we did not expect to find one. This is because strikers rarely meet the income and asset eligibility criteria of welfare programs. Although an effect may exist, we thought it unlikely that our statistical methods would be sensitive enough to discern it.

Our strategy for assessing whether welfare programs affect strike behavior was, however, identical to that used with the unemployment insurance program. In the first phase, we tested whether the availability of AFDC, general assistance, and food stamp benefits for strikers was related to strike behavior in 1970. Several combinations of control variables were tested during this phase of the work. In the second phase, we tested whether an interaction between availability of benefits and benefit levels was related to strike behavior in 1970. Finally, in the third phase we estimated cross-sectional models for different years as well as fixed-effects models.

Table 6.7
Fixed-Effects Regressions on the Frequency and Duration of Strikes, 1960-1974, with Welfare Variables Included (*t*-statistics in parentheses)

Independent variable	Frequency	Duration
[AFDCAID = 1] x max. UI benefit	.0001	.0001
	(0.5)	(0.6)
Food stamp coverage	.022	.044
	(0.4)	(0.7)
UI Rule 1 = 1	-.051	.229
	(0.5)	(2.2)
UI Rule 3 = 1	-.661	-.079
	(3.3)	(0.4)
[Either UI Rule 1 *or* UI Rule 3=1]	.010	-.003
x max. UI benefit	(4.3)	(1.1)
Unemployment rate	-.072	.061
	(6.7)	(5.0)
% establishments with 100+ employees	13.820	.590
	(1.5)	(0.1)
% labor force in unions	1.407	.331
	(1.8)	(0.4)
% females in labor force	-5.176	.170
	(3.2)	(0.1)
% urban in labor force	1.623	2.673
	(1.5)	(2.3)
% of population in poverty	-.020	-.009
	(3.7)	(1.4)
Intercept	2.516	.349
	(2.7)	(0.3)
N	763	763
R Square	.782	.305
F	41.291	5.031

Definition of variables:

AFDCAID = 1 if the state has an AFDC Unemployed Father Program and that program permits strikers to collect benefits.

Food stamp coverage measures the percent of the poor in the state who reside in counties that participate in the food stamp program.

Other variable definitions are at the bottom of table 6.1.

In no case did we find a consistently significant relationship between a measure of welfare aid to strikers and strike behavior. Although the estimated coefficients often took a positive sign, in most cases they were not statistically significant. Nor did we obtain consistent results when we attempted to replicate the results for 1970 in other years. Table 6.7 illustrates this point. This table adds two welfare variables to the fixed-effects specification in table 6.6. The first variable is the real level of AFDC benefits in the state multiplied by AFDCAID. As noted in chapter 5, table 5.6, AFDCAID is a binary (0,1) variable indicating that the state allows strikers to receive AFDC-U benefits. The second variable is the percent of poor people in the state that reside in counties that provide food stamp benefits. The table reveals that neither variable is significantly related to either strike frequency or strike duration. We conclude that either there is no relationship between AFDC, general assistance, food stamps and strike behavior, or the relationship exists but is too subtle for our statistical tools to reveal.

Conclusion

This chapter establishes a link between the unemployment insurance system and strike behavior. A more generous unemployment insurance program is related to a higher strike frequency in states that use "innocent bystander" or "stoppage-of-work" disqualification rules. This relationship is evidently not a minor one. The regressions indicate that for such states a 1 percent increase in the maximum unemployment benefit is associated with a .5 percent increase in strike frequency, *ceteris paribus*. Moreover, in our best judgment, the most plausible explanation for the association is causality, i.e., certain characteristics of the unemployment insurance system affect strike frequency.

In stating this conclusion, it is important to emphasize what was not found. We did not find evidence of a link between the provision of AFDC, food stamps, or general assistance to strikers and strike behavior. Moreover, our evidence on unemployment compensation is restricted to strike frequency; no conclusions are possible on whether the unemployment insurance program affects either strike duration or number of workers involved. Finally, no conclusions are possible on whether the New York- Rhode Island disqualification rule affects strike behavior. Either these relationships are nonexistent or our methods are insufficiently precise to discern them.

NOTES

1. We also tested the effect of the "lockout" rule and the "interim employment" rule on strike activity. In all of our experiments with 1970 data, these two rules appeared to have no discernible effect on any measure of strike activity. Consequently, in this chapter we concentrate on the effects of the three rules mentioned here.

2. We used the natural logarithm of the dependent variables because residual plots revealed problems of skew and outliers with the untransformed variables.

3. In a study that used bargaining unit data, Cynthia L. Gramm found that the size of the bargaining unit was positively and significantly related to several measures of strike activity. Similarly, she found that the percent of unionized workers in the bargaining unit's industry who were male had a positive and significant effect on the probability of a strike. See, Cynthia L. Gramm, "The Determinants of Strike Incidence and Severity: A Micro-Level Study," *Industrial and Labor Relations Review,* Vol. 39, No. 3 (April 1986), pp. 361-76. In a study that used a pooled time series cross-sectional sample of bargaining units in Canada, Swidinsky and Vandercamp also found that the propensity to strike increased with the size of the bargaining unit. See, Robert Swidinsky and John Vandercamp, "A Micro-Econometric Analysis of Strike Activity in Canada," *Journal of Labor Research,* Vol. III, No. 4. (Fall, 1982), pp. 455-71. In the United States in the 1970s, the mean duration of all strikes was about 23 days; in bargaining units with 1,000 or more workers, however, the mean duration of strikes was 51 days. (Calculations for all strikes based on our own data; for the mean duration of strikes in large bargaining units, see Gramm.)

4. The coefficients on the interaction between program generosity and the UI Rule 2 dummy variable would be the equivalent of a regression line fitted to two points. The residuals on New York and Rhode Island would be forced to zero, implying an implausible model that perfectly explains strike frequency in New York and Rhode Island.

5. We also tested a model that was identical to the one in column 3 except that the maximum UI benefit was included as a regressor. The coefficient on this additional variable was negative and statistically insignificant. The result is consistent with the hypothesis that in states with neither UI Rule 1 nor UI Rule 3, a more generous UI program does *not* influence strike behavior.

6. The construction industry is known to be a particularly strike-prone industry. Since the end of World War II, the construction workforce has constituted about 5 percent of the nonagricultural labor force; but about 20 percent of the nation's strike activity has been in the industry. See, David B. Lipsky and Henry S. Farber, "The Composition of Strike Activity in the Construction Industry," *Industrial and Labor Relations Review,* Vol. 29, No. 3 (April 1976), pp. 388-404.

7. We chose 1960 because the 1960 Census provided demographic data that were not available for other years. We chose 1974 because that was the last year in which we had good strike data. We chose 1966 because we did not have data on the labor dispute disqualification rules for 1965. In each of these years some variables had to be interpolated. Interpolation of the data is dealt with below in the discussion of the fixed-effects models.

8. Note that the coefficient on the interaction variables tends to decline over time. This is in part because the models were run with the maximum benefit measured in nominal dollars. When the maximums were deflated by a price index, these differences nearly disappeared. Of course, signs and *t*-statistics would not be affected by a price index.

9. A good reference on fixed effect models is Yair Mundlak, "On the Pooling of Time Series and Cross Section Data," *Econometrica*, Vol. 40, No. 1, (January 1978), pp. 69-86 and the citations therein.

10. The regressions were run on 763 observations rather than 765 because data on the unemployment rate were missing and could not be interpolated for Oregon in 1970 and 1971.

11. For example, if UI Rule 1 = 1 in 1960 and UI Rule 1 = 0 in 1962, we set UI Rule 1 equal to 1/2 in 1961. Variables such as the percent female or percent urban in the labor force had to be interpolated from 1960 and 1970 census data. Other variables, such as the percent of establishments with 100+ employees, were missing for only a few years and could be interpolated in the same way as the UI Rules.

12. The table 6.6 results led us to wonder whether the same would be found in univariate plots. That is, suppose one looks at a state that changed rule 1 during the 1960–1974 period. Would one observe a discrete change in strike frequency at precisely that point in time when the rule changes? The plots were disappointing. There is no evidence of a discrete jump. Our result is then a multivariate result. A number of factors affect strike frequency, one of which is the unemployment insurance program. Only by holding other factors constant can one observe the effect of the UI program.

13. More concretely, the evidence on strike frequency indicates that an increase in the interaction variable induces some bargaining units to go on strike. If those bargaining units have unobserved characteristics associated with short strike durations, then an increase in the interaction variable would cause a change in sample composition that precipitates a *decline* in average strike duration. Thus, even if, with sample composition held constant, an increase in the interaction variable *increases* strike duration, we may not observe that increase because when the interaction variable changes sample composition changes. We obtained some evidence consistent with this line of argument. We estimated the table 6.6 fixed-effects model using the following three dependent variables:

FDUR30 = % of all strikes in the state that exceed 30 days
FDUR56 = % of all strikes in the state that exceed 56 days
FDUR80 = % of all strikes in the state that exceed 80 days

The coefficients on the interaction variable for these dependent variables were as follows:

Dependent variable	**Coefficient on interaction variable**	***t*-statistic**
FDUR30	.00003	.043
FDUR56	-.00057	.445
FDUR80	-.00068	1.503

Thus, roughly speaking, it appears that an increase in the interaction variable changes sample composition by increasing the share of all strikes that are short strikes and reducing the share of very long strikes.

14. To see this, let Y_{1i} represent strike duration for firm i. We seek to estimate parameters in a model of the form,

(1) $Y_{1i} = X_{1i}B_1 + U_{1i}$,

where X_{1i} is a 1 x K vector of exogenous regressors, B_1 is K x 1 vector of parameters, and

U_{1i} is an error term with mean zero and finite variance. Suppose that the probability that strikes occur is of the form,

(2) Prob of strike $= Pr(Y_{2i} \geq 0)$,

(3) $Y_{2i} = X_{2i}B_2 + U_{2i}$, where X_{2i}, B_2, and U_{2i} are defined in a manner analogous to X_{1i}, B_1, and U_{1i}.

Now, we only observe duration when strikes occur. Letting Y_{1i}, represent observed duration we have

$Y_{1i} = Y_{1i}$ iff $Y_{2i} \geq 0$
$Y_{1i} = 0$ iff $Y_{2i} < 0$

Following Heckman, the expected value of Y_{1i} in our data is

(4) $E(Y_{1i} \mid X_{1i}, Y_{2i} \geq 0) = X_{1i}B_1 + E(U_{1i} \mid U_{2i} \geq - X_{2i} B_2)$.

In Heckman's words, "Regression estimators of the parameters of equation (1) fit on the selected sample omit the final term of equation (4) as a regressor, so that the bias that results from using nonrandomly selected samples to estimate behavioral relationships is seen to arise from the ordinary problem of omitted variables." (James Heckman, "Sample Bias as a Specification Error," *Econometrica,* Vol. 47, No. 1, [January 1979], pp. 153-162).

Heckman goes on to present techniques for obtaining consistent parameter estimates. Those cannot be used in our data because we are estimating models with aggregate data. In essence we estimate

$$(5) \quad \frac{1}{N_S} \sum_{j=1}^{N_S} Y_{1jS} = \frac{1}{N_S} \sum_{j=1}^{N_S} X_{1jS} B_1 + \frac{1}{N_S} \sum_{j=1}^{N_S} U_{1jS}$$

Where N_S is the number of observations in state S.

The analogue to (4) in this case is

$$(6) \quad \frac{1}{N_S} \sum_{j=1}^{N_S} E(Y_{1jS}) = \frac{1}{N_S} \sum_{j=1}^{N_S} X_{1jS} B_1 + \frac{1}{N_S} \sum_{j=1}^{N_S} E(U_{1jS} \mid U_{2i} \geq -X_{2i}B_2)$$

There is no simple transform of Mills' ratio that acts as a proxy for the last term.

7
What is the Proper Policy?

When is it appropriate to provide government transfer payments to workers who are involved in a labor dispute? One could claim that it is never appropriate; the transfer payments favor one of the disputants and thereby violate a doctrine of governmental neutrality. Others might counter that a fundamental function of government is assisting the needy. When a family is in dire straights because its breadwinner is engaged in a strike (an eminently legal activity), then it is appropriate for the state to assist that family. Clearly, the question raises difficult issues. At its heart is a philosophical question about the proper role of the modern state in what are usually distinct spheres: government transfers and industrial relations. To the extent that people differ in their perceptions of the appropriate goals of public policy in these two spheres, their answers to the question differ.

In consequence, this chapter begins with a discussion of goals. The first section discusses goals underlying current government policy in the two spheres. With regard to transfer policy the key goals are alleviating hardship and compensating workers for earnings lost due to involuntary unemployment. In industrial relations the key goals are promotion of industrial peace and governmental neutrality in labor disputes. Clearly, it is difficult to formulate policies that simultaneously attain all of these goals. Policy must strike a balance between them. Given that, the second section examines tradeoffs between the goals as well as policies implicit in the tradeoffs. For example, if the society wishes to emphasize industrial peace and deemphasize alleviation of hardship, what kinds or policies are appropriate? What form should transfer programs take? Finally, we present our position including our judgments about the proper role of the state, and a proposed package of policies consistent with those judgments.

Goals for Public Policy

It is not always easy to discern the goals of either transfer or industrial relations policy. Policy may be motivated by an array of goals, some manifest and some latent. Here we focus on manifest goals that have unambiguously motivated past policy and around which there appears to be a broad consensus.

Goals for Transfer Programs

Government transfer programs are usually divided into two categories: public assistance and social insurance. Different goals underlie each category. Public assistance programs are the oldest form of government transfer program. Their goal is to *alleviate hardship*—to provide a floor of protection so that people do not have to starve or beg. Children are of particular importance for such programs. Since they are not responsible for their poverty, and since poverty may affect their future development, children are viewed as particularly deserving of government aid. The food stamp and Aid to Families with Dependent Children (AFDC) programs are examples of public assistance programs. The latter program is restricted to families with children. Both programs are only available to families that can pass a "means test" and thereby demonstrate material hardship.

Social insurance programs seek to compensate workers for an adverse event such as disability, old age, on-the-job injury, or involuntary unemployment. In comparison to public assistance, these are new programs. In the United States they gained prominence after passage of the 1935 Social Security Act. For purposes of the present study it is sufficient to focus on the goals of one of the social insurances, unemployment insurance.

The primary goal of unemployment insurance is to *compensate workers for income lost due to involuntary unemployment.* For example, a laid-off worker is usually considered involuntarily unemployed and thus eligible for benefits. In general, benefits are a fraction of previous wages up to a maximum. They are usually not adjusted for family size.[1] It is important to recognize that unlike a public assistance program, unemployment insurance does not simply assist people in dire need. In

1970, more than 40 percent of the payments went to people with annual family incomes greater than the median. Only 11 percent of the payments went to families living in official poverty.[2]

Of course, the two goals of transfer programs have implications for strike-related transfers. Single-minded pursuit of the goal of alleviating hardship implies payment of government transfers to workers involved in a labor dispute whenever the workers suffer severe material hardship. Special emphasis would be placed on providing benefits to families with children. Single-minded pursuit of the goal of compensating income lost as a result of involuntary unemployment implies government transfers to workers involved in a labor dispute whenever the workers are involuntarily unemployed. Therein lies the vexing issue of whether strikers are ever involuntarily unemployed. We address that in the Policy Options section.

Goals for Industrial Relations

Government policy regarding collective bargaining has undergone a significant evolution in the last century, moving from outright prohibition of unions and strikes to explicit guarantees for both. Two goals appear basic to today's policy: *promotion of industrial peace,* and *governmental neutrality in labor disputes.*

Industrial peace has been a goal of public policy since the industrial revolution. Unions and strikes were banned in the nineteenth century because they interfered with the free flow of commerce. Later, in the debate over the 1935 Wagner Act, it was argued that only by assuring the presence of trade unions and prohibiting unfair labor practices by employers could the nation minimize disruptive industrial strife. In a sense, over the course of a century the goal of promoting industrial peace remained fixed, while the strategy for attaining that goal shifted dramatically. Of course, history is more complex than that. Not only strategies but also perceptions have changed. At one point strikes were viewed as criminal acts and at another as institutionalized (legal) actions. The point is, however, that throughout history the government sought to minimize strike-related disruptions of commerce.[3]

The nation's present strategy would seem to be one of minimizing strike activity by encouraging collective bargaining. While strikes are a necessary and legal mechanism through which workers express disaffection with employers, the government encourages both workers and employers to find less disruptive avenues for voicing and resolving differences.

The second goal—governmental neutrality in labor disputes—is more difficult to document. The goal was articulated in the debate over the Taft-Hartley Act of 1947. It was claimed that the federal government had gone too far with the 1935 Wagner Act, and that a more even-handed approach was requisite. The idea was for the government to act like a referee in a boxing match. It should enforce the rules (no unfair practices), and stop the fight if the situation gets out of hand. As with any good referee, the government should not favor either party.

The two goals of industrial relations policy have implications for strike-related transfers. Single-minded pursuit of the goal of industrial peace implies that strike-related transfers are only appropriate to the extent that they do not disrupt industrial peace. Single-minded pursuit of the goal of governmental neutrality implies limiting strike-related transfers to those cases where they either do not favor one of the disputants, or where they counterbalance some other policy of the government.

Policy Options

While a discussion of goals is useful for establishing a context, there remains the original question of the conditions under which strike-related transfers are appropriate. At the outset, it is important to recognize that a single-minded pursuit of one of the above goals is unlikely. A more realistic view would be that we seek to attain two, three, or even all four goals simultaneously. That raises the problem of tradeoffs. It may be quite difficult to satisfy the goal of alleviating hardship while at the same time maintaining state neutrality in labor disputes. A tradeoff may exist whereby an emphasis on one goal means deemphasis of another. That implies a somewhat more focused question: in light of the society's desire to attain more than one of the goals, when are strike-related transfers appropriate?

This section addresses that question. It examines the range of feasible policy options that strike a balance between the goals. To keep the exposition manageable, we deal with pairs of goals. The section begins with a discussion of policies designed to strike a balance between the goal of promoting industrial peace and the goal of compensating income lost due to involuntary unemployment. Next we discuss policies that balance the goals of promoting industrial peace and alleviating hardship. The section closes with a discussion of policies that balance the goal of governmental neutrality against the twin goals of transfer programs. Clearly, each discussion is related to the other. In consequence, the first examines issues in some detail, while the subsequent discussions build on that and are briefer as a result.

Balancing the Goal of Promoting Industrial Peace Against the Goal of Compensating Involuntary Unemployment

At the outset, it is useful to be concrete about the kinds of transfer policies that are compatible with the goal of compensating strike related involuntary unemployment. Chapter 2 introduced a number of policies that may be justified in these terms, i.e., unemployment insurance provisions regarding innocent bystanders, work stoppages, lockouts, interim employment and extended waiting periods (the New York-Rhode Island rule). Clearly, some of these provisions come closer to compensating involuntary unemployment than others. The unemployment of innocent bystanders would seem unambiguously involuntary. Innocent bystanders do not vote on and are not participating in the strike. The employer has laid them off; they did not choose to withdraw their labor services. Similarly, the lockout provision could be justified in terms of involuntary unemployment, since lockouts are initiated by the employer. Of course, there may be ambiguities here. A lockout may be a response to union tactics.

More difficult to justify are provisions regarding work stoppages, interim employment, and extended waiting periods. In a sense workers who receive benefits under these provisions are voluntarily unemployed because they choose to go on strike. In another sense, however, the unemployment is involuntary. In each case an employer has in some way contributed to the unemployment. Moreover, the unemployment is part of a collective action. To see how this complicates the issue, suppose a worker votes against a strike, but the majority of union members vote for it. Even though he would prefer to continue working, he participates in the strike because the collective has chosen to do so. Is that voluntary unemployment? In such cases the distinction between voluntary and involuntary is fraught with ambiguities.

The larger point is that one can conceive of transfer policies that are arguably consistent with the goal of compensating strike-related involuntary unemployment. Given that, there remains the question of whether there exists a tradeoff between the goal of promoting industrial peace and the goal of compensating such unemployment. In our view, the answer depends upon how the transfer payments are financed.

If the cost of the transfer payments are fully borne by the disputing parties, then in accordance with our interpretation of Reder and Neumann (see chapter 5), there need be no tradeoff. When the striking parties bear the full cost of the payments, the payments should not affect either strike frequency or duration. In consequence, if the costs are fully borne by the parties, the society can both compensate income lost due to strike-related involuntary unemployment *and* promote industrial peace. In this case *it is appropriate* to provide government transfer payments to workers who are involved in a labor dispute. Financing is the key. There are at least four policy options for insuring that the parties bear all of the costs:

(1) *Perfect Experience Rating.* Under this provision the employer would bear the full cost of the transfers payments. The option is clearly feasible. It would simply require refinement of the current financing system. At present the principal reasons for imperfect experience rating are minimum and maximum tax rates on employers. The main route to perfect experience rating is elimination of these minimums and maximums.[4]

(2) *Worker Repayment of Benefits Received.* Under this provision workers who receive strike-related benefits would repay the benefits to the government. In a sense, this would put the government in the

business of making loans to workers during a strike and collecting repayments afterwards. Administrative feasibility may be a problem here. It is not clear precisely how the government would collect money from the workers after the strike. For example, if the government used a payroll tax, that tax would have to be targeted on the strikers and not levied on new workers or workers who did not participate in the strike.

(3) *Union Repayment of Benefits Received.* Here the striking union would repay the benefits. While perhaps easier to enforce than worker repayment, if the union represents other workers, some of the costs could be shifted to workers outside of the bargaining unit.

(4) *Income Taxation of Unemployment Insurance Benefits.* Policy has already moved in this direction. As of 1987 unemployment insurance benefits are fully taxable under the federal income tax. All four policies insure that the parties to the dispute bear the cost of the transfer benefits.

Suppose, however, it is deemed appropriate for the larger society to share in the cost of strike-related transfer payments. This is the status quo. At present, when workers receive compensation for involuntary unemployment associated with a labor dispute, the payments are financed out of imperfectly experience rated taxes on the employer. That means the larger society shares in the cost. In this case our theory predicts a tradeoff between the two goals: greater compensation for involuntary unemployment associated with a labor dispute leads to increased strike activity and less industrial peace.

The evidence in chapter 6 is consistent with this theoretical proposition. We find that in states with a work-stoppage and/or innocent bystander provision, more generous unemployment insurance benefits are associated with an increase in strike frequency. Of course, still stronger empirical evidence is conceivable. It would be particularly impressive if it could be shown that more perfect experience rating attenuates the tradeoff between program generosity and strike activity.[5] Although more evidence is always better, there are good reasons for claiming that if the parties to the dispute do not bear the full cost of strike activity, then the goal of compensating involuntary unemployment comes in conflict with the goal of industrial peace.

In this case, one is forced to choose between the goal of compensating workers for strike-related involuntary unemployment and the goal of promoting industrial peace. If, on the one hand, it is believed that the society should do more in terms of promoting industrial peace, then several policy options appear viable. Certainly one option is to eliminate some or all provisions under which workers involved in labor disputes receive benefits. An alternative would be to reduce the level of unemployment insurance benefits paid to such workers. This could be done in many ways;

(1) *Use a different, lower benefit schedule or maximum for such workers.*

(2) *Extend the waiting period.* This is essentially what is done in New York and Rhode Island. Workers involved in labor disputes can only receive benefits after an eight-week waiting period. Note also that several states use the strategy of an extended waiting period for workers who are unemployed due to a quit.

(3) *Reduce the duration of benefits.* For example, workers involved in a labor dispute might receive 12 rather than 26 weeks of unemployment insurance benefits.

If, on the other hand, it is believed that society should do more in terms of compensating strike-related involuntary unemployment, then policy would move in the other direction. States might consider additional provisions for compensating workers involved in labor disputes (e.g., provisions dealing with lockouts, interim employment, and innocent bystanders). An alternative would be to increase the level of benefits paid to such workers. For example, workers involved in labor disputes could have a higher maximum benefit or be guaranteed 40 rather than 26 weeks of unemployment insurance benefits. The appropriate policy in this case depends upon value judgments about the relative importance of promoting industrial peace versus compensating workers for strike-related involuntary unemployment.

Balancing the Goal of Promoting Industrial Peace Against the Goal of Alleviating Hardship

Our assessment of policy options designed to strike a balance between the goals of promoting industrial peace and alleviating hardship is similar to the above in both form and substance.

To be concrete about possible policies, note that the goal of alleviating hardship is usually associated with public assistance programs. It follows that one way to alleviate the hardship of workers involved in labor disputes is to grant them eligibility for public assistance benefits. The workers and their families might, for example, receive food stamps, AFDC-U, general assistance or benefits from some new program, e.g., a negative income tax. In keeping with the goal of alleviating hardship, only those who can demonstrate hardship would be eligible for benefits. Like any recipient of public assistance, the families have to pass a means test.

Is there a tradeoff between the goals of alleviating hardship and promoting industrial peace? Our answer is much as before. Financing is the key. If the cost of the transfer payments are fully borne by the parties to the dispute, then there need not be a conflict between the goals. If, however, it is deemed appropriate for the larger society to share in the cost of such transfers, then there may be a tradeoff. In the latter case, greater payments to alleviate strike-related hardship can lead to increased strike activity and less industrial peace.

The government has several options for insuring that the parties to the dispute bear the full cost of the transfer payments. The options are parallel to those in the previous section. The workers, the union, or the employer could repay the government for the cost of such payments. Moreover, the payments could be subject to the federal income tax. This would obviously go against tradition. Public assistance benefits have historically been financed out of general revenues and not subject to the income tax. There is no precedent for levies on employers or repayment by recipients. In the case of strike related transfers, however, a reassessment of that tradition may be in order.

If the tradition is maintained and the larger society shares in the cost of alleviating hardship associated with strikes, then increased government transfers may lead to more strike activity. In this case, one is forced to choose between the goal of alleviating strike-related hardship and the goal of promoting industrial peace. The policy options are similar to those discussed above. If it is believed that the society should do more in terms of promoting industrial peace, then workers involved in labor disputes could either be prohibited from receiving public assistance benefits or could be paid reduced benefits (perhaps as a result of a waiting period). In contrast, if it is believed that the society should do more in terms of alleviating strike-related hardship, then policy would move in the opposite direction. For example, workers involved in labor disputes could (if they passed the means test) receive food stamps and AFDC-U; eligibility requirements for AFDC-U could be loosened; and states could be encouraged to use their general assistance programs to aid workers involved in labor disputes.

It should be emphasized that we have no hard empirical evidence indicating a tradeoff between strike activity and public assistance transfers. Although we tested for a relationship, we did not obtain statistically significant results. That may mean that the tradeoff is minuscule (or even nonexistent) and that society could provide public assistance to workers involved in labor disputes without experiencing a noticeable increase in strike activity. Alternatively, our results may simply indicate that our statistical methods are not precise enough to discern the effect of existing policy; a more generous policy of alleviating strike-related hardship could conceivably lead to a substantial change in strike activity. The point is that our empirical results can not guide policy in this case. We do not know the magnitude of the tradeoff.

Balancing the Goal of State Neutrality in Labor Disputes Against the Goals of Transfer Programs

As before, we would argue that there is a form of tradeoff between these goals. Policies that compensate strike-related involuntary unemployment or that alleviate strike-related hardship favor workers and thereby affect neutrality. To see this, consider the problem of the government remaining neutral in labor disputes while at the same time compensating workers for strike-related involuntary unemployment. More concretely, suppose the government introduces a provision whereby workers obtain unemployment insurance in the event of a lockout. While arguably consistent with the goal of compensating involuntary unemployment, this provision will surely strengthen the hand of workers. This is true even if the benefits are not financed out of taxes on the employer. If the government were neutral in labor disputes before introduction of this provision, then the provision would violate neutrality.

Only if the government favored employers before introduction of the provision, could this policy be consistent with the goal of governmental neutrality. For example, one might argue that employers can rely upon the police powers of the state to constrain strikers from closing plants. Moreover, when an employer loses profits during a strike, his corporate profits tax liability is reduced, implying a form of government subsidy to the employer. From this perspective the government favors employers, and introduction of the lockout provision helps to restore neutrality.

A parallel argument applies to alleviating hardship. Suppose the government introduces a provision whereby striking workers obtain AFDC-U benefits. Once again, since this provision can strengthen the hand of the workers, it is only neutral if it serves to counterbalance some other policy that favors employers.

What about the innocent bystander provision in unemployment insurance? Is there a tradeoff here? Since the benefits do not flow to the strikers, why would this provision affect neutrality? As argued in chapter 5, if in the absence of this provision the employer would have compensated the innocent bystanders anyway, the employer benefits from the provision. This is because of imperfect experience rating. Without the provision he pays the full cost of compensating innocent bystanders out of his own funds. With the provision part of that cost is shifted to the larger society.[6]

There is then a form of tradeoff between the goals of state neutrality in labor disputes and the transfer program goals of compensating involuntary unemployment and alleviating hardship. If we assume that at present the government is neutral in labor disputes, then *any new policy that either increases or decreases strike-related transfer payments* will move the society away from neutrality. An increase in transfer payments strengthens the hand of workers while a decrease weakens it. Similarly, any policy that increases or decreases the taxes that finance transfer payments will alter neutrality. Of course, the conclusion changes if one assumes that at present the government favors one side. In that case increases or decreases in transfers or taxes can be an appropriate palliative for unbalanced policy. In a sense, this reveals the weakness of the concept of neutrality. There is a troubling "anything goes" aspect to it. Any government decision could be justified in terms of maintaining or restoring neutrality.

A Proposal

The previous section partially answers the original question of when strike-related transfers are appropriate. It indicates that if the society chooses to pursue specific goals, then certain types of strike-related transfers are called for. There remains, of course, the question of which goals the society should pursue. That is a question of value judgments, and the social sciences have little to say about such questions. Ultimately, it is a question that each person must answer for himself or herself. Having devoted a great deal of thought and effort to this project, the authors have developed their own views of what goals the society should pursue and what policies are appropriate. We would be remiss to not state those views.

In our opinion the goals that deserve greatest emphasis are alleviation of hardship and promotion of industrial peace. With regard to the first goal, in a modern industrial state it is a fundamental responsibility of government to provide a minimum level of income support such that people do not have to starve or beg. This responsibility extends to strikers and nonstrikers alike, and is of particular importance for families with children. When people can demonstrate material hardship by passing a means test, they deserve assistance irrespective of the reason for that hardship. Although compensation of income lost due to involuntary unemployment is important, we place a higher priority on alleviating hardship.

With regard to the second goal, the modern state is properly concerned about promotion of industrial peace. Strikes imply a costly loss of output and should be minimized. Of course, that does not mean that they should be eliminated. Some level of strikes may be necessary to resolve conflicts and to enhance the effectiveness of other conflict resolution mechanisms. However, to the extent that there are feasible alternatives to strikes—alternatives that are consistent with worker rights and democratic institutions—the government should promote those alternatives. We place a higher priority on attaining this goal than on some nebulous notion of neutrality.

These goals lead us to the following proposals.

(1) Public assistance (AFDC, food stamps, and general assistance) should be available to families suffering financial hardship irrespective of their involvement in a labor dispute.

(2) Unemployment insurance benefits should be paid to innocent bystanders.

(3) All strike-related transfers should be financed out of taxes on the employer.

This policy addresses the problem of hardship suffered by strikers and their families by providing public assistance to workers involved in labor disputes. It promotes industrial peace by placing the cost of strike activity squarely upon the parties involved. Finally, the proposal includes payment of unemployment insurance to innocent bystanders. Their unemployment is unambiguously involuntary and thus worthy of compensation.

We would like to see the benefits financed out of taxes on the struck employer. This is a simpler administrative mechanism than worker repayment. Moreover, the workers who receive benefits under our plan would be quite poor, and would probably find it difficult to repay the government for the benefits. Asking impoverished workers to repay government benefits seems inconsistent with the goal of alleviating hardship. In our view, however, how the costs are divided between the disputing parties is not as important as making certain that the larger society does not share in that cost.

Our proposal is silent on other strike-related provisions of the unemployment insurance program, i.e., lockout, work stoppage, etc. Even if the parties bear the full cost of strikes, we find little advantage to such provisions. They are administratively cumbersome, e.g., the lockout rule, and they are difficult to justify in terms of either compensating involuntary unemployment or alleviating material hardship, e.g., the work-stoppage rule. In our opinion, the most desirable of these provisions is the New York-Rhode Island rule whereby strikers receive benefits if the strike lasts eight weeks. This provision has the twin virtues of being simple to administer and of providing aid to people who are almost certainly experiencing material hardship. If it is decided that workers involved in labor disputes should continue to receive unemployment insurance, then we would propose extending the above proposal as follows.

(4) Provide unemployment insurance benefits to workers who satisfy the New York-Rhode Island rule.

(5) Eliminate other provisions that provide unemployment insurance benefits to workers involved in labor disputes (except for the innocent bystander rule).

(6) Finance these strike-related benefits through taxes on the disputing parties. Consideration should also be given to having the workers or their union share in the cost of these unemployment insurance benefits.

Once again, these proposals would move government policy toward the goals of alleviating hardship and promoting industrial peace. Whether the reader agrees or disagrees with our proposals, we hope this work leads to a public discussion of the merits of the present system of strike-related transfer payments. In our view, that system is flawed. It does not make sense to provide unemployment insurance to workers when the involuntary nature of their unemployment is so fraught with ambiguity. It does not make sense to have the larger society share in the cost of strike-related benefits and thereby effectively subsidize strike activity. It does not make sense to deny public assistance benefits to the child of a law-abiding striker, and yet provide benefits to the child of a jailed felon. In our view the present system is difficult to justify and in need of reform.

NOTES

1. Eleven states make small adjustments for family size through dependents' allowances.

2. Ronald Ehrenberg, Robert Hutchens and Robert Smith, "The Distribution of Unemployment Insurance Benefits and Costs," U.S. Department of Labor, Technical Analysis Paper No. 58, 1978.

3. For a discussion of the goal of industrial peace in general and the Wagner Act in particular, see Douglas V. Brown and Charles A. Myers, "Historical Evolution," in Joseph Shister, Benjamin Aaron, and Clyde W. Summers, eds., *Public Policy and Collective Bargaining* (New York

and Evanston: Harper and Row, 1962); Charles O. Gregory and Harold A. Katz, *Labor and the Law,* 3rd edition (New York and London: W.W. Norton & Co., 1979); Benjamin J. Taylor and Fred Witney, *Labor Relations Law,* 5th edition (Englewood Cliffs, NJ: Prentice-Hall, 1987); Thomas A. Kochan and Harry C. Katz, *Collective Bargaining and Industrial Relations,* 2nd edition (Homewood, IL: Richard D. Irwin, 1988).

4. For a discussion of this see Daniel Hamermesh, *Jobless Pay and the Economy* (Baltimore: Johns Hopkins University Press), 1977.

5. As indicated in chapter 6, we looked into this. Due to problems with collinearity, we failed to obtain meaningful results. Moreover, our measures of the extent of experience rating were less than ideal.

6. If experience rating were perfect, then the provision would simply codify the status quo. The employer would continue to bear the full cost of compensating innocent bystanders (who would have been compensated in the absence of the provision). In this case the provision would be consistent with governmental neutrality. It would also be without teeth.

Appendix A
People Who Contributed to This Book

This project has benefited from the efforts and thoughts of numerous people. We would like to take this opportunity to thank them for their contributions.

Several people provided us with information on data and policies. Included are:

George Abbott
Edna Biederman
Virginia Chupp
Judith Coulter
Don Glenn
Karen Goudreau
Edward Hanlon
William Heartwell
John Hickey
J. Eldred Hill
Carol Jackson
Claudine Jennings
Fred Kniesler
Kathy Lazckay
Roslyn Lindsay
Charles Little
Cecil L. Malone
Charles McGlew
Steve Marsten
George R. Michaud
C. Harvey Monk
Walter Neece
Betty Norton
Tom Palumbo
Murray Rubin
Mark Sanders
Bert Seidman
Joseph Sieber
Sylvia Small
Karen Smith
Tom Snover
Bernard Street
Dawn Van Hall
William J. Yost
John Zallsky
Meyer Zitter

In addition the representatives of 46 out of 54 jurisdictions responded to our survey of state unemployment insurance policies. The following people provided particularly detailed information:

Norman J. Brooks
Frank O. Heintz
Thomas Malek
Agaliece W. Miller
Wendell K. Pass
A. G. Zillig

We presented preliminary versions of our ideas in several forums. Included are the ILR Associates, a graduate seminar run by John Burton and Stewart Schwab, the ILR School's collective bargaining seminar, as well as seminars at Boston University and the University of British Columbia. In each case we benefited from the criticisms, comments, and encouragement of the participants.

Finally, the project could not have been executed without the help of secretaries, research assistants, computer programmers, and coders. We gratefully acknowledge their contributions.

Secretaries

Jean Brown
Amy Dawson
Gail Hendrix
Barbara Lanning
June Niblock
Jean Morano
Diane Porter

Research Assistants

Nancy Hanks
Damian Mullin
Tim Schmidle
Joshua Schwarz
Kate Squire
John Williams

Computer Programmers

Clarence Henderson
Gary Laske

Coders

Amy Babat
David Block
Daniel Ciminelli
Andrew Glassman
Cynthia Hewitt
Patricia Kallett
David Lester
Teri Loeb
Janice Mackey
Ellen Madow
Maria Mejia
Andrea Parks
Steven Paulson
Sandra Porges
Scott Schnipper
Meryl Seltzer
David Speyer
Maria Troiano
Deborah Watts
John Williams
Karen Woolf

Appendix B
Sources of Variables

Sources of Variables Measuring Characteristics of Transfer Programs

Variable		Description
UI RULE 1	=	1 if strikers receive benefits when employer continues to operate; else = 0 *Comparison of State Unemployment Laws*
UI RULE 2	=	1 if New York and Rhode Island; else = 0 *Comparison of State Unemployment Laws*
UI RULE 3	=	1 if "innocent bystanders" receive benefits; else = 0 *Comparison of State Unemployment Laws*
UI RULE 4	=	1 if strikers laid off from "interim employment" job receive benefits; else = 0 *Comparison of State Unemployment Laws*
UI RULE 5	=	1 if workers receive benefits during a lockout; else = 0 *Comparison of State Unemployment Laws*
UNIMAX	=	maximum weekly UI benefit in state *Comparison of State Unemployment Laws*
UIMETH1	=	benefits as a percent of weekly covered earnings for benefits below the maximum in state *Comparison of State Unemployment Laws*
AVEBEN1	=	UIMETH1* AHEMAN (see table 5.7 for AHEMAN) *Comparison of State Unemployment Laws*
UITAX	=	taxable wage base for employers in state *Comparison of State Unemployment Laws*
TAXEMAN	=	UITAX/(AHEMAN*2000) *Comparison of State Unemployment Laws*
UIMAXRAT	=	maximum UI tax rate in state *Comparison of State Unemployment Laws*

Variable		Description
UIMINRAT	=	minimum UI tax rate in state *Comparison of State Unemployment Laws*
UIDIST	=	Experience Rating Index from Becker Joseph Becker, *Experience Rating in Unemployment Insurance: Competitive Socialism,* John Hopkins Press, 1972
COVPC	=	percent of workers in state covered by state UI laws calculated from data in *Comparison of State Unemployment Laws*
DURAT	=	maximum number of weeks of benefits in state *Comparison of State Unemployment Laws*
PCTPOOR	=	percent of poverty population in state participating in Food Stamp Program U.S. Department of Agriculture, Food and Nutrition Service, March 31, 1975. Memorandum indicating when U.S. counties initiated Food Stamp Program 1970 U.S. Census data on County poverty populations
AFDCAID	=	1 if state allows strikers to receive AFDC-U payments; else = 0 Office of Family Assistance, Social Security Administration, HHS
AFDCPROG	=	1 if state has an AFDC-U program; else = 0 U.S. Bureau of Family Services. *Characteristics of State Public Assistance Plans Under the Social Security Act, General Provisions (Eligibility Assistance Administration)* National Center for Social Statistics. *Public Assistance Statistics.* 1971
AFDCMAX	=	AFDC maximum weekly payment for a family of four in state *Public Assistance Programs; Standards for Basic Needs*

AFDCBEN	=	AFDCMAX*AFDCAID Office of Family Assistance, Social Security Administration, HHS National Center for Social Statistics, *Public Assistance Statistics*
GENAID	=	1 if state provides general assistance to strikers; else = 0 U.S. Bureau of Family Services, *Characteristics of State Public Assistance Plans Under the Social Security Act, General Provisions (Eligibility Assistance Administration)* 1962

Sources of Control Variables Employed in the Analysis

Variable		Description
UNMEMLAB	=	# of union members/LFTOT *Directory of National and International Labor Unions in the United States,* 1959, 1961, 1963, 1965, 1967, 1968 *Directory of National Unions and Employee Associations,* 1971, 1973, 1975, 1977 Geographic Profile of Employment and Unemployment, 1976
MINELAB	=	# of workers in mining/LFTOT Geographic Profile of Employment and Unemployment, 1976 *Employment and Earnings*
CONSTLAB	=	# of workers in construction/LFTOT Same as MINELAB
MANULAB	=	# of workers in manufacturing/LFTOT Same as MINELAB
TRANLAB	=	# of workers in transportation/LFTOT Same as MINELAB
TRADELAB	=	# of workers in trade/LFTOT Same as MINELAB

FINLAB = # of workers in finance/LFTOT
Same as MINELAB

SERVLAB = # of workers in services/LFTOT
Same as MINELAB

PCTURB = LFTOT in urban areas/LFTOT
1960, 1970 Census of Population
Geographic Profile of Employment and Unemployment

PCTPAMALE= males between age 25 and 55/LFTOT
1960, 1970 Census of Population
Geographic Profile of Employment and Unemployment

PCTFEM = # females in labor force/LFTOT
1960, 1970 Census of Population
Geographic Profile of Employment and Unemployment

AFLMEMLAB= # AFL-CIO members/LFTOT
Directory of National and International Labor Union in the United States, 1959, 1961, 1963, 1965, 1967, 1968
Directory of National Unions and Employee Associations, 1971, 1973, 1975, 1977
Geographic Profile of Employment and Unemployment, 1976

PCTMIG = net civilian migration 1960-1970/civilian resident population 1970
Current Population Reports

SOUTH = 1 if state is in South Census Division; else = 0
Current Population Reports

RTTOWORK = 1 if state has right to work law; else = 0
State Right To Work Laws With Annotations

VALADPC = value added by manufacturing/total - of employees in manufacturing
1977 Census of Manufacturers;
Annual Survey of Manufacturers, 1975-76;
Annual Survey of Manufacturers, 1966

ESIZE100	=	# establishments with 100+ employees/# establishments County Business Patterns
ESIZE20	=	establishments with 20+ employees/# establishments *County Business Patterns*
AVESIZE	=	# employees in state/# establishments Employment and Earnings; *County Business Patterns*
AHEMAN	=	average hourly earnings of production workers on manufacturing
WCH6970	=	percent change in AHEMAN between 1969 and 1970 *Handbook of Labor Statistics,* 1978
WCH6870	=	percent change in AHEMAN between 1968 and 1970 *Handbook of Labor Statistics,* 1978
MEDINC	=	median income of families in state in 1969 *Employment and Earnings*
POVRTY	=	percent of families with money income below poverty line in state *City and County Data Book,* 1972
URAT	=	unemployment rate in state Manpower Report/Employment and Training Report
LFTOT	=	number of people in state's labor force
INDUST	=	State Industrialization Index
AFFLUENC	=	Affluence Index

Source of INDUST and AFFLUENC is David R. Morgan and William Lyons, ''Industrialization and Affluence Revisited: A Note on Socioeconomic Dimensions to the American States, 1970,'' *American Journal of Political Science,* Vol. 19, No. 2 (May 1975), pp. 270-271.

References

Abowd, John and Orley Ashenfelter, "Anticipated Unemployment, Temporary Layoffs and Compensating Wage Differentials," in Sherwin Rosen, ed., *Studies in Labor Markets* (Chicago: University of Chicago Press, 1981), pp. 141-170

Ahrens, Richard A., "Labor Dispute Disqualification: The Function of 'Grade or Class' Provisions in State Unemployment Compensation Statutes," *St. Louis University Law Journal* 18, 4 (Summer 1974), pp. 629-640.

Arnold, James A., III, "Unemployment Compensation: Denial of Benefits for Participation in a Labor Dispute," *Arkansas Law Review* 30 (Winter 1977), pp. 551-556.

Ashenfelter, Orley and George Johnson, "Bargaining Theory, Trade Unions, and Industrial Conflict," *American Economic Review* 59, 1 (March 1969), pp. 35-49.

Becker, Joseph M., *Experience Rating in Unemployment Insurance: Virtue or Vice* (Kalamazoo, MI: W.E. Upjohn Institute, 1972), pp. 22-23.

Bernstein, Irving, *Turbulent Years* (Boston: Houghton Mifflin, 1971), p. 158.

Bloch, Frank S., "Cooperative Federalism and the Role of Litigation in the Development of Federal AFDC Eligibility Policy," *Wisconsin Law Review* 1979, 1 (1979), pp. 48- 50.

Britt, David and Omer Galle, "Industrial Conflict and Unionization," *American Sociological Review* 37 (February 1972), pp. 46-57.

Britt, David and Omer Galle, "Structural Antecedents of the Shape of Strikes: A Comparative Analysis," *American Sociological Review* 39 (October 1974), pp. 642-651.

Letter from Norman J. Brooks, Commissioner, Washington State Employment Security Department, to the authors, December 14, 1981.

Buck, Andrew, "A Reexamination of British Strike Activity," *Atlantic Economic Journal* 10 (September 1982), pp. 38-39.

Carney, James T., "The Forgotten Man on the Welfare Roll: A Study of Public Subsidies for Strikers," *Washington University Law Quarterly* 3 (Summer 1973).

Chamberlain, Neil W. and James W. Kuhn, *Collective Bargaining*, 2nd ed. (New York: McGraw-Hill, 1965).

Chaplin, Josephine and J. Brown, *Public Relief: 1929-39* (New York: Henry Holt, 1940).

Coase, Ronald H., "The Problem of Social Cost," *Journal of Law and Economics* 3 (October 1960), pp. 1-44.

Comment, "Strikers' Eligibility for Public Assistance: The Standard Based on Need," *Journal of Urban Law* 52, 1 (1974), p. 125.

Confer, David R. "Pennsylvania's Lockout Exception to the Labor Dispute Disqualification from Unemployment Compensation Benefits: Federal Challenges and Issues," *Dickinson Law Review* 80 (1975), p. 72.

Cooter, Robert, "The Cost of Coase," *Journal of Legal Studies* 11 (January 1982), p. 15.

Cutler, Michael E. "Balancing in Labor Law Preemption Cases: New York Telephone Co. v. New York State Department of Labor," *Stanford Law Review* 32 (April 1980), pp. 827-844.

Congress of the United States, Joint Economic Committee, *Handbook of Public Income Transfer Programs: 1975,* Paper No. 20, Studies in Public Welfare, 1974.

Daniel, Cletus, *Bitter Harvest: A History of California Farmworkers 1870-1941* (Ithaca, N.Y: Cornell University Press, 1981).

Edwards, P.K. *Strikes in the United States, 1881-1974* (New York: St. Martin's Press, 1981).

Edwards, P.K., "The Strike-Proneness of British Manufacturing Establishments," *British Journal of Industrial Relations* 19 (July 1981), pp. 135-148.

Ehrenberg, Ronald, Robert Hutchens, and Robert Smith, "The Distribution of Unemployment Insurance Benefits and Costs," U.S. Department of Labor, Technical Analysis Paper No. 58, 1978.

Eisenberg, Stephen G., "Policy Considerations Underlying the Payment of Unemployment Insurance to Strikers," *New York State Bar Journal* 56, 5 (July 1984).

Letter from Henry Eschwege, Director, GAO, to Senators Helms and Thurmond and Congressmen Coleman and Dickinson, March 26, 1981, p. 1.

Fierst, Herbert A. and Marjorie Spector, "Unemployment Compensation in Labor Disputes," *The Yale Law Journal* 49, 3 (January 1940), pp. 483-486.

Flaherty, Sean, "Contract Status and the Economic Determinants of Strike Activity," *Industrial Relations* 22 (Winter 1983), pp. 20-33.

Gartner, Manfred, "Strikes and the Real Wage-Employment Nexus: A Hicksian Analysis of Industrial Disputes and Pay," *Journal of Labor Research* 6 (Fall 1985), pp. 323-336.

Gennard, John, *Financing Strikers* (New York: John Wiley, 1977).

Interview with Roger Gerby, New York State Department of Labor, Division of Research and Statistics, October, 1981.

Gramm, Cynthia, "The Determinants of Strike Incidence and Severity: A Micro-Level Study," *Industrial and Labor Relations Review* 39, 3 (April 1986), pp. 361-376.

Griffith, Larry J., Michael E. Wallace and Beth A. Rubin, "Capitalist Resistance to the Organization of Labor Before and After the New Deal: Why? How? Success?" *American Sociological Review* 51 (April 1986), pp. 147-167.

Gross, Thomas Brian, "A Possible Cure for a Case of Mistaken Identity: Unemployment Benefits for Nonstriking Workers Who Have Failed to Cross a Picket Line," *University of Pittsburgh Law Review* 42 (Fall 1980), pp. 94-99.

Haber, William and Merrill G. Murray, *Unemployment Insurance in the American Economy* (Homewood, IL: Richard D. Irwin, 1966), pp. 76-89

Hamermesh, Daniel, *Jobless Pay and the Economy* (Baltimore: Johns Hopkins University Press, 1977).

Heckman, James, "Sample Bias as a Specification Error," *Econometrica* 47, 1 (January 1979), pp. 153-162.

Hetherington, W. Joseph, "Federal Preemption of State Welfare and Unemployment Benefits for Strikers," *Harvard Civil Rights and Civil Liberties Law Review* 12, 2 (1977).

Hicks, John R., *The Theory of Wages* (London: MacMillan, 1932), pp. 136-158.

Hutchens, Robert M., "Layoffs and Labor Supply," *International Economic Review* 24 (February 1983), pp. 37-55.

Joe, Tom and Cheryl Rogers, *By the Few, for the Few: The Reagan Welfare Legacy* (Lexington, MA: Lexington Books, 1985), pp. 33-57, 50-57.

Kaufman, Bruce, "The Determinants of Strikes in the United States, 1900-1977," *Industrial and Labor Relations Review* 35 (July 1982), pp. 473-490.

Kaufman, Bruce, "Interindustry Trends in Strike Activity," *Industrial Relations* 22 (January 1983), pp. 45-57

Kennan, John, "The Effect of Unemployment Insurance on Strike Duration," *Unemployment Compensation: Studies and Research* 2, National Commission on Unemployment Compensation, July 1980, pp. 467-486.

Kerr, Clark and Abraham Seigel, "The Interindustry Propensity to Strike: An International Comparison," in Arthur Kornhouser, Robert Dubin, and Arthur Ross, ed., *Industrial Conflict* (New York: McGraw-Hill, 1954), pp. 189-212.

Kochan, Thomas A., Lee Dyer, and David B. Lipsky, *The Effectiveness of Union-Management Safety and Health Committees* (Kalamazoo, MI: W.E. Upjohn Institute, 1977).

Kretzschmar, Lisa, "New York Telephone Co. v. New York State Department of Labor: Limiting the Doctrine of Implied Labor Law Pre-Emption," *Brooklyn Law Review* 46 (Winter 1980), pp. 297-320.

Interview with Robert Langlais, Rhode Island Department of Employment Security, February 21, 1985.

Leamer, Edward A. "Let's Take the Con Out of Econometrics," *American Economic Review* 73 (March 1983), pp. 31-43.

Leigh, J. Paul, "Risk Preference and the Interindustry Propensity to Strike," *Industrial and Labor Relations Review* 36, 2 (January 1983), pp. 271-285.

Lesser, Leonard, "Labor Disputes and Unemployment Compensation," *Yale Law Journal* 55, 1 (1945), pp. 172-176.

Levitan, Sar A., Garth L. Mangum and Ray Marshall, *Human Resources and Labor Markets*, 3rd Edition (Cambridge, MA: Harper and Row, 1973).

Lewis, Willard A., "The Concept of 'Labor Dispute' in State Unemployment Insurance Laws," *Boston College Industrial and Commercial Law Review* 8, 1 (Fall 1966), pp. 29-54.

Lewis, Willard A., "The 'Lockout as Corollary of Strike' Controversy Reexamined," *Labor Law Journal* 23, 11 (November 1972), pp. 659-670.

Lewis, Willard A., "The Law of Unemployment Compensation in Labor Disputes," *Labor Law Journal* 113, 2 (February 1962).

Lewis, Willard A., "The 'Stoppage of Work' Concept in Labor Dispute Disqualification During Industrial Disputes," *Monthly Labor Review* 51, 6 (December 1940), pp. 1380-1382

Lipsky, David B. and Henry S. Farber, "The Composition of Strike Activity in the Construction Industry," *Industrial and Labor Relations Review* 29, 3 (April 1976), pp. 388-404.

"Loopholes Give Extra Aid to Strikers," *Business Week,* September 9, 1972 p. 26.

MacDonald, Maurice, *Food, Stamps, and Income Maintenance* (New York: Academic Press, 1977).

Letter from Cecil L. Malone, Director, Unemployment Insurance, Arkansas Employment Security Division, to the authors, December 2, 1981.

Mauro, Martin J., "Strikes as a Result of Imperfect Information," *Industrial and Labor Relations Review* 35, 4 (July 1982), pp. 522-538.

McCarthy, John D. and Mayer N. Zald, "Resource Mobilization and Social Movements: A Partial Theory," *American Journal of Sociology* 82 (May 1977), pp. 1212-1242.

Michaud, George A., Chief Hearing Officer for the Alaska Employment Security Division, in telephone interviews and correspondence in December 1984 and January 1985.

Letter from Agaliece W. Miller, Employment Security Administrator, Illinois Bureau of Employment Security, to the authors, December 11, 1981.

Moore, William and Douglas Pearce, "Comparative Analysis of Strike Models During Periods of Rapid Inflation, 1967-1977," *Journal of Labor Research* 3 (Winter 1982), pp. 39-53.

Mundlak, Yair, "On the Pooling of Time Series and Cross Section Data," *Econometrica* 40, 1 (January 1978), pp. 69-86.

Myers, Robert J., *Social Insurance and Allied Government Programs* (Homewood, IL: Richard D. Irwin, 1965), pp. 20-22.

"How Your Tax Dollars Support Strikes," *Nation's Business,* March 1973, p. 25.

New York State Department of Labor, *The Industrial Controversy Provision of the New York State Unemployment Insurance Law, 1935-1975,* Labor Research Report No. 1, April 1976, p. 2.

Northrup, Herbert R., "The Rise and Demise of PATCO," *Industrial and Labor Relations Review* 37, 2 (January 1984), p. 178.

Paldum, M. and P.J. Pederson, "The Macro-Economic Strike Model: A Study of Seventeen Countries, 1948-1975," *Industrial and Labor Relations Review* 35, 4 (July 1982).

Letter from Wendel K. Pass, Acting Executive Director, Office of Employment Security, Pennsylvania Department of Labor and Industry, to the authors, December 17, 1981.

Perry, Charles R., Andrew M. Dramer, and Thomas J. Schneider, *Operating During Strikes* (Philadelphia, PA: Industrial Relations Unit of the Wharton School, University of Pennsylvania, 1982).

Letter from Eldon E. Peterson, Unemployment Insurance Director, Division of Employment, Nebraska State Department of Labor, to the authors, November 25, 1981.

Ray, Robert David, "Unemployment Compensation During Labor Disputes: Qualifying the 'Direct Interest' Disqualification," *Missouri Law Review* 46 (Summer 1981), pp. 694-707

Reder, Melvin and George R. Neumann. "Conflict and Contract: The Case of Strikes," *Journal of Political Economy* 88 (October 1980), pp. 867-886.

Rejda, George E., *Social Security and Economic Security,* 2nd Edition (Englewood Cliffs, NJ: Prentice-Hall, 1984).

"Review of Food Program Developments in 1981," *Clearinghouse Review* (January 1982), p. 776.

Ringer, James M. "Effect of Participation in a Labor Dispute Upon Continuation of Unemployment Benefits," *Cornell Law Quarterly* 52 (Spring 1967), pp. 738-752.

Ross, Arthur, *Trade Union Wage Policy* (Berkeley, CA: University of California Press, 1948).

Royback, Joseph G., *A History of American Labor* (New York: The Free Press, 1966), pp. 351.

Sapsford, David, "The Theory of Bargaining and Strike Activity," *International Journal of Social Economics* 9 (February 1982).

Shadur, Milton I., "Unemployment Benefits and the 'Labor Dispute' Disqualification," *The University of Chicago Law Review* 17, 2 (Winter 1950).

Siebert, Stanley, Phillip Bertrand and John Addison, "The Political Model of Strikes: A New Twist," *Southern Economic Journal* 52 (Summer 1985), pp. 23-33.

Singh, Davinder, Glyn Williams, and Ronald Wilder, "Wage Determination in U.S. Manufacturing 1958-1976: A Collective Bargaining Approach," *Journal of Labor Research* 3 (Spring 1982),pp. 223-337.

Skeels, Jack, "The Economic and Organizational Basis of Early United States Strikes, 1900-1948," *Industrial and Labor Relations Review* 35 (July 1982), pp. 491-503.

"Social Welfare—Effect of Eligibility for Unemployment Compensation on AFDC Benefits," *West Virginia Law Review* 78, 2 (February 1976), pp. 268-277.

Steiner, Gilbert Y., *The State of Welfare* (Washington, D.C.: Brookings, 1971), pp. 198-213.

Stern, Robert N., "Intermetropolitan Patterns of Strike Activity," *Industrial and Labor Relations Review* 29, 2 (January 1976), pp. 218-235.

Swidinsky, Robert and John Vandercamp, "A Micro-econometric Analysis of Strike Activity in Canada," *Journal of Labor Research* 3, 4 (Fall, 1982).

Taylor, Benjamin J. and Fred Witney, *Labor Relations Law,* 4th ed. (Englewood Cliffs, NJ: Prentice-Hall, 1983).

Thieblot, Armand J. and Ronald M. Cowin, *Welfare and Strikes: The Use of Public Funds to Support Strikes* (Philadelphia, PA: University of Pennsylvania Press, 1972).

Thomas, Marc E., "Strikers' Eligibility for Public Assistance: The Standard Based on Need," *Journal of Urban Law* 52, 1 (1974).

Tilly, Charles, *From Mobilization to Revolution* (Reading, MA: Addison-Wesley, 1978).

UAW Washington Report 20, 36, September 26, 1980, p. 1.

U.S. Department of Health and Human Services, Social Security Administration, *Public Assistance Statistics, January 1980* (September 1980).

U.S. Department of Health and Human Services, Social Security Administration, *Public Assistance Statistics, November 1980* (September 1981).

U.S. Department of Health and Human Services, Social Security Administration, *Public Assistance Statistics, December 1980* (November 1981).

U. S. Department of Health and Human Services, Social Security Administration, *Characteristics of State Plans for Aid to Families with Dependent Children*, 1982 Edition (Washington, D.C.: Government Printing Office, 1982).

U.S. Department of Health and Human Services, Social Security Administration, *Characteristics of State Plans for Aid to Families with Dependent Children*, 1984 Edition.

U.S. Department of Labor, *Handbook of Labor Statistics* (Washington, D.C, 1983).

U.S. Department of Labor, Employment and Training Administration, *Comparison of State Unemployment Insurance Laws*, Washington, D.C., 1984.

U.S. Social Security Board, *Draft Bills for State Unemployment Compensation of Pooled Funds and Employer Reserve Account Types*, Washington, D.C., 1936.

U.S. Social Security Board, "Issues Involved in Decisions on Disputed Claims for Unemployment Benefits," *Social Security Yearbook, 1940*, Washington, D.C., June 1941.

Walsh, Kenneth, *Strikes in Europe and the United States* (New York: St. Martin's Press, 1983).

Whitehead, Brian R., "Unemployment Benefits, Laid-Off Workers, and Labor Disputes: The Unemployment Benefit Conflict," *Willamette Law Review* 19 (Fall 1983), pp. 737-756.

Witte, Edwin E., "Development of Unemployment Compensation," *Yale Law Journal* 55, 1 (December 1945).

Yost, William, the Hearing Officer in the case, in a telephone interview, December 10, 1984.

Letter from A.G. Zillig, Director of the Alaska Division of Employment Security, to the authors, December 9, 1981.

INDEX

Aaron, Benjamin, 200n.3
Abel, I.W., 82
Abowd, John, 163n.38
Addison, John, 162nn.16, 25
AFDC. *See* Aid to Families with Dependent Children (AFDC)
AFDC-U. *See* Aid to Families with Dependent Children-Unemployed Parent (AFDC-U)
Ahrens, Richard A., 57-58, 74n.74, 75nn.75-79, 86
Aid to Families with Dependent Children (AFDC): before 1961, 8; analysis of effect on strike behavior of availability of, 181-83; eligibility requirement changes under, 81-84
Aid to Families with Dependent Children-Unemployed Parent (AFDC-U): court cases related to state neutrality in labor disputes, 86, 89-94; court cases related to state options to grant benefits for strikers, 86-89; estimated aid to strikers under, 2, 100; program to assist unemployed parents and strikers, 84-85; regulation concerning unemployed striker's eligibility, 88; state-federal administration, 86; statutory implications for payment of strikers' benefits, 86, 94-100
Air traffic controllers strike, 2, 59, 62, 66-68
Aragon decision effect, 63
Arnold, James A., III, 74n.65
Ashenfelter, Orley, 135, 136, 161n.2, 162n.11, 163n.38

Becker, Joseph, 154, 163n.40
Bernstein, Irving, 79, 121nn.11, 12, 14-17, 26
Bertrand, Phillip, 162nn.16, 25
Bituminous Coal Operators Association strike, 2
Bloch, Frank S., 123n.51, 53, 126-27n.114
Brennan, William, 74n.73
British Unemployment Insurance Act of 1911, 18, 26, 41-42
Britt, David, 162nn.19, 22
Brooks, Norman, 75n.85
Brown, Josephine C., 121nn.16, 18
Buck, Andrew, 162n.18

Carney, James T., 35n.44, 36n.46, 37nn.64, 66, 69, 73, 48, 72nn.33, 34, 77, 94, 105, 121nn.1, 3, 5, 6, 13, 15-17, 122n.27, 31, 36, 41, 124n.84, 129nn.138-40, 131n.159
Chamberlain, Neil W., 82, 122n.28
CIO. *See* Congress of Industrial Organizations (CIO)
Clark, Robert W., III, 125n.97
Coase, Ronald, 140-41, 162n.35
Coase Theorem, 140-42, 146
Coleman, E. Thomas, 108
Collective bargaining: government policy for, 189-90; neutral framework in Taft-Hartley Act for, 90
Community Services Program of CIO, 83
Confer, David R., 36nn.52, 56
Congress of Industrial Organizations (CIO), 83
Cooter, Robert, 163n.37

Cowin, Ronald M., 127n115, 2, 10, 82, 88, 100-101, 109, 121nn.4, 15-18, 121-22nn.24-27, 122nn.30, 32, 33, 123-24n.66, 127n.115, 129n.140, 130nn.157-58, 131n.159
Creel, George, 78-79
Cutler, Michael E., 73n.50

Daniel, Cletus, 78-79, 121nn.7-11
Data for analysis, 11-12, 147-59, 177
Dickinson, William L., 108
Disqualification for benefits: by grade or class, 57-59; under innocent bystander provision, 51-57; willful misconduct as condition for, 62, 66-68
Dow Chemical Company strike, 1
Dramer, Andrew M., 42, 71nn.8-10
Dyer, Lee, 36n.61

Edwards, P. K., 137, 161nn.1, 3, 162n.23
Ehrenberg, Ronald, 132n.185, 200n.2
Eisenberg, Stephen G., 39, 70n.1
Employee replacements, permanent, 42
Employment, interim or temporary, 31-33
Eschwege, Henry, 130nn.152-54
Establishment: differing definitions at state level of term, 23-24; *See also* Functional integration test

FAA. *See* Federal Aviation Administration (FAA)
Farber, Henry, 184n.6
Federal Aviation Administration (FAA): air traffic controllers strike against, 2; role in air traffic controllers strike, 59, 62
Federal Emergency Relief Administration (FERA) relief policy, 77-80
Federal Unemployment Tax Act, 21
FERA. *See* Federal Emergency Relief Administration (FERA)
Fierst, Herbert A., 27, 36nn.45, 48, 49, 70n.3, 123n.62
Flaherty, Sean, 135, 162n.12
Food Stamp Act of 1964: attempts to limit recipients through amendment, 105-7; establishment and development of program for, 104-5; test of constitutionality of 1981 amendment, 110-12
Food stamp program: court interpretation of legality of exclusion of strikers from, 109-12; effect of availability of benefits on strike behavior, 181-83; eligibility rules for, 102-4; estimated aid to strikers under, question of eligibility of strikers for, 8-9, 104-7; strikers limited in access through OBRA legislation, 107
Functional integration test, 23-24

GA. *See* General assistance (GA)
Galle, Omer, 162nn.19, 22
Gartner, Manfred, 134, 162n.10
General assistance (GA): analysis of effect on strike behavior, 181-83; diversity of programs and eligibility rules for, 113; eligibility of strikers for, 9; provisions and administration of, 112; welfare assistance to strikers at state level, 82
Gennard, John, 10
Gerby, Roger, 76n.101
Good cause condition, 97-98
Grade or class of worker, 57-59

Gramm, Cynthia, 161n.5, 184n.3
Gregory, Charles, 200-201n.3
Griffith, Larry, 138, 162n.29
Grinnell Corp. v. *Hackett*, 9
Gross, Thomas B., 55, 74nn.57, 58, 60-62, 65

Haber, William, 33n.1
Hamermesh, Daniel, 201n.4
Hansen, Alvin, 161n.1
Heckman, James, 186n.14
Helms, Jesse, 3, 108
Hetherington, W. Joseph, 18, 34nn.4, 7, 36n.60, 41, 43-44, 70n.3, 71nn.7, 12, 72n.33
Hicks, John R., 134, 136, 161n.7
Hodory v. *Ohio Bureau of Employment Services*, 52-53, 56
Hopkins, Harry, 77-78, 80
Hutchens, Robert, 132n.185, 163n.38, 200n.2

Income maintenance programs, Social Security Administration, 80-81
Industrial conflict models. *See* Strike behavior models
Industrial peace: as goal of government collective bargaining policy, 189-90; and involuntary unemployment, 191-92; and society's responsibility for, 194
Industrial relations, 187, 189
Information, imperfect, 134
Innocent bystander: conditions for unemployment eligibility benefits, 6, 7, 17, 53-54; definition of, 51-52; failing to cross picket lines, 54-55; in &2Hodory&1 case, 52-53; ineligibility under Ohio law of, 52; under New York state law, 47; under Rhode Island state law, 48; *See also* Grade or class of worker
Interim or temporary employment. *See* Employment, interim or temporary

Javits, Jacob, 90
Joe, Tom, 13n.8, 122n.38, 127n.123
Johnson, George, 135, 136, 161n.2, 162n.11
Joint-choice model, 11, 138-42, 157-59, 161; *See also* Coase Theorem; Industrial conflict models

Katz, Harold A., 200-201n.3
Katz, Harry C., 200-201n.3
Kaufman, Bruce, 135, 137, 162nn.13, 19-20
Kennan, John, 10, 162n.36
Kennedy, John F., 104
Kerr, Clark, 138, 161n.3
Kochan, Thomas, 200-201n.3
Kochan, Thomas A., 36n.61
Kretzschmar, Lisa, 73n.50
Kuhn, James W., 82, 122n.28

Labor dispute: analysis of effect of disqualification policies, 165-68; analysis of effect of unemployment insurance generosity on, 169-74; conditions for unemployment benefits in, 5-7; differing interpretations of term, 21-23; states paying unemployment benefits in employer-caused, 30; *See also* Lockout by employer

Langlais, Robert, 72n.32
Leamer, Edward, 159, 163n.43
Leigh, J. Paul, 137, 162n.24
Lesher, Richard, 3
Lesser, Leonard, 36n.45
Levin, Carl, 4
Levitan, Sar, 121n.22, 122nn.35, 37
Lewis, Willard A., 22, 26, 30, 34nn.12, 13, 21, 35nn.27-29, 33, 42-43, 36n.59, 70n.3, 74-75n.74, 75nn.75, 86
Lipsky, David, 36n.61, 184n.6
Lockout by employer: as condition for unemployment benefit eligibility, 6, 7, 17; conditions for legality of defensive and offensive, 25-26; court determination in *Sunstar*, 28-29; effect of state lockout exceptions rule, 27-28; states paying unemployment benefits when, 26-30; under Taft-Hartley Act, 24; *See also* National Labor Relations Board
Long, Russell, 90

McCarthy, John, 162n.26
MacDonald, Maurice, 128nn.125, 128, 129nn.132-35, 137

McGlew, Charles, 76n.94
Malek, Thomas S., 37nn.67-68
Malone, Cecil, 75n.91
Mangum, Garth, 121n.22, 122nn.35, 37
Marshall, Ray, 121n.22, 122nn.35, 37
Mauro, Martin J., 134, 161n.8
Meany, George, 4
Michaud, George A., 71n.16, 17
Michigan: definition of establishment, 34-35n.25; temporary job conditions for benefits, 31-33
Minnesota: interpretation of lockout rule, 28-29; lockout rule in, 27-28
Models of industrial conflict. *See* Industrial conflict models
Models of strike behavior. *See* Strike behavior models
Moore, William, 135, 162n.15
Mundlak, Yair, 185n.9
Murray, Merrill G., 33n.1
Myers, Charles, 200n.3
Myers, Robert J., 122n.34

National Labor Relations Act, 21-22
National Labor Relations Board (NLRB), 24-25
Neiman, Kenneth, 132n.184
Neumann, George, 11, 138-42, 157-59, 161, 162nn.31-34, 163n.42, 192
Neutrality, government: as goal of government policy, 189-90, 196-98; at state level, 89-94, 120
New York state: conditions for paying unemployment benefits, 68-69; unemployment benefits for strikers, 5, 6, 17, 39-40, 47-48; unemployment compensation law of, 46-48
New York Telephone case, 20, 51, 56
NLRB. *See* National Labor Relations Board (NLRB)
Norris-LaGuardia Act, 21
Northrup, Herbert, 75nn.87, 88

OBRA. *See* Omnibus Budget Reconciliation Act (OBRA)
Ohio: definition of establishment, 34-35n.25; innocent bystanders under law in, 52-53
Omnibus Budget Reconciliation Act (OBRA), 7, 85, 102; amendment limiting striker access to food stamps and AFDC-U, 107-8, 112; changes in eligibility test for food stamps, 1981, 103-4; legal challenges to, 7; *See also* Reagan administration

Paldum, M., 161n.4
Pass, Wendel K., 36nn.53, 57
PATCO. *See* Professional Air Traffic Controllers Organization (PATCO)
Pattern bargaining, 139
Pearce, Douglas, 135, 162n.15
Pennsylvania: interpretation of lockout rule, 29-30
Perl, Lewis, 13n.17
Perlis, Leo, 83
Perry, Charles R., 42, 71nn.8-10
Peterson, P.J., 161n.4
Policy options, 194, 198-200
Priban, K., 70n.4
Professional Air Traffic Controllers Organization (PATCO), 59
Protocol theory: function and purpose of, 138-40, 159; predictions of, 180, 181
Public aid: for strikers, 82-83; to strikers, 2-3; to strikers under FERA policy, 77-80, 82

Railroad Unemployment Insurance Act, 1
Ray, David, 74n.65
Rayback, Joseph G., 121n.26
Reagan administration: policy to change AFDC expenditures, 7, 101-2; role in air traffic controllers strike, 59
Reder, Melvin, 11, 138-42, 157-59, 161, 162nn.31-34, 163n.42, 192
Reder-Neumann model. *See* Joint-choice model
Rejda, George, 121n.19
Rhode Island: question of unemployment benefits for strikers in *Grinnell*, 9; unemployment benefits for strikers, 5, 6, 17, 39-40, 48-49
Ringer, James, 74n.65
Rogers, Cheryl, 13n.8, 122n.38, 127n.123
Rolph, James, 78
Rubin, Beth, 162n.29

Sapaford, David, 162n.17
Schlesinger, Arthur M., 77, 121nn.2-3
Schneider, Thomas J., 42, 71nn.8-10
Shadur, Milton I., 23, 34n.4, 34n.23, 35n.26, 70n.5
Shister, Joseph, 200n.3
Sieber, Joseph, 75n.90
Siebert, Stanley, 137, 162nn.16, 25
Siegel, Abraham, 138, 161n.3
Singh, Davinder, 134, 161n.9
Skeels, Kack, 162n.21
Smith, Robert, 132n.185, 200n.2

Social Security Act of 1935, 5, 18, 80-82; AFDC amendment in 1961, 84-85; AFDC-U amendment in 1968, 87; amendment to prohibit AFDC-U benefits to strikers, 102; state-administered unemployment compensation systems, 18
Social Security Board Draft Bill, 18-19, 26, 57
Society's goals, 194, 195-96
Spector, Marjorie, 27, 36nn.45, 48, 49, 70n.3, 123n.62
State employment security agencies, 15
States: administration of food stamp program, 102; autonomy in setting conditions for unemployment benefits, 68; development of policies for unemployment compensation, 17; differing provisions for strikers' unemployment benefits, 5-6, 62, 66-68; discretion in AFDC programs, 81; laws for unemployment compensation, 15; legality of option to decide ADFC-U payments for strikers, 86-89; neutrality in labor disputes, 89-94, 120; sole administrators of general assistance, 86; with stoppage-of-work, lockout, and innocent bystander provisions, 69; as unit of analysis for strike behavior, 133, 147, 149
Steiner, Gilbert Y., 129nn.134, 137
Stern, Robert, 161n.6
Stevens, John Paul, 51, 56-57
Stockman, David, 101
Stoppage-of-work provisions: effect on level of strike activity of, 40-41, 43-44; as exception to nonpayment of striker benefits, 39; generosity of state, 69; implications of and rationale for, 40-42; in Rhode Island state law, 48; and unemployment benefits, 5-7, 15, 69
Strike: distinct from lockout, 27; and unemployment benefits, 41
Strike behavior: factors affecting, 12; link to unemployment insurance of, 12; state as unit of analysis for, 133
Strike behavior model, state analysis: data for, 147-59, 165; hypotheses for, 143-46, 153, 161
Strike behavior models, 134, 157; analysis of political, social and organizational elements in, 135-36; bargaining-power theory of strikes, 136; explanation of strike school of, 134-35; joint-choice model of, 138-41
Strikers: effect of implied prohibition to obtain public aid on, 94-102; eligibility eliminated for some programs, 7; eligibility for benefits under General Assistance (GA), 112-14; eligibility under AFDC-U program, 85; eligibility under current government transfer programs, 1; legal questions of eligibility for ADFC-U and GA, 86-100; under New York state law, 47-48; question of eligibility under food stamp programs, 104-7; question of unemployment benefits under AFDC-U, 87; as recipients of food stamps, 105, 109; under Rhode Island state law, 48-49; welfare assistance in 1940s and 50s, 82; *See also* Aid to Families with Dependent Children-Unemployed Parent (AFDC-U); General assistance (GA); Unemployment insurance
Summers, Clyde, 200n.3
Supreme Court: interpretation of state stoppage-of-work provisions, 45; position on involuntary nature of unemployment in labor dispute, 55-57; significance of ruling in *New York Telephone*, 49-51
Surplus commodity programs, 104
Swidinsky, Robert, 184n.3

Taft, Robert A., 90
Taft-Hartley Act of 1947, 90; goal to ensure government neutrality, 190; Section 7, 24
Taylor, Benjamin J., 35nn.27-28, 30, 32, 200-201n.3
Temporary employment. *See* Employment, interim or temporary

Texas: innocent bystander provision, 54
Thieblot, Armand J., 2, 10, 82, 88, 100-101, 109, 121nn.4, 15-18, 121-22nn.24-27, 122nn.30, 32-33, 123-24n.66, 127n.115, 129n.140, 130nn.157-58, 131n.159
Thomas, Marc E., 13n.14, 39, 70n.1
Thurmond, Strom, 107, 108
Tilly, Charles, 162n.27
Transfer payments: effects on strikes of, 141-42; financing of, 142-43; policy options for costs of, 192-93
Transfer programs, government: goals for public assistance and social insurance as, 188; public assistance and social insurance, 188; role of state in policy for, 187; striker eligibility under current, 1

Unemployment benefits: conditions for payment with interim job, 31; payment in employer lockout, 24-30; state financing of, 154; at state level, 5; state provisions for, 5-7; *See also* New York; Rhode Island; States
Unemployment (definition), 87
Unemployment insurance laws, state: court cases related to disqualification for benefits under, 87-89; interpretation of lockout rules in, 24-30; lockout exception rule, 27; provisions related to benefits for strikers of, 15-17; stoppage-of-work provisions, 5-6, 40
Unemployment insurance system: goals of government policy for, 188-89; link to strike activity of, 12, 178-79, 183; state authority for rules of, 5; and strike activity, 12
United Mine Workers strike, 2, 52
United Steel Workers strike, 2, 52
USX strike, 2, 6

Vandercamp, John, 184n.3

Wage determination model (Hicks), 134
Wagner Act of 1935, 189, 190
Wallace, Michael, 162n.29
Walsh, Kenneth, 161n.4
Welfare programs, government: Aid to Families with Dependent Children (AFDC and AFDC-U), 80-102; effect of liberalization on strikers' benefits, 3; food stamps, 102-12; and strike activity, 12; *See also* Public aid; Transfer programs, government
White, Byron, 112
Whitehead, Brian R., 34n.14
Wilder, Ronald, 161n.9
Williams, Glyn, 161n.9
Witney, Fred, 35nn.27-28, 30, 32
Witte, Edwin E., 18, 33nn.1, 3, 6
Work Stoppage Historical File, 147-48, 150, 159
Work-stoppage provisions. *See* Stoppage-of-work provisions

Yost, William, 75n.92

Zald, Mayer, 162n.26
Zillig, A.G., 71n.16, 17

INDEX OF CASES

Abbott v. *Employment Security Department*, 27 Wash. App.619, P.2d 734 (1980), 58, 75n.84
Abuie v. *Ford Motor Co.*, 194 N.E. 2d 136 (1963), 23, 34n.22
Adamski v. *BUC*, 161 N.E. 2d 907 (Ohio 1959), 24, 34-35n.25
Aero Design & Engineering Co. v. *Board of Review*, 356 P.2d 344 (Okla.1960), 44, 71n.14
Ahne v. *Department of Labor and Industrial Relations*, 53 Hawaii 185, P.2d 1397 (1971), 23, 34n.22, 41, 70n.4
Albuquerque-Phoenix Express, Inc. v. *Employment Security Commission*, 544 P.2d 1161 (N.M.1975), 44, 71n.15
American Shipbuilding Company v. *NLRB*, 380 U.S. 300 (1965), 25, 26, 35n.33

Baker v. *General Motors Corp.*, 106 Sup.Ct. 3129 (1986), 18, 33n.1, 55-56, 65, 74nn.66-73
Batterton v. *Francis*, 432 U.S. 416 (1977), 87, 89, 118, 121nn.21, 23, 122n.43, 123nn.56-61
Bethea v. *Mason*, 384 F.Supp.1274 (D.Md.1974), 88, 123n.55
Bethlehem Steel Co. v. *Board of Review (In re Rusynko)*, 402 Pa. 202, 166 A.2d 871 (1961), 58, 75n.81
Betts Cadillac-Olds,Inc., 96NLRB 268 (1951), 25, 35n.31
Birkenwald, Inc., 282 NLRB 130 (1987), 26, 35n.40
Board of Review v. *Mid-Continent Petroleum Corp.*, 141 p.2d 69 (Okla.1943), 44, 71n.14
Borchman Sons v. *Carpenter&1, 166 Neb. 322, 89 N.W. 2D 123 (1958), 58, 75n.83*
Brechner v. *Ind. Comm'n.*, 148So.2d 567 (1963), 31, 37n.64
Bruly v. *Ind. Com.*, 100 So.2d 22 (Fla.1958), 31, 37n.63
Bsaker v. *General Motors Corp.*, 106 s Ct 3129 (1986), 33nn.1, 2
Burgoon v. *Board of Review*, 100 N.J. Super. 569, 242 A.2d 847 (1968), 58, 75n.8
Burns v. *Alcala*, 420 U.S. 575 (1975), 81, 121n.21

Carleson v. *Remillard*, 46 U.S. 598 (1972), 89, 123n.61
Charbonnet v. *Gerace*, 457 So.2d 676 (La.1984), 67, 76n.99
Chrysler Corp. v. *Smith*, 297 Mich.438, 298 N.W. 2d 87 (1941), 24, 34n.25
City of Spring Valley v. *County of Bureau*, 115 Ill.App. 545 (1904), 113, 132n.183
Continental Oil Co. v. *Board of Labor Appeals*, 582 P.2d 1236 (Mont.1978), 44, 71n.15
Conway v. *Federal Aviation Administration*, appeal docketed Mich. Employment Security Board of Review, No. UCF81-89419-R01-94173 through UCF81-89630-R01-94343, Fe.15,1985, 66, 75-76n.93
Copen v. *Hix*, 130 W.Va. 343, 43 S.E.2d 382 (1947), 75n.82
Cruz v. *Department of Employment Security*, 22 Utah 393, 453 P.2d 894 (1969), 31, 37n.64

Darling & Co., 171 NLRB 801 (1968), 26, 35n.37
Department of Transportation, Federal Aviation Administration v. *Iowa Department of Job Services*, 341 N.W.2d 752 (Iowa Sup. Ct. 1983), 66, 75n.92
Dienes v. *Holland*, 78 Ill.2d 8, 397 N.E.2d 1358 (1979), 31, 37n.62
Douglas v. *Brown*, 189, 200n.3
Dow Chemical Co. v. *Taylor*, 57F.R.D.105 (1972), 32-33, 37nn.72, 73
Dravo Corp. v. *Bd. of Rev.*, 187 Pa.Super. 246, 144 A.2d 670 (1958), 58, 75n.83

Eaton v. *Lyng*, 669 F.Supp. 266 (N.D. Iowa 1987), 111, 118, 131nn.171-74
Employment Sec. Adm'n v. *Browning-Ferris, Inc.*, 438 A.2d1356 (Md.1982), 44, 71n.15

Evans v. *Ind. Com.*, 361 S.W.2d 332, (Mo.1962), 31, 37n.64
Ex parte McCleney, 286 Ala. 288, 239 So.2d,311 (1970), 55, 74n.64
Federal Aviation Administration v. *Administrator, Unemployment Compensation*, 494 A.2d 564 (Conn.1985), 67, 76n.95
Federal Aviation Admin. v. *Montana State Dept. of Labor and Industry*, 685 P.2d 365 (Mont. 1984), 67, 76n.96
Francis v. *Davidson*, 379 F.Supp. 78 (D.Md.1974) [*Francis II*], 88-89, 118, 122n.43, 123n.54
Francis v. *Davidson*, 340 F.Supp. 351 (1972) [*Francis I*], 87-89, 118, 122n.43

Great Lakes Steel Corp. v. *Michigan Employment Security Commission*, 381 Mich. 249, 161 N.W.2d 14 (1968), 31-32, 37n.65
Grinnell v. *Hackett*, 475 F.2d 449; *cert. denied*, 414 U.S. 858 (1973), 9, 13n.12, 48, 64, 72n.31

Haley v. *Board of Review*, 106 N.J. Super. 420, 256 A.2d 71 (1969), 58, 75n.81
Harter Equipment, 280 NLRB 130 (1987), 26, 35nn.38, 39
Hawaii Telephone Co. v. *Hawaii Department of Labor and Industrial Relations*1, 405 F. Supp. 275, 90 LRRM 2854 (1975), 41, 70nn.5, 6
Hessler v. *American Television & Radio Co.*, 258 Minn. 541, 104 N.W. 2d 876 (1980), 28, 36n.50
Hodory v. *Ohio Bureau of Employment Services*, 408 F. Supp.1016 (1976), 52, 64, 74nn.52-55, 112
Holland Motor Expresss, Inc. v. *Michigan Employment Security Commission*, 42 Mich.App. 19, 201 N.W. 2d 308 (1972), 27, 36n.47

Inland Trucking Company v. *NLRB* 1,440 F.2d 562 (1971), 35n.36
In re Curatala, 10 N.W.2d 10, 173 N.E. 2d 1397 (1971), 23, 34n.22
In re Ferrara, 217 N.Y. 2d 11, 176 N.E. 2d 43 (1961), 23, 34n.22
In re Hatch, 130 Vt.218, 290A.2d180 (1972), 31, 37n.64
In re Kennecott Copper Corp., 13 Utah 262, 372 P.2d 987 (1962), 58, 75n.83
Iron Workers' Union v. *Ind. Comm'n*, 194 Utah 242, 139 P.2d208 (1943), 58, 75n.82
ITT Lamp Div. of Int. Tel.& Tel. Corp. v. *Minter*, 439 F.2d 989 (1970), 93, 124n.82
ITT Lamp Division v. *Minter*, 318 F.Supp. 364 (1970), 10, 13n.13, 93, 97-100, 117, 120, 125nn.95, 103-5, 126n.111, 127n.121

Jaramillo v. *County of Santa Clara*, 91 LRRM 2755 (1976), 109-110, 118, 131nn.160-63
Johns-Manville Products Corp., 223 NLRB 189 (1976), 25, 35n.34

Kimbell, Inc. v. *Employment Security Commission*, 429 U.S. 804 (1976), 44, 64, 71n.13
King v. *Smith*, 392 U.S. 309 (1968), 89, 123n.61

Labinsky v.*Ind. Com.*, 167 So.2d 620 (Fla.1964), 31, 37n.63
Lane v. *NLRB*, 418 F.2d 1208 (1969), 26, 35n.37
Lascaris v. *Wyman*, 340 N.Y.S.2d 397 (1972) [*Lascaris II*], 93-94, 96, 99, 118, 124n.74, 125nn.93, 94, 126n.110
Lascaris v. *Wyman*, 305 N.Y.S.2d 212(N.Y. S.Ct. 1969) [*Lascaris I*], 92, 95-96, 99, 117, 124n.72, 125n.90
Lawrence Baking Co. v. *Michigan Unemployment Compensation Commisswion*, 308 Mich. 198, 113 N.W.2d 260 (1944), 41, 70n.5
Ledesma v. *Block*, 825 F.2d (6th Cir. 1987)1046, 111, 118, 131nn.175-76

Lee National Corp. v. *Board of Review*, 187 Pa. Super. 96, 211 A.2d 124 1(1965), 29, 36n.54
Local 730 v. *Unemployment Compensation Review Board*, 480 A.2d 1000 (1984), 36n.55
Lyng v. *UAW*, 108 Sup.Ct. 1184 (1988), 7, 13n.10, 111-12, 118, 131nn.177-81

McAllister v. *Board of Rev.*, 197 Pa.Super. 552, 179 A.2d 121 (1962), 31, 37n.64
McAnallen v. *ESC*, 26 Mich.App. 621, 182 N.W. 2d 753 (1970), 24, 35n.25
Mackintosh-Hemphill Div., E.W.Bliss Co. v. *Board of Review*,, 205 Pa. Suoer. 9, 106 A.2d 23 (1965), 29, 36n.54
Magner v. *Kinney*, 141 Neb. 122, 2N.W. 2d 689 (1942), 41, 70n.6
Mark Hopkins, Inc. v. *Employment Comm'n.*,, 24 Cal.2d 744, 151 P.2d 229 (1944), 31, 37n.64
Matter of Burger, 277 App. Div.234 (Third Dept.), aff'd. 303 N.Y. 654 (1950), 47, 72n.24
Matter of Heitzenrater, 19 N.Y.2d 1 (1966), 47, 72nn.24, 27
Meadow Court Dairies v. *Wiig*, 50 Hawaii 225, 437 P.2d 317 (1968), 41, 71n.6

Nash v. *Florida Industrial Commission*, 389 U.S. 235 (1967), 22, 34n.20, 63
Nestle v. *Johnson*, 68 Ill.App.3d 17, 385 N.E.2d 793 (1979), 54, 74n.58
New York Telephone Co. v. *New York State Department of Labor*, 566 F. 2d 388 (2d Cir.1977), 50, 73nn.44-50
New York Telephone Co. v. *New York State Department of Labor*, 434 F. Supp.810, 95 LRRM 2487 (1977), 73nn.36-43
New York Telephone Co. v. *New York State Department of Labor*, 440 U.S. 519, 100 LRRM 2896 (1979), 30, 32, 34n.11, 36n.62, 37nn.70, 71, 46, 49, 53, 65, 71nn.21-30, 73n.35
NLRB v. *American National Insurance Co.*, 343 U.S. 395 (1952), 90, 123n.64
NLRB v. *Brown, et al d/b/a/ Brown Food Store et al*, 380 U.S. 278 (1965), 25, 35n.35
NLRB v. *McKay Radio & Telegraph Co.*, 304 U.S. 333 (1938), 26, 35n.41
NLRB v. *Truck Drivers Local Union No, 449 (Buffalo Linen Supply Co.)*, 353 U.S.85 (1959), 25, 35n.32
Northwest Airlines v. *App. Bd.*, 378 Mich. 119, 142 N.W. 2d 649 (1966), 23, 34n.22

Ohio Bureau of Employment Services v. *Hodory*, 431 U.S. 471 (1977), 53, 74n.56
Oil,Chemical and Atomic Workers Union, Local 1-1978 v. *Employment Security Division*, 659 P.2d 583 (Alaska 1983), 44-45, 71nn.15-20
Operating Engineers Local No.3 v. *Ind. Comm'n*, 7 Utah 2d 48, 318 P.2d 336 (1957), 58, 75n.83
Outboard Marine & Manufacturing Co. v. *Gordon*, 403 Ill. 523, 87 N.E. 2d 610 (1949), 58, 75n.80

Park v. *ESC*, 353 Mich. 613, 94 N.W. 2d 407 (1959), 24, 35n.25
Penn Manufacturing Corp. v. *Board of Review*, 215 Pa. Super.310, 264 A.2d 126 (1969), 29, 36n.54
Philbrook v. *Glodgett*, 421 U.A. 707 (1975), 100, 126n.114

Ramone v. *Department of Employment Security, Board of Review*, 474 A.2d 748 (R.I.1984), 68, 76n.99
Russo v. *Kirby*, 453 F.2d 548 (1971), 111, 117, 124n.83, 131n.165

San Diego Building Trades v. *Garmon*, 359 U.S. 236 (1959), 51, 73n.50
Scott v. *Unemployment Comp. Comm'n.*, 141 Mont.230, 376 P.2d 733 (1962), 37n.64
Shell Oil Co. v. *Brooks*, 567 P.2d 1132 (Wash.1977), 44, 71n.15
Spielman v. *Industrial Comm'n.*, 236 Wis. 240N.W. 1 (1940), 23, 34n.24

State of Montana v. *Department of Public Welfare*, 136 Mont. 283 (1959), 99, 126n.109
Strat-O-Seal Manufacturing Co. v. *Scott*, 72 Ill.App.2d 480 (1966), 91, 95, 99, 117, 124nn.67-71
Sun Oil Co. of Pennsylvania v. *Unemployment Compensation Review Board*, 440 U.S. 977, 100 LRRM 3055 (1979), 29-30, 36n.55, 65
Sunstar Foods, Inc. v. *Uhlendorf*, 310 N.W. 2d 80 (1981), 36n.51
Super Tire Engineering v. *McCorkle*, 412 F.Supp. 192 (1976), 99, 125-26n.108
Swiecicki v.*Dept. of Employmenmt Security*, 667 P.2d 28 (Utah 1983), 68, 76n.99

Teamsters Union v. *Oliver*, 358 U.S. 283 (1959), 90, 123n.64
Townsend v. *Swank*, 404 U.S. 282 (1971), 89, 123n.61

UAW v. *Lyng*, 648 F.Supp. 1234 (D.D.C. 1986), 7, 13n.9, 100, 110-11, 118, 131nn.166-70, 126n.112
Unemployment Compensation Board of Review v. *G.C. Murphy Co.*, 19 Pa. Commw. Ct. 572, 339 A.2d 167 (1975), 55, 74n.63
Unemployment Compensation Commission v *Aragon*, 329 U.S. 143, 91L Ed 136 (1946), 21-22, 34nn.15-19, 63
U.S. Department of Agriculture v. *Moreno*, 102, 127n.126
United Steel Workers of America v. *Meierhenry*, 608 F. supp. 201 (1985), 51, 73n.50

Vrotney Unemployment Compensation Case, 400 Pa. 440, 163 A.2d 91 (1960), 29, 36n.54

Warner Press, Inc. v. *Review Board*, Ind.App., 413N.E.2d 1003 (Ind.1980), 44, 71n.15
Wilson v. *Employment Security Commission*, 74 N.M. 3, 389 P.2d 855 (1963), 58, 75n.81
Wolf v. *FAA*, 461 N.Y.S.2D 573 (n.y. 1983), 68, 76n.99